AMERICAN SOUL

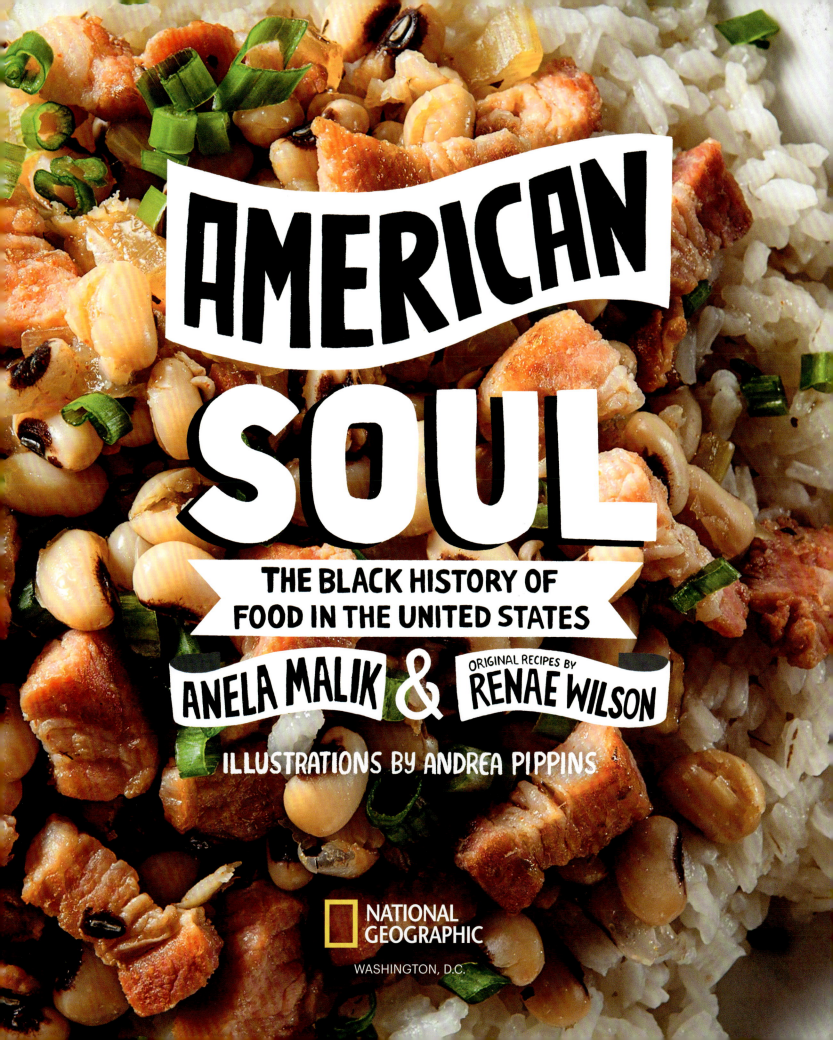

Contents

INTRODUCTION
The Stories We Tell 6

CHAPTER ONE
The Diverse Roots of American Cuisine 14

CHAPTER TWO
Enslaved Black Labor & Wealth Generation 40

CHAPTER THREE
Nationalizing Black Cuisine 104

CHAPTER FOUR
Looking Ahead 144

CHAPTER FIVE
A Celebratory Feast 182

EPILOGUE
Where Do We Go Now? 294

Acknowledgments 298
Select Sources 299
Maps & Illustrations Credits 302
General Index 306
Recipe Index 315

OPPOSITE: A serving of fried shrimp and shark, green beans, red rice, and potato salad from renowned restaurant Gullah Grub in South Carolina
PAGES 2-3: Try a plate of hoppin' John, a hearty dish often eaten on New Year's Day to bring good luck in the coming year.

INTRODUCTION

The Stories We Tell

Do the stories we tell about food really matter? • I believe so. Food is a part of who we are and how we relate to others. Food features prominently in the stories and memories that form our personal, communal, and even national identities. My mother's pan-fried tofu and my father's seafood gumbo are just as much a part of my story as my education, my travel experiences, my race, and my gender. I can easily recall the smell and taste of those family dishes as if they were sitting on the table in front of me. They are part of my core childhood memories—some hilarious and others benign—with my siblings, all of which are important to who I am, who I have become.

Take gumbo, for example. Gumbo has a long history that traces back to West Africa. This raises the questions: Is my father's gumbo a representation of his personal food preferences and his own family's dinnertime traditions, or is it a dish that reflects his Blackness and his ties to the diaspora? And how does that singular dish—and the knowledge he imparted to me about how to make it—also connect me to the diverse experiences of other Black Americans and the diaspora?

These questions, and the stories found in their answers, show how food plays a vital role in understanding who we are and how we relate to each other. And that understanding is what brought me quite unexpectedly to the world of food media.

Today, I make my living as an influencer and writer who focuses on nuanced and thoughtful explorations of food, travel, identity, history, and more. I never set out to be an influencer—if you had asked me five years ago if I thought I would be making a career writing and telling stories about food, I would have laughed. I had envisioned myself working in politics, pursuing a career in government.

Ironically, it was that very serious path that led me here. After receiving my master's degree, I joined the U.S. Foreign Service and became a diplomat. I was working at the American Embassy in Amman, Jordan, when I started creating digital content. I used food—and the stories food told—to learn about local culture and meet new people. And over time what began as a fun hobby grew into a new career that has taken me around the world and taught me so much.

Food opened the door to new dialogue, a conversation that continues today: When I visit a restaurant to create a social media video, the conversations start. From restaurateurs, chefs, and servers, I hear about the food they make and serve and how it's connected to their dreams for the future, how the recipes are inspired by

---

Author Anela Malik

> Along with our own personal identities, food—the way we talk about, produce, consume, and distribute it—is deeply connected to ideas about who is truly American, who deserves credit, who belongs, and even what the United States stands for.

their families and communities, and how the connections they make with their regular customers keep them going.

Online, I receive comments that a post made someone else feel seen; that their mother makes something similar and now they have broader context for the history of the dish I shared; how much it means to them to see their heritage represented.

I once asked my digital community what food means to them. Their replies illustrate how vital food is to our memories, identities, and communities:

To me, food indicates a shared experience. Even if you eat alone in a restaurant, you are still dining in community by default. Any time you provide food, you connect with those who receive it. Food is a universal way for us to offer and receive a connection that transcends language. —Lauren, Washington, D.C.

Food bridges the gap from past to present, connecting me to my family's village in China to growing up in the U.S. It is how I share my heritage, through the different specialty foods eaten during different holidays and the more humble dishes that my grandmother prepared for me throughout my life—it is how I remember and honor her memory. —Wilma, Washington, D.C.

As a Black woman, I've battled imposter syndrome in so many different spheres of my life. Food and cooking is my way of taking back what society tries to tell me I'm not good enough to achieve. My kitchen is my world and the food that comes out of it is my love letter to my friends and family. —Sarah, Virginia

Along with our own personal identities, food—the way we talk about, produce, consume, and distribute it—is deeply connected to ideas about who is truly

---

Focus On: "United States" Versus "America"

"America" can be an ambiguous term. In some contexts and cultures, "American" can refer to anyone or anything from North or South America. I use "America" or "American" to mean the United States of America or of/from the United States. I recognize the U.S.-centric use of "American" that I'm adopting here and the critiques it evokes as imperialist and colonialist. However, "American" is the most common way that people from the United States refer to themselves, which is why I use it that way throughout this book.

American, who deserves credit, who belongs, and even what the United States stands for. That's why the stories in this book matter. That's why the conversations within this book are more than just a recounting of history—they are an exploration of who we are as Americans.

Vital Yet Obscured

Black peoples are culture makers in the United States. Their impact has long been recognized as such, especially in the spheres of art and music. Black knowledge, expertise, culture, and contributions extend into all aspects of American life, from fashion to language. They also extend into foodways.

Black food is American food. The opposite is also true.

No examination of the nation's food traditions and practices is complete without exploring the extent that Black peoples have impacted what and how we eat. But the deep and enduring contributions of Black folks to American cuisine are often obscured. Early Black history in the United States is rooted in enslavement and systems that legally barred Black peoples from learning to read or write. Few written records from the innumerable Black cooks, chefs, domestic laborers, agricultural workers, pitmasters, fishermen, hunters, game herders, gardeners, oystermen, and caterers from the first 200 to 300 years of colonial and American history survive today. And so, until recently, Black food history and traditions passed from generation to generation largely through word of mouth. That has made it harder, though not impossible, to trace the impact of Black peoples on American cuisine.

Early food writing was the work of the highly educated, largely white elite and often left out any mention of Black contributions. Though the profession has become decidedly more diverse in recent decades, a gap remains. Today, media coverage of Black food is often concentrated around holidays such as Black History Month and Juneteenth—a specific and limiting context. Less common are stand-alone pieces examining Black foodways and how they're interwoven with American cuisine.

The nature of professional cooking, too, has changed, but in a way that further obscures Black contributions to American foodways. Beginning in the early 1900s, more white Americans began cooking as a profession, taking on roles that had largely been the purview of Black laborers. The trade evolved into a celebrated career that now often requires formalized—and very expensive—training. While many kitchens—both domestic and professional—used to be run by Black chefs and cooks, many of them women, the leadership of

A dishwasher takes his break outside a waterfront restaurant in Washington, D.C., in 1942.

professional kitchens in the United States today is largely made up of predominantly white, male chefs. As Marcus Samuelsson has said, "Black people had to work really hard to get out of the kitchen … and now they have to work really hard to get back in."

Historians like Jessica B. Harris, Frederick Douglass Opie, Adrian Miller, Michael W. Twitty, and a cadre of other researchers are filling knowledge gaps in the Black history of America's foodways. Food writers, editors, bloggers, chefs, bakers, and restaurateurs around the country are also highlighting Black contributions to domestic cuisine, drawing lines between the African continent, diaspora communities, and America's cuisine today.

This book is a celebration of and accompaniment to their works. It would be impossible to produce a single comprehensive history of Black contributions to American cuisine. This is not an attempt to do that. Instead, I will walk you through key moments in the history of the United States, particularly Black history, that helped shape our cuisine. You will read stories about the vital voices working on issues surrounding Black food in America and find recipes rooted in history and community. Ultimately, *American Soul* considers this irrefutable

Nigerian author Chimamanda Ngozi Adichie (center) joins a dinner party with her friends (from left) actor Osas Ighodaro, comedian Chigul, rapper Phyno, visual artist Victor Ehikhamenor, and television host Ebuka Obi-Uchendu.

> ### *Focus On:* Uppercase-B "Black"
>
> *"The designation 'black American' no longer means up from the South.*
> *It can also encompass folks from the Caribbean, Central and South America, and the African continent itself."*
> —Historian Jessica B. Harris in *High on the Hog: A Culinary Journey From Africa to America*
>
> I use uppercase "Black" to refer to the peoples and cultures of the African diaspora. There are numerous Black cultures and subcultures in the United States, dynamic and changing over time, influenced by migration (forced and unforced), geography, proximity to others, and a multitude of factors that affect identity and cultural formation. Yet, despite this diversity, Blackness remains a distinct marker, particularly in a nation where race so strongly impacts the social, political, and economic landscape.
>
> I also use "African American" as a synonym for "Black." However, particularly during the early periods of colonial and national history, Black peoples were not American citizens. They did not have equal protections and rights under the Constitution. It wasn't until the late 1800s when the Emancipation Proclamation and 14th Amendment guaranteed their status as free citizens that Black peoples began the difficult and ongoing transition to full and equal citizenship and fair treatment within the United States.
>
> I also deliberately use "Black peoples" in the plural form to emphasize the diverse roots of Black history in the United States. During enslavement, Africans were forcibly imported from a variety of communities and nations, each with their own belief systems and traditions. Using the plural "peoples" emphasizes that they carried their own histories and practices to their new homes, over time forming and reforming new communities and cultures. Black migration into and within the United States persisted after the end of the Transatlantic Slave Trade, resulting in a variety of Black cultures and subcultures across the country. This is evident in the diversity of culinary influences in Black communities throughout the nation. Even today, there is no singular monolithic Black culture.

fact: The development of American cuisine is inextricable from the innovation, labor, expertise, and cultures of the Black diaspora.

Wait, What Is American Cuisine?

The term "cuisine" is all at once broad—encompassing innumerable dishes and techniques—and severely limited. Some define a cuisine by its regional inflections: the common ingredients and techniques used in a particular area. In the context of the United States, southern food and cornbread are examples of regional takes on cuisine. Others point toward identity, situating cuisine as an important, though contested, symbol that helps define a group in relation to others. Soul food embodies this identity—and conflict—for many African Americans. Cuisine can also be framed as a vehicle of shared knowledge and experience, emphasizing the ways in which food and its preparation connect the present to the past.

Cuisine can reflect a deeply personal and everyday nature, conveying the ways food is prepared at home, whether alone

> America's cuisine reflects the nature of the United States itself, a relatively young nation founded and molded by waves of immigration.

or with close relations. When contemplating this personal side of cuisine, we often think of simpler—some would say "homey"—dishes such as stews, casseroles, or even pastas. Comfort foods and celebratory foods are often remarkably personal in this way.

On the other hand, cuisine can be cosmopolitan. It may reflect all the pomp and circumstance of professional food made for profit. Professional cuisine often utilizes ingredients and techniques that are uncommon for the household cook. Molecular gastronomy and small-plate menus, though divisive, are prominent examples.

Debate persists over what is considered American cuisine. For some, American cuisine defies definition. The United States is geographically vast, containing multitudes of regions and subregions. At least 350 languages are spoken within its borders. This diversity, some critics say, defies the very concept of a singular American cuisine. Those critics characterize American cuisine as inflected by the foreign, by imported ingredients, by French techniques, and by immigrant hands. To them, these qualities dilute American cuisine beyond recognition.

If you ask someone outside the United States what they think of as American food, the likely answer will involve pizza, hamburgers, hot dogs, and a few fast-food chains. Informed by mass media and the marketing of large food companies with global brand recognition, American food is often reduced to a shallow stereotype in the eyes of others.

Despite the difficulty in drawing neat boundaries around it, America does have a cuisine. I define "American cuisine" quite simply as the common ingredients, flavors, dishes, and techniques that most Americans recognize. This definition is deliberately broad, intended to cover everything from fried chicken to American Chinese food, in recognition of the diverse array of cultural and regional contributions to the food landscape of the United States. In a sense, this definition of "American cuisine" relies on qualities that are hard to describe, but ones we know when we see them or taste them.

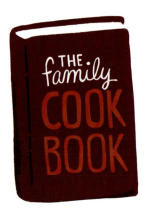

America's cuisine reflects the country's diversity. Italian immigrants introduced pizza to the United States, and in less than 200 years the hot, bubbly pies became one of the most popular foods in the country (the average American eats 46 slices of pizza a year). The hamburger, considered "American" across the globe, has roots in Germany. Cashew chicken was popularized by a Chinese immigrant restaurateur and chef seeking to blend flavors of his Cantonese heritage with techniques familiar to diners in Springfield, Missouri.

Black pepper, ubiquitous on American dinner tables, is native to India and grown predominantly in tropical nations. Vanilla, one of the most common ingredients in U.S. baked goods, comes predominantly from the islands of Madagascar and Réunion, off the east coast of Africa. Gumbo, sriracha and other hot sauces, macaroni and cheese, MSG, and even the California roll—all common dishes or ingredients in American cooking—have complex, multicultural, and often international histories.

And of course, the nation's cuisine has changed over time, evolving in response to agricultural, technological, and societal changes. No cuisine is uniform or stagnant. Including America's.

America's cuisine reflects the nature of the United States itself, a relatively young nation founded and molded by waves of immigration. The last century has seen the rise of fast food and industrialized food products; technological advances such as the microwave; constantly changing conceptions of what constitutes "healthy" food; the waning but still important influence of French culinary techniques; and the growth of a "New American," California-inflected, locally focused emphasis on flavor and seasonality. American cuisine is a vibrant, dynamic, and ever changing canon of preferences, knowledge, and techniques.

Diving In

Consider this book a sampling of important moments in the development of American foodways through the lens of Black history. It does not represent the totality of that history but rather a starting point. Within, you will find recipes, explorations of cookbooks as repositories of food and cultural knowledge, highlights of Black food institutions, and profiles of historians, chefs, mixologists, writers, and creators who are examining and renewing Black and American cuisine today.

Most of the recipes in this book were developed by Renae Wilson using historical records, oral histories, and historic cookbooks. Others, found in chapter five, were contributed by Black chefs, bakers, writers, and historians. Some rely on ingredients tied to Black history, migration, and culture. Others are simply dishes made by Black peoples, emphasizing the breadth of Black expertise and labor in the varied culinary spheres of the United States. Through the profiles, recipes, and reflections in *American Soul,* we can begin to get a broader understanding of Black foodways and the issues faced by Black food professionals. We can also paint a fuller picture of the dynamic and evolving canon that is American cuisine.

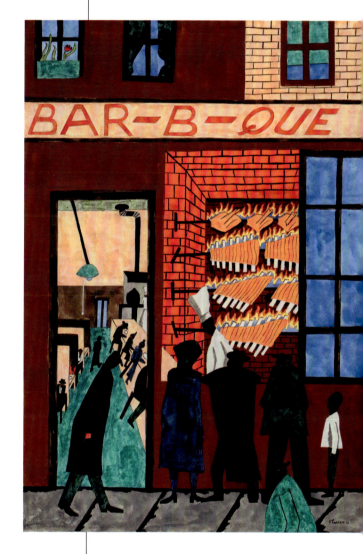

"Bar-b-que," painted in 1942 by Jacob Lawrence, depicts a busy Harlem restaurant scene.

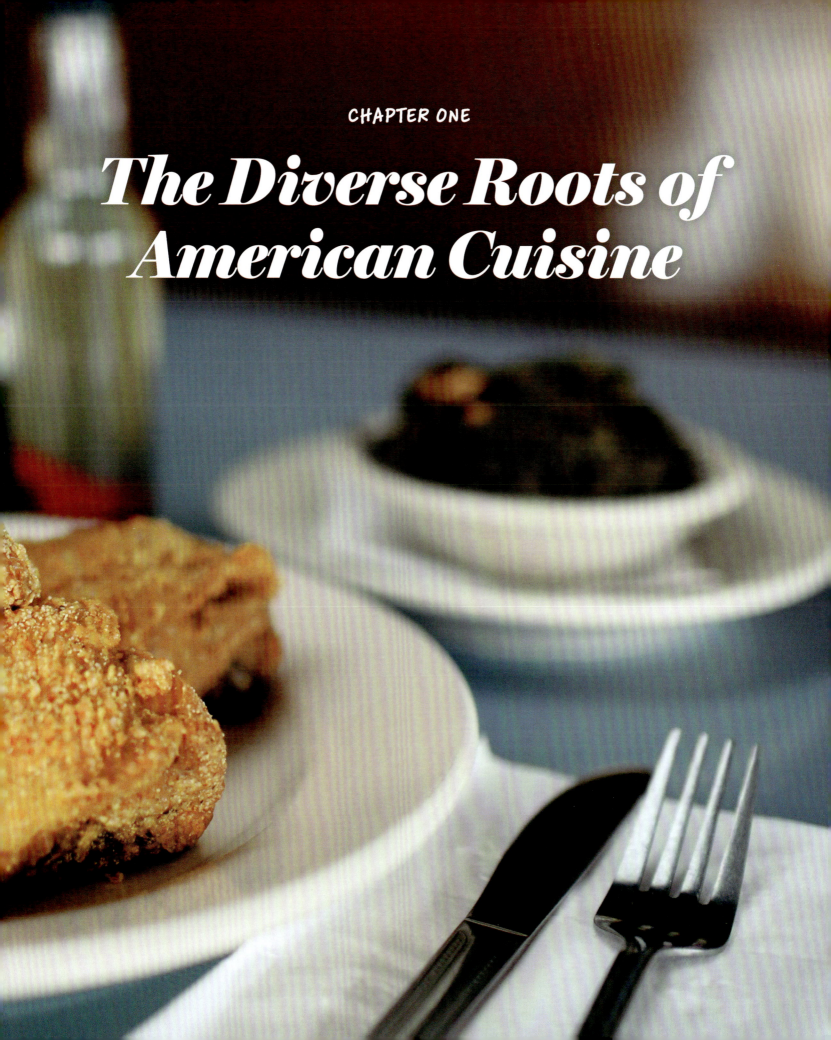

CHAPTER ONE

The Diverse Roots of American Cuisine

Where We Began

Before we get to the enduring Black contributions to American cuisine, it's imperative to note how our Indigenous communities shaped the culinary foundation we all now share.

- *Communities and cultures do not exist in isolation. Rather, they feed off each other, teach each other, and often adapt and innovate using information and tools shared with each other. Fusion cuisines like American Chinese food or Ethiopian soul food (which*

I recently tried in Washington, D.C.) are examples of how this process of cultural diffusion, communication, and innovation can play out in the food space.

American cuisine rests on a host of complex food beliefs, practices, technologies, and traditions that reflect the diversity of the nation, as well as its many regions and communities. Exploring common ingredients, flavors, dishes, and techniques helps us begin to understand the varied histories that have impacted American cuisine and paints a deeper picture of America's food landscape—one that's more colorful and detailed than would exist without this diversity. There is always a deeper, more nuanced story to be told, but these histories offer a starting point.

This book does not approach cuisine and culture as a zero-sum game. Highlighting and exploring Black foodways and their connections to American cuisine is not meant to erase or obscure the contributions of others. American cuisine is a vast and complex system of knowledge and practices, one in which many peoples and cultures have made their mark. There is space to acknowledge them all as parts of that interwoven tapestry.

For all those reasons and more, we begin here with an exploration and acknowledgment of Indigenous contributions to American cuisine, as it would be impossible to start at the "beginning" without them. Black culinary labor, expertise, and contributions to American foodways did not begin in a vacuum, in a pristine land unmarked by other communities, histories, or cultures. Though some narratives of the colonization of the Americas represent this land as empty, ripe for the taking upon the arrival of the first colonists, this is far from the truth. Indigenous peoples were here long before European intervention and in many cases were vital to the survival of the communities that developed as a result of colonization. They remain an integral, though often unrecognized, part of societies in the Americas and around the world today.

OPPOSITE: **In 1950, Diego Rivera painted the Huastec civilization in his mural "Cultivation of Maize and Preparation of Pancakes."**
PAGES 14–15: **A diner serves plates of southern classics: fried chicken, macaroni and cheese, and collard greens.**

Indigenous Roots

Much of American cuisine rests on Indigenous foodways, whether commonly acknowledged or not. Indigenous populations throughout the Americas have declined dramatically since their peak before colonial contact, and many of their foodways were disrupted by colonialism. Estimates of the size of Indigenous populations in North America at the time of colonial contact vary dramatically, with some estimates ranging from 60 million people up to 112 million people. Today, there are around 7.4 million Indigenous people in the United States.

Colonial settlers in North America, Black peoples among them, absorbed many food practices and habits after coming in contact with Indigenous communities. Their subsequent adaptations helped shape the foundation of American cuisine.

The stories of how and when ingredients made their way from one community to the next are complex, spanning hundreds of years and stretching across continents. As people move, so do ingredients and food knowledge. For example, potatoes—brought to Europe in the 1500s—are, in fact, indigenous to the Andes, a region in South America where they were domesticated by Indigenous communities approximately 8,000 years ago. Tomatoes are native to Central America. Imagine American food today without potatoes or tomatoes. Likewise, ingredients now considered standard in American cooking—maple syrup, squash, beans, salmon, and blueberries, for example—have Indigenous roots, though we may now think of them as simply a part of American cooking.

Historic Indigenous food practices were influenced by location and the environment, the immediate community and neighboring communities, and access to materials and trade relationships, among other factors. Food cultivation, hunting, gathering, cooking, and preservation differed from community to community—encompassing varying agricultural legacies, diverging roles of women in food production and preparation, and more. Given this vast diversity, it can be difficult

to trace Indigenous contributions from any one particular group to American cookery. Indigenous food history is further complicated, obscured, and lost because of colonialism, land theft, displacement, cultural erasure, and other destructive forces.

In many ways the development of American cuisine depended on a process of knowledge transfer from Indigenous communities to colonial settlers and enslaved Africans. Native peoples sometimes lived and worked side by side with Black enslaved peoples in a variety of contexts, at times as enslavers themselves. Enslaved Africans learned Indigenous food practices—from specific dishes and ingredients to methods of cooking, agricultural practices, and knowledge of local food sources—as a means of survival in the Americas, as they were forced to labor on plantations, in cities, and throughout early American society.

Early colonial North American food practices involved the cultivation, foraging, and preparation of indigenous ingredients such as sassafras and squash. Look to some of the earliest American cookbooks and you'll find recipes such as Baked

Potato varieties are the backbone of many dishes that stem from Indigenous cultures.

Indian Meal Pudding in *The Virginia Housewife* (1824) and an Indigenous dish called sofky, a corn-based custard included in *The Carolina Housewife* (1847), along with other dishes such as Seminole Soup.

We can still see this culinary influence today. In the American Southwest, prickly pear—a traditional food of the Hualapai peoples—often flavors drinks or candies and is widely marketed on local menus. Throughout the Pacific Northwest, you'll find pies and treats made with huckleberry, a sacred food of the Coast Salish people. Or consider the ubiquity of maple across the United States. Ojibwa Indians, along with other Indigenous communities, collected maple sap and made syrup and sugar long before the arrival of colonial settlers. Indigenous peoples then taught colonial settlers the practice.

Corn, or maize, is indigenous to what is now the state of Oaxaca in Mexico. It's estimated that corn has been grown there as a domesticated crop for 9,000 years. Corn-based flatbreads eaten with fillings were part of the diets of the Aztec and Maya and had spread throughout North and South America by the time of colonial contact. Sound familiar? The modern parallel is the taco. Today, across the United States and around the globe, tacos are employed in almost any type of meal, from an egg breakfast to a dinner of regional barbecue.

Colonialism brought violence, cultural destruction, and death to many Indigenous peoples in the "New World." America is still reckoning with the impacts of that legacy, which ultimately set the stage for a nation founded on immigration. Over time, foundational Indigenous knowledge coalesced with the food traditions newcomers carried with them to American shores. This hybrid created a new cuisine that is distinctly American, yet uniquely multicultural.

Currently, there are more than 500 recognized Indigenous tribes in the United States, more than 600 First Nations groups in Canada, and 68 Indigenous groups in Mexico. Many of these communities have struggled with the loss of their traditional foodways due to colonization, forced assimilation, and food inequity. However, Indigenous scholars, activists, cooks, families, communities, and chefs continue to preserve and revitalize their food traditions. Indigenous chef–led restaurants, such as the award-winning Owamni in Minneapolis, among many other Indigenous food projects throughout the U.S., use traditional and culturally meaningful ingredients not only to feed people but also to educate them.

ABOVE: A page from *The Virginia Housewife* cookbook by Mary Randolph, published in 1824
OPPOSITE: Corn has been growing beneath the mountains of Oaxaca, Mexico, since Aztec and Maya times.

Food for Thought

Cornbread

"Whatever color it was, cornmeal was the primary ingredient of the primary bread that nourished millions of Black people in the plantation South."
—Adrian Miller, *Soul Food: The Surprising Story of an American Cuisine, One Plate at a Time*

Cornbread illustrates how America's food has emerged as a creolized national cuisine, one that draws on elements from multiple cultural traditions. Today, cornbread's rich, comforting flavors have come to define, for many, southern regional cuisine. But it's a popular staple on restaurant menus and family dining tables throughout the nation. Though southern in origin, cornbread is now a truly national food.

Cornbread simultaneously draws on Indigenous foodways, enslavement in the United States, and African food traditions. Corn is indigenous to North America and was domesticated as early as 7000 B.C. A staple crop of many Indigenous peoples, corn was central to religious beliefs, origin stories, and understandings of time.

Corn was originally brought to Africa by European traders in the 16th century, before the Transatlantic Slave Trade began. Both Native American and West African food traditions evolved to utilize corn in similar ways in the precolonial era. It was often made into porridges, mashes, or cakes.

Corn was an important part of the North American diet during the colonial period, particularly in the southern United States. In early southern regions, Black and Indigenous peoples, along with poor whites, often lived in shared communities or in close contact, resulting in an exchange of foodways. Corn was a staple of enslaved rations and was also commonly used both at home and in professional cooking for the plantocracy class. Corn shucking was a celebrated event that marked the changing of seasons and, like other harvest festivals, was an opportunity for enslaved laborers to gather and enjoy a break from often brutal and monotonous work routines.

Black enslaved peoples were largely responsible for growing corn on large plantations. They also continued cooking with corn, drawing on West African traditions, mixed with the Indigenous foodways they had been exposed to in the colonies. Names differed, but techniques and methods often mirrored one another and overlapped: Fufu, kush, sofky, corn mush, cornbread, and hoecakes are all part of this complicated legacy.

Cornbread is thought of as quintessentially southern and also as part of the soul food canon. When you consider its legacy as a dish historically made by Black hands out of ingredients grown by enslaved Africans, with roots in Indigenous foodways and agricultural knowledge, cornbread emerges as a quintessential American dish.

OPPOSITE: "Corn Shucking in the Moonlight" by Mary Lyde Hicks Williams depicts the life of the freed enslaved peoples she saw on her uncle's plantation during Reconstruction in North Carolina.

Immigrant Influences

Colonization itself involves migration—of people, of goods, and of knowledge systems. Along with the voluntary migration of Europeans during the colonial era, the Trans-atlantic Slave Trade forced more than 10 million enslaved Africans to migrate to North America, the Caribbean, and South America. Each subsequent period of American history witnessed additional migrations—from the wave of Chinese immigrants in the 1800s to the millions of Mexican immigrants who have come to the United States since 1965. The hundreds of languages spoken in the country today are a testament to that legacy.

To understand how American cuisine was created, remember that each community, culture, and family brings their own preferences, recipes, food knowledge, and favored ingredients with them. In their new communities, everything from the purchases made in local markets to the recipes shared with new neighbors makes an impact on the people and systems surrounding them. Conversely, the food landscapes of new communities, as well as availability of ingredients, changes the food practices for migrants. The result is a process of culinary mixing and adaptation.

Consider the taco I mentioned earlier. This corn-based flatbread has been in the Americas for thousands of years. Traditional indigenous toppings likely included wild game such as turkey, venison, and bison. Today, tacos are often made with chicken, beef, or pork fillings—proteins that are native to Europe or Asia, rather than North or South America. How did that happen? Colonization. As food systems, migration, and cooks' preferences changed through colonization, new toppings subsumed the traditional. Flour tortillas, rather than corn, utilized wheat introduced to the Americas in the colonial period and became common taco bases. These food evolutions were often imposed via violence and displacement. America's widespread love for tacos is a reminder of the deep, often unrecognized histories of Indigenous peoples interwoven in our modern food system.

Similar processes of culinary adaptation occurred as other immigrant groups arrived in the colonies and later the United States. Historical records show that colonial cuisine incorporated "New World" ingredients, some imported foodstuffs, and techniques borrowed from Indigenous and Black peoples. American Chinese food offers another more recent example of this process: The cuisine evolved from Chinese immigrants looking to make familiar dishes with new, American ingredients. Now, the style of cuisine is considered quintessentially American by many.

We can also look at sriracha sauce. Widely used in American cuisine today, the spicy condiment has international roots. Huy Fong Foods produces and distributes its sriracha hot sauce in California. The red jalapeño peppers used to make Huy Fong sriracha are also grown in California, just a few hours from the factory. Huy Fong Foods was founded in 1980 by David Tran, a refugee from Vietnam. The beloved sriracha is an interpretation of a hot sauce originally created in Thailand and popular throughout Southeast Asia. In the span of less than 50 years, Huy Fong sriracha has become a potent symbol of popular American food culture and is found on the menus of some of the biggest food chains in the United States. The company reportedly made up to $150 million in annual revenue in 2019. Yet, its roots lie in a refugee's 1978 escape on a boat from Hong Kong.

Tex-Mex is another result of this process of culinary adaptation. "When Texas became part of the United States, the people that lived there had a culture that became part of the American story, just like the *Mayflower*," says Sarah Lohman in *Eight Flavors: The Untold Story of American Cuisine*. "A bowl of chili, drawn from Mexican heritage, influenced by the Germans, and made famous in the state of Texas, is a true American dish."

As people have migrated, so have seeds, favorite meals, food stories and beliefs, agricultural knowledge, and dining preferences. These interwoven threads form the complex tapestry of American cuisine.

The outside of Chop Suey, a Chinese restaurant in New York City's Lower East Side during the 1930s

Food for Thought

Creole Cuisine & Gumbo

Creole food is one of America's most widely recognized regional cuisines and has a towering presence among Louisiana's varied culinary traditions. "No other part of the United States has preserved its regional cuisine to the degree that Louisiana has," says Paul Freedman in *American Cuisine: And How It Got This Way.* • New Orleans was established on lands utilized by numerous Indigenous nations who called it Bulbancha, or "place of many tongues." La Nouvelle-Orléans was founded in the early 1700s as the French colonized the area. The colony passed from French to Spanish control, then eventually joined the United States in 1803 as part of the Louisiana Purchase. New Orleans was home to many migrants, both forced and unforced, during this early period of its history. And it operated as a major slave port—in the 1800s it was home to the largest slave market in the United States. By the 1830s, one-third of New Orleans' population was enslaved.

Creole cuisine developed in this urban environment of diverse communities. While Creole cuisine is similar to, and in some cases overlaps with, Cajun cuisine—a distinct Louisiana food culture associated with a more rural, game-and-meat-inflected bayou cooking tradition—Creole food is distinguished from Cajun cuisine by rich sauces, "more bread, butcher's meats and fancy desserts," says Freedman. Creole cooking draws on Indigenous, French, Spanish, and Black influences, as well those from Portuguese, Italian, German, Caribbean, and, more recently, Vietnamese populations.

Gumbo offers an example of this fusion of influences and culinary traditions. (It's also an important dish in both Creole and Cajun cuisines.) The name itself is believed to tie gumbo's heritage to the African diaspora, as multiple West African languages utilize terms that include or sound similar to "gombo" as the word for okra. Some historical texts use the term alongside "okra" as a synonym. Recipes for gumbo from the 1800s include okra as a staple ingredient, adding weight to the belief that the development of this stew is intrinsically tied to the labor, skills, and expertise of Black peoples. Okra is believed to have made its way to the Americas through the Transatlantic Slave Trade, where the knowledge and labor of Black peoples in the colonies ensured it became a mainstay of southern cuisine. Gumbo's common pairing with rice is another nod to the African diaspora: It mirrors the many meals in West Africa that are structured around a savory stew served alongside a starch. Rice's presence in the Americas is also deeply tied to Black labor and expertise.

TOP: "The Old Plantation," painted between 1785 and 1795, portrays enslaved peoples in South Carolina playing music and dancing at a plantation. BOTTOM LEFT: Workers tirelessly lug oysters off a packet boat in New Orleans, Louisiana. BOTTOM RIGHT: Raw whole okra—an essential ingredient in Creole cuisine

ABOVE: **A streetcar rolls past restaurants and shops on Canal Street in New Orleans.** OPPOSITE: **Sizzling hot shrimp and vegetable gumbo**

The roux, a mixture made of flour and fat that we so strongly associate with gumbo today, is believed to be a later addition to gumbo preparation, in many cases replacing okra to give the stew thickness. Roux's addition indicates French and Creole culinary influences, populations that lived in, worked in, and colonized Louisiana before it became part of the United States. Some gumbos, particularly those in Louisiana, utilize the dried, powdered leaves of the sassafras plant, called filé, as a thickening agent as well. Sassafras is indigenous to North America and has long been used by native peoples, including the Choctaw, as a thickener and for other therapeutic purposes. Some narratives even claim that gumbo is an interpretation of French bouillabaisse, though there's more limited evidence for that claim.

Debate about gumbo persists: Which version of gumbo came first, okra or filé? Whose influence is more prominent in the dish? Maybe the answer is that gumbo comes from not one distinct group or individual tradition but rather is an amalgamation of many cultural inputs and food practices over time. Even today there is no one way to make gumbo. Every region, city, and even cook maintains their own interpretation. As with many dishes, gumbo included, history and evolution are complex and tied to many cultures and peoples.

Food Regions of the United States

Food historians, cookbook authors, and passionate eaters often try to categorize "American food" geographically. While the lines are often blurred, there are still some distinctive regional flavors and ingredients: You can count on locals to defend Maine lobster, Texas beef, and Georgia peaches, for example. The map above divides the country into a few broad, traditional regions based on climate and topography and the common plant and animal foods grown or raised there. Many of those foods—from salmon and crab to maize, squash, and maple syrup—can be traced back to Native American foodways. Cities that have led the way in food innovation are also highlighted.

Black History

American history is, in part, Black history. For as long as European settlers have lived on the land that is now the United States, so have Black peoples. • If we consider Black peoples as one of the earliest groups of immigrants to come to the Americas during the colonial era—by forced migration and human trafficking of the enslaved—we can also consider Black peoples to be one of the foundational groups that helped create what we now know as America, and subsequently see them as shapers of American cuisine. Though rarely credited, Black peoples have been cultural and culinary tastemakers in the country for centuries—even before its founding.

Black hands cleared stumps and performed much of the hard physical labor that helped claim the land that became the United States. Black labor and Black bodies, governed by a system of enslavement that some historians describe as systematized torture of Black peoples, generated immense wealth that helped fuel America's industrialization and ultimately global power. Black innovation and creativity also fueled musical genres and social movements that transformed the United States, from the blues to the civil rights movement.

And in that complex interplay of cultural exchange, physical labor, expertise, political and social revolution, and innovation, Black foodways have left an undeniable mark on American cuisine. Black contributions to American cuisine are often oversimplified, rely on stereotypes, or are simply absent from popular narratives. Yet Black contributions to American cuisine are all-encompassing. The history of the Black cultural influence on our foodways certainly includes the stereotypical roles of big house cooking and plantation work. But there are less recognized contributions, too: Famed Black caterers and tastemakers who built culinary empires. Black cowboys and cooks who fed the trail drives of the American West and made their mark on the fledgling nation as it expanded. The Black peoples in Appalachia, in the North, and beyond. Black American culinary history is robust and diverse. That's what we're here to explore together. So let's get into it!

OPPOSITE: **Three young women prep their ingredients before cooking a meal together.**

Southern Skillet Cornbread (left), p. 36, Hot-Water Cornbread (above), p. 37

Southern Skillet Cornbread

Cook time: 35 minutes | *Makes 8 to 10 servings*

2 slices thick-cut bacon

½ cup (1 stick) butter, plus more for serving

1¼ cups cornmeal

¾ cup all-purpose flour

2 teaspoons baking powder

2 teaspoons salt

1 teaspoon baking soda

1½ cups buttermilk

2 large eggs, beaten

Preheat oven to 450°F.

In a 10-inch cast-iron skillet, cook bacon over medium-high heat, turning often, until crispy, 7 to 8 minutes. Using a slotted spoon, transfer bacon to a paper towel–lined plate to drain (save for another use); reserve bacon grease in the pan.

Add butter to skillet and let melt.

In a large bowl, whisk together cornmeal, flour, baking powder, salt, and baking soda. Add buttermilk and eggs and stir until just combined.

Swirl skillet until fully coated with butter and bacon grease. Pour in the batter and place skillet in the oven. Bake until cornbread is browned on top and edges pull away from sides of pan, 20 to 25 minutes.

Top with pats of butter, slice, and serve hot.

Hot-Water Cornbread

Cook time: 20 minutes | Makes 12 servings

- 1¾ cups plus 2 tablespoons finely ground cornmeal, plus more as needed
- 2 tablespoons baking powder
- 2 teaspoons granulated sugar
- ½ teaspoon kosher salt
- 2 cups boiling water
- 2 tablespoons salted butter, plus more for serving
- 1 large egg yolk, beaten
- 1½ cups vegetable oil, for frying

In a large bowl, use a fork to stir together cornmeal, baking powder, sugar, and salt. In a separate medium bowl, stir boiling water and butter together until butter is melted.

Add beaten egg yolk to ½ cup of the butter mixture, then slowly pour mixture into the dry ingredients. Continue adding ½ cup at a time of the butter mixture to the dry ingredients, until cornmeal is the texture of wet sand and is moistened enough to form a damp patty. If mixture is still dry, add 1 tablespoon at a time of hot water; and if too wet, stir in up to 1 tablespoon more cornmeal.

Heat oil in a high-sided 10-inch cast-iron skillet over medium-high heat until it begins to ripple. Form cornmeal batter into 12 patties about 2 inches wide and 1 inch thick. Working in batches to avoid crowding the pan, add patties to hot oil and cook, turning halfway through, until golden brown on each side, 2 to 3 minutes per side.

Transfer patties to a paper towel–lined plate to drain. Serve hot with butter.

Gumbo

Cook time: 4 hours | Makes 6 to 8 servings

- 1½ pounds bone-in beef shank
- ½ pound boneless short rib, cut into 1½- to 2-inch cubes
- 1 pound stew meat, cut into 1½- to 2-inch cubes
- ½ teaspoon salt
- 1½ teaspoons freshly ground black pepper, divided
- 7 tablespoons extra-virgin olive oil, divided
- 2 medium onions, 1 rough chopped, 1 finely chopped
- 2 medium carrots, peeled, 1 rough chopped, 1 finely chopped
- 2 stalks celery, 1 rough chopped, 1 finely chopped
- 1 pound okra, tops and ends removed, sliced on an angle into 1-inch pieces
- 1 pound andouille sausage, cut on an angle into ½-inch slices
- 1 tablespoon butter
- 4 tablespoons flour
- 1 green bell pepper, seeded and finely chopped
- 3 cloves garlic, smashed
- 1 (14.5-ounce) can diced tomatoes
- 2 tablespoons Cajun seasoning
- 1 teaspoon dried thyme
- 2 bay leaves
- 8 ounces lump crabmeat
- Steamed rice, for serving

Season shank, short rib, and stew meat with salt and ½ teaspoon black pepper.

In a large Dutch oven or stockpot, heat 2 tablespoons olive oil over high heat. Add shanks to pot and cook until crisp and browned, about 4 minutes per side. Transfer to a plate.

Add 1 tablespoon more oil to the pot. In batches, sear short rib until crisp and browned on all sides, about 6 minutes. Transfer to a plate. Add stew meat and sear until browned on all sides, about 6 minutes. Add beef shanks back to the pot, along with 8 cups water, roughly chopped onions, roughly chopped carrots, and roughly chopped celery; bring to a boil. Reduce heat and let simmer, uncovered, for 1½ to 2 hours, skimming any impurities off the top with a strainer.

Meanwhile, bring a separate large pot of salted water to a boil. Add okra and blanch for 45 seconds. Drain and run under cool water until okra is cold and some of the slime has rinsed away. Set aside.

Transfer meat from the pot onto a work surface, then strain beef stock into a large bowl, discarding any solids. When cool enough to handle, pick meat from shank bones and set aside. Discard the fat and bones.

Bring the Dutch oven back to high heat and add 2 tablespoons of oil. Add the andouille and cook, stirring occasionally, until browned, 3 to 5 minutes. Using a slotted spoon, transfer andouille to a plate.

Add remaining 2 tablespoons of oil to the Dutch oven, along with butter and flour. Cook, stirring often, until flour is deep brown in color, about 5 minutes. Add finely chopped onions, carrots, celery, and bell pepper. Cook, stirring often, until vegetables are softened, about 6 minutes. Add garlic and stir until aromatic, about 2 minutes more. Stir in tomatoes, Cajun seasoning, thyme, remaining 1 teaspoon of black pepper, and bay leaves, and stir to combine.

Add beef stock and shank meat, stew meat, and short rib with any juices back to the pot. Let everything simmer for 30 minutes. Stir in okra and andouille, and simmer until thickened and okra is tender, about 30 minutes more, adding more water or stock if mixture gets too dry. Remove bay leaves. Stir in crabmeat. Adjust seasoning to taste.

Serve over steamed rice.

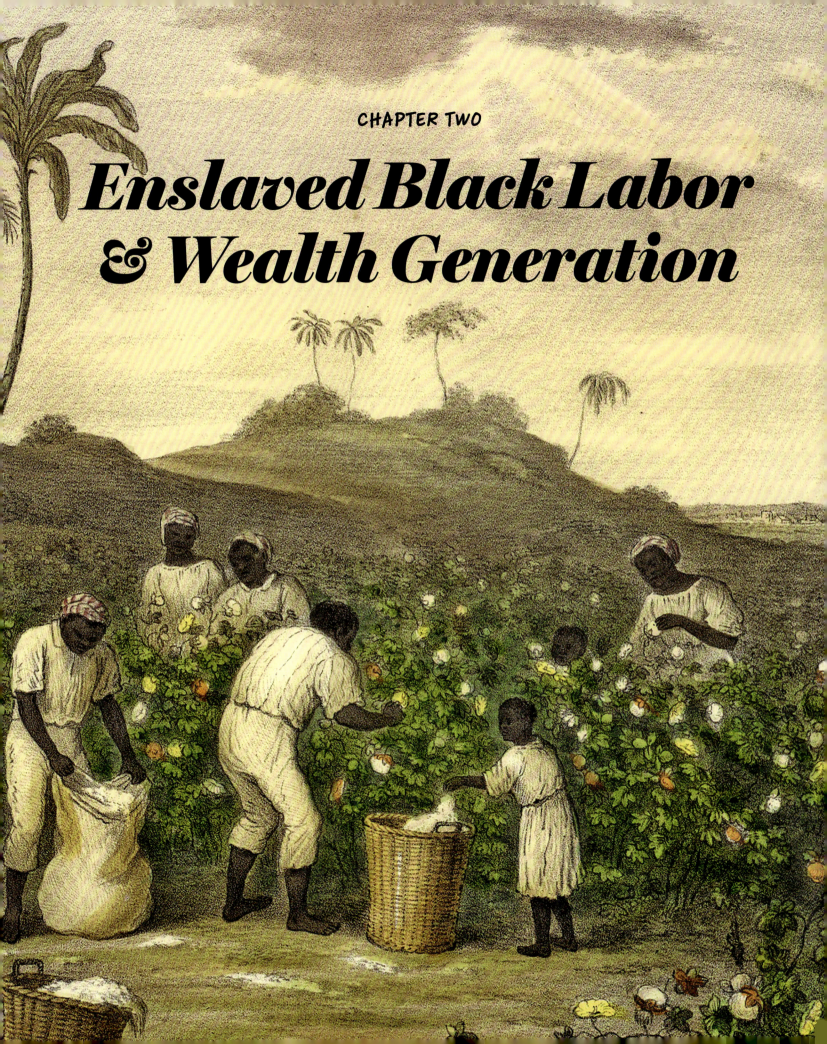

CHAPTER TWO

Enslaved Black Labor & Wealth Generation

The Building of America's Food System

In 2023, I spent a week in South Carolina and Georgia learning about the Gullah Geechee, descendants of enslaved Africans brought to the lower Atlantic region in what is now the United States. Over time, these enslaved peoples from West and Central Africa developed a unique culture and language in their new home while maintaining elements of their heritage from their ancestral communities. Gullah Geechee cuisine evolved in this environment, blending African culinary practices with new inputs. The Gullah Geechee story offers one example of how Black labor, expertise, and cultural practices came to influence foodways in America.

My experience learning about the Gullah Geechee encouraged me to look closely at American history, even the painful and shameful parts. On St. Helena Island in South Carolina I sat in a praise house, a small wooden shack more than 100 years old that was used as a segregated place of worship during enslavement. There, I listened to local pastors trace the importance of such sites for their communities. As they did, they emphasized that though American history is often dark, to understand the United States we have to acknowledge where we come from. That was a message repeated again and again on different stops of that trip. The history of the Gullah Geechee is part of the foundational story of the United States, a nation founded on colonization and slavery and where new cultures were created from many disparate parts. As painful as that history is, it's one we shouldn't look away from, and one that has shaped the U.S. today.

That history guides this exploration of food as well. To trace the enduring contributions of Black peoples to American cuisine, we have to start at the beginning, which encompasses enslavement, violence, displacement, and immense horrors. It's a history that begins with a system of forced labor and human trafficking for the sake of generating wealth and fueling profits. That's where this journey starts, but as you'll see, it also encompasses incredible innovation, resilience, and creativity.

OPPOSITE: **Martin Luther King, Jr., stayed at Gantt Cottage on St. Helena Island, South Carolina, when working on his "I Have a Dream" speech.**
PAGES 40–41: **"Cotton Plantation, Progress of Cotton No. 1" is the first of 12 lithographs from 1840 detailing life on a cotton plantation.**

Colonial Expansion & Enslavement: A Brief Overview

The story of the Transatlantic Slave Trade is a complex tale of colonization and expansion. Armed with new knowledge brought by 15th-century exploration, European powers raced to lay claim to land and resources in North and South America, as well as the Caribbean. Incredible profits and power were at stake as colonial forces sought to expand their areas of control and extract resources. Initially, Spain and Portugal laid claim to parts of the American continents. By the 1700s a host of European powers were engaged in the struggle for territory, setting up British, Danish, Dutch, Norwegian, Russian, Scottish, and Swedish colonies. This brutal race for land, resources, and profits fueled the Transatlantic Slave Trade.

The work of colonial expansion and claiming new lands required immense labor. Clearing trees and plants to make way for agricultural production, producing goods, and developing the structures of these new societies required resources, especially people. As colonial expansion decimated Indigenous populations through disease and conflict, enslaved Africans became a means to that end.

The Portuguese enslaved Africans and brought them to Europe to perform labor in the 15th century. By the mid-1500s the Spanish had also made the trip across the Atlantic, transporting enslaved Africans to North American colonies. Other European powers began engaging in the trade, and soon a brutal forced mass migration began.

The vast majority of the enslaved were taken from West and Central Africa, from coastal and connected interior regions—today's Senegal, Gambia, Mali, Guinea-Bissau, Angola, Congo, Ghana, Nigeria, Cameroon, and beyond. This

Shackles were used as torturous tools of oppression during the Transatlantic Slave Trade.

was in part due to expediency; those regions were most accessible to the forts and enslavement prisons along the western African coastline frequented by slave-trading vessels. This system of sourcing was also an economic strategy—enslaved peoples from those regions had prized agricultural experience. They were sought after for their familiarity with cultivating rice, indigo, tobacco, and corn, as well as livestock farming and other specialized labor needs.

From the coast of Africa, traders would depart for the colonies with their cargoes of enslaved Africans. This Middle Passage could take months. Enslaved Africans were separated by sex and chained in cramped and unsanitary conditions belowdecks for extended periods of time—brought above for food only in small groups to prevent mutiny, as enslaved peoples typically outnumbered the crew. The heat belowdecks was so intense that ship doctors would faint when tending the sick. Disease and infection were rampant. Many died from

Enslaved Africans were chained, whipped, and beaten before boarding ships for a terrifying, forced journey across the Atlantic.

82

INVENTORY OF NEGROES upon Berry Plain Plantation 1st Feb. 1855 / Plantation, taken 31st December, 18 / Manager

No.	Names	Age	Occupation	Value	1858-9 No. Value	Names	Age	Occupation	Value
1	Thornton	58		$100	100	George Son of Betty, born March 1857		Polly daughter of Sally born Apl 1st 1858	
2	Leannah	44	Cook	300	300				
3	Andrew	48		350	350				
4	Betty	17		700	800	Henry. Second Son born October 1858			
5	Sally gone	14	to Yankees	550	800				
6	Frank	35		700	850				
7	Bob	34		700	1000				
8	Magnus	26	Dinsroom servant	1000	1100				
9	Ann	20		400	—	Jef Davis Son of Betty, born 15th Nov. 1861			
10	Judy	10	Nurse	450	900				
11	Milford	3	Gone to Yankees	300	650				
12	Sam	56	Drayman	750	200 Sold				
13	Jinny	48	Washer	350	350				
14	Matilda	35		300	350				
15	Sidney gone	6	to Yankees	300	500				
16	Alex	2		175	400				
17	Anthony	19		825	Sold for 1270				$7735
18	Martha	7 months		Died 1856	$8550				
	Ann's Baby	2 week		Died do					

1859
Sam Sold — $200.
Anthony do. 1370

dysentery, smallpox, or other ailments. Some accounts describe a "melancholy" when enslaved peoples lost the will to live and subsequently died. The death rate on the Middle Passage is estimated to have ranged from 10 to 40 percent of those who were forced onto the journey. The dead were unceremoniously thrown overboard.

At the end of this long and dangerous journey, enslaved Africans were sold in the colonies, where they were sought after as forced laborers. Meanwhile, the ships, now emptied of their human cargo, headed back to Europe carrying the products of enslaved labor such as tobacco, sugar, rice, and cotton. Though this trade is often described as triangular, it was in fact global: North American colonies connected with the Caribbean to exchange goods and enslaved peoples, Caribbean goods made their way back to Africa to be used as currency to traffic more enslaved peoples, and goods from Asia were also regularly used in this system of trade. Those who successfully completed the multistop trading trip reaped immense profits.

It's estimated that in three centuries more than 10 million people were forcibly transported from Africa, trafficked for labor, and forced to endure the Middle Passage. Of those millions of enslaved Africans, an estimated 400,000 were brought to the North American colonies and later to the independent United States of America.

In 1619 Africans arrived in Point Comfort (known today as Fort Monroe) in Hampton, Virginia, marking the first *documented* arrival of African peoples to a permanent English settlement in North America. Their numbers were small, initially in the dozens. They arrived at a colony that was less than 20 years old, one that was still negotiating with Indigenous groups who inhabited the same territory. Over time a racial caste system was codified and chattel slavery cemented. "By 1670, custom and law insisted that children were slaves if their mothers were slaves, that enslaved Africans were to be treated as rights-less, perpetual outsiders (even if they converted to Christianity), that they could be whipped to labor, and that they could be sold and moved," writes Edward E. Baptist in *The Half Has Never Been Told: Slavery and the Making of American Capitalism*.

By 1775 one-fifth, or 20 percent, of the population in the 13 colonies was enslaved. After the American Revolution, through both purchased and forcible land acquisition, the fledgling nation claimed more territory from Indigenous peoples, as well as from Britain, France, Spain, and Canada. The institution of slavery expanded with the growing country, moving into South Carolina, Georgia, Kentucky, and beyond. The expansion of slavery was a contentious domestic political issue: Enslaved populations contributed greatly to states' power

> "Yet throughout the colonial history of the country, many of the hands that turned the spits in the massive hearths and brought the tankards filled with ale to the lusty patriots and founding fathers were black."
>
> —JESSICA B. HARRIS, *HIGH ON THE HOG: A CULINARY JOURNEY FROM AFRICA TO AMERICA*

OPPOSITE: A page from the "Inventory of Negroes at Berry Plain Plantation," written in 1855, lists the enslaved peoples living and working on the estate.

> *No matter that some stories note kind and benevolent "masters"—enslaved peoples still lacked basic rights. They were sold, their families were torn apart, and they were subject to brutal violence that some historians characterize as a regime of systematic torture.*

OPPOSITE: Enslaved families—like the one depicted in this 1861 drawing—were often cruelly separated during slave auctions.

despite the sad irony that enslaved peoples couldn't vote and weren't considered citizens. Violent conflicts over the legality and morality of slavery took place, even while the institution steadily expanded in the South and West. This lasted until 1861, when tension between Confederate and Union forces began the Civil War.

And though importation of enslaved peoples from abroad was officially banned in 1808, the enslaved population continued to grow in the United States, fueled by a population increase and an illicit slave trade. By 1860, census records place the domestic slave population at almost four million people, about 8 percent of the total population.

Labor Conditions & Treatment of the Enslaved

The purpose of this book isn't to expound on the well-documented horrors of the system of racialized chattel slavery that persisted for nearly 90 years after America declared its independence. However, because this period of American history has frequently been whitewashed, a note about the treatment of enslaved Africans is necessary before we begin to dig into how enslaved labor impacted the development of American cuisine.

In North America, the treatment, work regimes, and availability of food for enslaved Africans varied from location to location, plantation to plantation. Slavery was a complex social institution: There are some accounts of enslavers who treated enslaved peoples "well," though many did not. Ultimately, "slaves remained slaves," writes Eugene D. Genovese in *Roll, Jordan, Roll: The World the Slaves Made*. "They could be bought and sold like any other property and were subject to despotic personal power." No matter that some stories note kind and benevolent "masters"—enslaved peoples still lacked basic rights. They were sold, their families were torn apart, and they were subject to brutal violence that some historians characterize as a regime of systematic torture. Women were often raped and the targets of sexual violence; many were chronically malnourished. And of course, there was little to no recourse for mistreatment perpetrated by white people or by the larger society as a whole. That was the system in which enslaved peoples lived and worked.

Throughout this horrific period of American history, enslaved peoples were inextricably entwined with economic development, agriculture, cooking, and food service. Black peoples cultivated gardens, harvested crops, herded and slaughtered animals, processed food, cooked for themselves and for their enslavers, and did so much more. Through their labor, both explicitly and implicitly, Black peoples imparted knowledge, skills, and preferences on the development of early American cuisine.

Not Just Labor

◆◇◆◇◆◇◆

Enslaved Africans were brought to the Americas for labor. They grew, tended, processed, and preserved tobacco, rice, indigo, cotton, sugar, corn, and a host of other crops. Agricultural labor, and the goods it produced, formed the primary pillar of the colonial economy, generating immense wealth for enslavers and industries. In antebellum North America, slave-grown rice exports made Charleston, South Carolina, one of the world's wealthiest cities. In 1840, the value of slave-grown cotton reached an estimated $8 million, creating a class of white millionaires and spawning related industries. As a whole, enslaved labor was vital to the early economic growth of North American colonies and the United States.

Beyond agricultural production, enslaved peoples were often tasked with food preparation. This labor was typically designed to impress and uphold the social standing of the plantocracy class. Skilled enslaved cooks were artisans and considered valuable assets. Most enslaved cooks were women, though men also fulfilled the role at times. During the early North American colonial project and later in the newly independent United States, nearly every household of means had Black cooks, butlers, and servants charged with managing food service and entertainment, including preparing and serving food for guests.

On large southern plantations, owned by a small minority of southern farmers who wielded outsize political and social power, this likely involved a team of enslaved laborers working in a kitchen building set apart from the primary residence to protect against possible fire damage. Historical accounts of lavish plantation meals note dishes such as macaroni pie, bread pudding, ice creams, grilled fowl, roast turkey, boiled ham, oysters, venison, and turtle soup. On smaller farms and in cities, limited space and/or means ensured that enslaved Africans lived, worked, and cooked in close quarters with small-

The tag of an enslaved person from Charleston, South Carolina, in 1815

50 • AMERICAN SOUL

A detached kitchen—perhaps the oldest in Louisiana—at the Whitney Plantation near Wallace in St. John the Baptist Parish

holder enslavers. On both large and small operations, Black hands often stirred pots, created meals, and imparted their preferences on the seasoning and composition of dishes.

While most of the Black population in antebellum North America was enslaved, free Black men and women were also deeply entwined with the food space. Food service and catering were some of the few professional avenues open to Black peoples. Free Black laborers and entrepreneurs worked as peddlers and caterers, and were also part of the culinary elite in places such as Pennsylvania, New York, and Connecticut. They raised and sold livestock, brought produce and foodstuffs to market for sale, and built thriving food businesses.

Food offered avenues for economic advancement, and for some even a means to purchase their freedom or land. In Charleston in the early 1800s,

members of the free Black community owned confectionery shops and worked as street hawkers, butchers, and pastry sellers. In the North, enslaved, indentured, and free Black peoples also often worked in food service.

Black labor even made a lasting impact on the livestock industry. Americans consume, on average, more beef than people in any other nation, and in 2020 the beef industry produced more than 27 billion pounds of meat. How did beef come to play such a pivotal role in the American economy and cuisine?

In part because colonization offered vast lands for industry expansion and, paired with unpaid (forced) or cheap Black labor, allowed the industry in the United States to offer affordable meat that became widely accessible. Historical records and slave narratives demonstrate how important Black labor and knowledge were for the fledgling livestock industry in the antebellum South. Some legal codes even required that slaves be present to tend livestock in order for their enslavers to qualify for land grants.

Post emancipation, the livestock skills of enslaved peoples provided avenues for employment in cattle drives. In fact, though you rarely see them depicted in the media as such, Black peoples made up a significant portion of America's cowboys—up to 25 percent of the industry by some estimates. Historical accounts note numerous famed Black cowboys, cattle ropers, and even ranch owners who left their mark on the cattle industry.

Plants Cross the Atlantic

Local plant matter and foodstuffs were loaded onto slave-trading ships in Africa as supplies for the Middle Passage. These provisions served as a means for protecting the financial investment made by traders and enslavers, brought on board to keep valuable enslaved cargo alive for the journey. One British merchant is estimated to have made more than one million British pounds (in today's currency) on a single slave-trading journey.

Foods that were acquired for provisioning included large quantities of African staples. Animals that could be slaughtered on the Middle Passage, along with animal feed, were also purchased. Those supplies were selected in part out of convenience, but also because it was believed that enslaved Africans would be more likely to survive the journey if they were fed somewhat familiar foods. Often, enslaved African women were purchased as part of the provisioning process and were made to prepare food while on board the ships.

"African species were likely put aboard every single ship that crossed the Middle Passage," write Judith A. Carney and Richard Nicholas Rosomoff in *In the Shadow of Slavery: Africa's Botanical Legacy in the Atlantic World*. Examples of endemic plants include the kola nut, which is indigenous to West Africa. The

> "African newcomers not only transformed themselves into New World African Americans but also became vitally important agents in shaping the culinary tastes and a host of other customs of European Americans and Native Americans in the entire hemisphere."
>
> —ROBERT L. HALL, "FOOD CROPS, MEDICINAL PLANTS, AND THE ATLANTIC SLAVE TRADE" IN *AFRICAN AMERICAN FOODWAYS: EXPLORATIONS OF HISTORY AND CULTURE*

OPPOSITE: A woman holds a cotton hoe in New Madrid County, Missouri, in 1938.

kola nut was prized for flavoring water, which was stored in casks for long periods of time, susceptible to bacterial growth during the journey, and could taste foul.

According to William C. Whit in his chapter, "Soul Food as Cultural Creation," in *African American Foodways: Explorations of History and Culture*, "It is generally accepted that the following came across the Atlantic with slaves in one way or another: rice, yams, millet, cowpeas, black-eyed peas, sesame seeds, sorghum (Guinea corn), oranges, avocados, various bananas and plantains, okra, spinach, mustard greens, eggplant, cassava, maize, some squashes, sweet potatoes, peanuts, chilies, coconuts, and a variety of roots and tubers."

In addition to provisioning done by the enslavers, stories abound of enslaved Africans tucking grains and seeds into their hair for the journey across the Atlantic as they were being sold away. Though these stories are largely believed to be

Fresh kola nuts, an endemic plant of Africa

folklore, they "link plant transfers to the Transatlantic Slave Trade, African initiative and the dietary preferences of the enslaved," say Carney and Rosomoff.

Ultimately, as part of the Transatlantic Slave Trade numerous plants and foods made their way from Africa to the Americas. Some naming conventions reflect this origin: The Guinea squash (now more commonly called eggplant) and Guinea fowl reflect the term used for certain West African territories at the time, for example.

Along with the plants and seeds that made the journey to North America, the Transatlantic Slave Trade also carried the people who knew how to cultivate and harvest those crops: Enslaved peoples brought with them generations of agricultural knowledge; they were farmers, herders, and skilled craftspeople. Their knowledge was essential to the successful transition of plants and crops that were new to colonial communities and are today a staple of American cuisine.

Transmitting Knowledge Systems

At the start of the Transatlantic Slave Trade, African peoples had histories of plant and animal domestication that went back thousands of years, and they were already thoroughly connected to the global trade. The ancient Silk Road intersected part of the African continent and connected it to Europe, Asia, and the Middle East. In addition, African peoples adapted wild plants to their needs, drawing on the rich variety of indigenous plants, including yams, watermelons, millet, hibiscus, cowpeas, kola nuts, and coffee. Donkeys, an African domesticate, were commonly used for labor in the Old World. This was all part of the rich history mined by the slave trade.

It may never be possible to trace on which slave-trading ship and to what specific landing point each African plant made its way into the colonies, but raw material arrived alongside enslaved Africans, who, in their home countries, were herders, blacksmiths, farmers, rice growers, and craftspeople with lifetimes of experience. Their skills were essential in the process of agricultural experimentation that was ongoing in the colonies in the Americas.

Producing adequate food was of the utmost concern for the North American colonies. More than half the settlers in Jamestown died in the winter of 1609–1610 during a period called the Starving Time, a result of violence, disease, drought, and poor harvest. The Carolina colony was also in search of a profitable crop and relied on foodstuffs from England in its early days. Slave knowledge and labor were vital to successful harvests and survival.

The first colonial records of plants of African origin often point to gardens kept by enslaved Africans, termed "Negro plantations." When permitted, or at times in secret, enslaved peoples kept gardens in individual plots or in larger

> Black cooks made their mark on early American cuisine. They became known for an almost mythical cooking prowess, and through spicing, culinary techniques, the use of specific ingredients, and their very presence in the kitchen added to and changed the development of American food.

> *Over time, as Black peoples stirred cooking pots, served meals, created and re-created recipes, grew and traded produce, and made new homes, they passed along some of their cooking traditions, which were echoed in recipes, on dining tables, and throughout foodways of America.*

OPPOSITE: Nathaniel Gibbs's painting depicts two unidentified enslaved peoples tending a garden.

communal provision grounds that they tended late at night or when granted a day off, typically Sunday. The food they grew in those garden plots broke up the monotony of imposed rations, allowed them to regain some control over their diets, and ultimately ensured survival. At times they were able to sell excess produce or products such as eggs, enabling them some semblance of financial independence.

Historical accounts from the Caribbean, South American, and North American colonies explicitly credit enslaved peoples and their gardens for the introduction of plants such as okra, pigeon peas, sorghum, and millet. Accounts also suggest that the knowledge of how to grow and utilize these plants was passed from enslaved Black peoples to whites as well.

Consider cowpeas, of which the field pea and black-eyed pea are common varietals. Cowpeas originate from West Africa and are believed to have made it to North America during the slave trade. There, they made their way into the gardens of enslaved peoples and eventually into the awareness and onto the tables of enslavers. Soon cowpeas became a staple crop in the Carolina colony and were even exported to Caribbean islands for use as food rations for enslaved laborers on sugar plantations. Ultimately, cowpeas were widely consumed by Black and white peoples in the United States. Today, field pea and black-eyed pea varietals remain an important part of traditional Black—and more broadly southern—New Year's food traditions, retaining their importance in the modern era as part of dishes such as hoppin' John (see recipe on p. 265).

Creating New Food Systems

As Africans who were forcibly brought to North America continued their food traditions, adapted to a new country, and were exposed to new cooking methods by European and Native influences, a process of creolization ensued, one in which a new cuisine was built from multiple cultural inputs, including those of Black peoples.

In plantation kitchens, in inns and taverns, at catered events, and beyond, Black cooks made their mark on early American cuisine. They became known for an almost mythical cooking prowess, and through spicing, culinary techniques, the use of specific ingredients, and their very presence in the kitchen added to and changed the development of American food. As culinary historian Karen Hess writes in her introduction to *What Mrs. Fisher Knows About Old Southern Cooking: Soups, Pickles, Preserves, Etc.*: "Even when they conscientiously followed the recipe as read aloud by the mistress, certain subtle changes were bound to take place. The Chinese call this phenomenon *wok presence*, and it occurs even when cooks trained in the same kitchen make the same dish,

following the same recipe, even in well-run restaurants. It is all the more dramatic when cultural boundaries are crossed."

Early southern cookbooks illustrate this long process of culinary osmosis. Mary Randolph's *The Virginia Housewife,* published in 1824, was the first cookbook to depart from British traditions and showcase the diverse influences of early American cuisine. It contains a recipe titled "Egg plant," also known as Guinea squash at the time, a moniker denoting the ingredient's African genesis. Other recipes utilize African ingredients including okra and field peas. Randolph's field pea fritter is particularly indicative of how foodways of enslaved peoples had already begun to make their way into the canon of southern and American cuisine: The recipe takes an ingredient that likely arrived as slave provisions and prepares it in a manner similar to akara, a fritter made from field peas that originated in what is now Nigeria. The cookbook also includes pepper pot, a stew with debated origins that's history and arrival in North America are deeply entwined with the slave trade and Black labor.

Lowcountry okra soup, a classic comfort food of Gullah Geechee ancestry

Focus On: Food as a Means of Control & Investment

Food is an important vehicle for memory, culture, and community. In the case of Black history in the colonies and the United States, it was also a tool for social control.

Food and water consumption on the journey across the Atlantic to the Americas was strictly monitored. At times enslaved Africans would refuse to eat, likely a result of melancholy at being trafficked away from their homes and as a way to reclaim agency on the journey. Refusing food was often met with extreme violence including whippings, being forcibly burned, or throwing children overboard to encourage reticent mothers to eat. A device called a speculum oris was also used on recalcitrant enslaved Africans to pry open their jaws for forced feeding.

In the colonies, food continued to serve as a means of control. Rations provided to enslaved laborers were often scarce and monotonous. Generally, corn and pork were dietary staples. Historical accounts show how enslavers' views on food and rations differed, often connected to a desire to coerce or encourage enslaved laborers: Some felt that keeping slaves well fed was paramount to protecting their financial investment and their resale value, which could make up a significant portion of enslavers' net worth. Others carefully monitored rations and even kept them low as a way to keep enslaved laborers cooperative. Other accounts suggest that some enslavers did not provide adequate rations out of carelessness, malice, or financial pressures. In times of scarcity, rations were often cut to save money.

It is clear from the scale of food theft noted in historical accounts that many enslaved peoples suffered from malnutrition and hunger. In addition, enslaved peoples had high rates of illnesses related to nutritional deficits such anemia and scurvy. *Born in Slavery: Slave Narratives From the Federal Writers' Project, 1936–1938* (often called simply "The Slave Narratives") collected more than 2,300 accounts from formerly enslaved peoples and offers insight into how closely connected labor and food were for those enslaved. Some narratives note that children and the elderly were deliberately fed less or at times left to fend for themselves, as rations were tied to their ability to work. Narratives of children note that they suffered persistent hunger. Some enslavers also offered incentives such as additional rations to encourage young children into labor. In short: The more or less useful an enslaved person was as a laborer, the more or less food they may have been given access to.

The Carolina Housewife, published nearly three decades later, contains even more recipes that utilize ingredients or preparations tied to Black foodways. Those recipes include okra soup, groundnut soup, benne soup, pepper pot, New Orleans gumbo, hoppin' John, and Guinea squash (eggplant). *The Carolina Housewife* also has recipes that rely on ingredients grown predominantly by Black enslaved labor, such as rice, and dishes such as Macaroni à la Sauce Blanche, a French-style macaroni and cheese popularized in the United States through the labor of enslaved Black cooks.

Over time, as Black peoples stirred cooking pots, served meals, created and re-created recipes, grew and traded produce, and made new homes, they passed along some of their cooking traditions, which were echoed in recipes, on dining tables, and throughout foodways of America.

The Building Blocks of Southern Cuisine

Black peoples impacted the development of broader American foodways in a variety of ways that still affect American culinary practices today. That influence shines most brightly in southern cuisine. • Slavery was present in all 13 original colonies and remained a widespread phenomenon in the early days of the nation. However, over time slavery became concentrated in the American South owing to a variety of factors:

The northern states voted to abolish slavery in 1804, though some states took longer than others to end the practice. In 1808, importation of enslaved peoples from abroad was prohibited, though an illicit trade persisted. Once the international slave trade slowed, demand for labor spiked in the South as the cotton industry grew, and enslaved peoples from within the United States were used to fill the gap.

As a result, historians estimate that more than one million Black enslaved laborers were transported to the Deep South to work on cotton plantations between the late 1700s and the start of the Civil War. This second forced migration separated families, tore apart communities, and concentrated enslaved populations in the South.

Though the exact geographic definition of the area varies, the black belt of the American South is so named for its fertile black soil—the locus of cotton production in the antebellum period. It also became strongly associated with Black peoples: In the 1800s, Black populations in the black belt regions of Alabama, Mississippi, and Georgia outnumbered white populations. Southern states outside the black belt also had large enslaved populations that outnumbered white ones.

60 • AMERICAN SOUL

"Cotton Pickers," a 1945 oil painting by Thomas Hart Benton, portrays Black laborers picking cotton.

Creating Southern Cuisine

Given the concentration of Black peoples in the region, the antebellum American South was an area where they often did the growing, sourcing, selling, buying, trading, and preparing of food. Whether acting in service of the plantocracy class or for their own personal needs, Black peoples made an indelible mark on southern cuisine. We can look toward common ingredients in southern cuisine to begin to excavate this rich history.

Okra

Okra is indigenous to Africa, though its exact genesis within the continent is debated. It was brought to the colonies via the Transatlantic Slave Trade. In North America, it was often grown by enslaved workers and used by Black peoples to thicken soups and stews, mirroring traditional uses in West African cooking. Over time, okra made its way onto the planters' tables and into the earliest American cookbooks, such as *The Virginia Housewife* and *The Carolina*

A bundle of fresh peanuts pulled straight from the ground

Housewife. Both books were written in the 1800s by wealthy white women of the aristocratic planter class who had enslaved staff, likely including cooks. Today, okra is used in a variety of ways in southern cuisine, and is often stewed with tomatoes, battered and fried, or used in gumbo.

Peanuts

Peanuts are indigenous to South America and were introduced to the African continent before the Transatlantic Slave Trade began. They became a staple crop in West Africa, often used in soups and stews, and were brought to North America through the slave trade. Peanuts are another food that crossed the Middle Passage, likely as provisions, as they could be eaten raw or cooked and kept for long periods without spoilage. In North America, enslaved peoples grew peanuts in subsistence gardens, while white communities did not immediately embrace the crop. Colonial accounts note that enslaved peoples spread knowledge of uses of the peanut, and over time peanuts were embraced in the American South and beyond. In the 1800s, roasted peanuts were a common snack in cities, and by the 1900s peanut oil was a major commercial commodity. Today, peanuts remain a significant part of southern cuisine, often eaten as a snack, such as boiled peanuts, and used in treats such as peanut brittle.

Crop Migrations

Many indigenous African food crops migrated on the same ships as enslaved Africans. Plenty of these foods, including okra and black-eyed peas, were cultivated and used by Black cooks and are still identified as southern crops. Those same cooks also used African kola nuts as flavoring centuries before they were turned into the quintessential American drink, Coca-Cola. Millet and sorghum fed enslaved peoples on the long Middle Passage, and sorghum later became a favorite American sweetener. Coffee took a less direct route, making its way from Ethiopia to the Middle East and Europe before landing in the Americas.

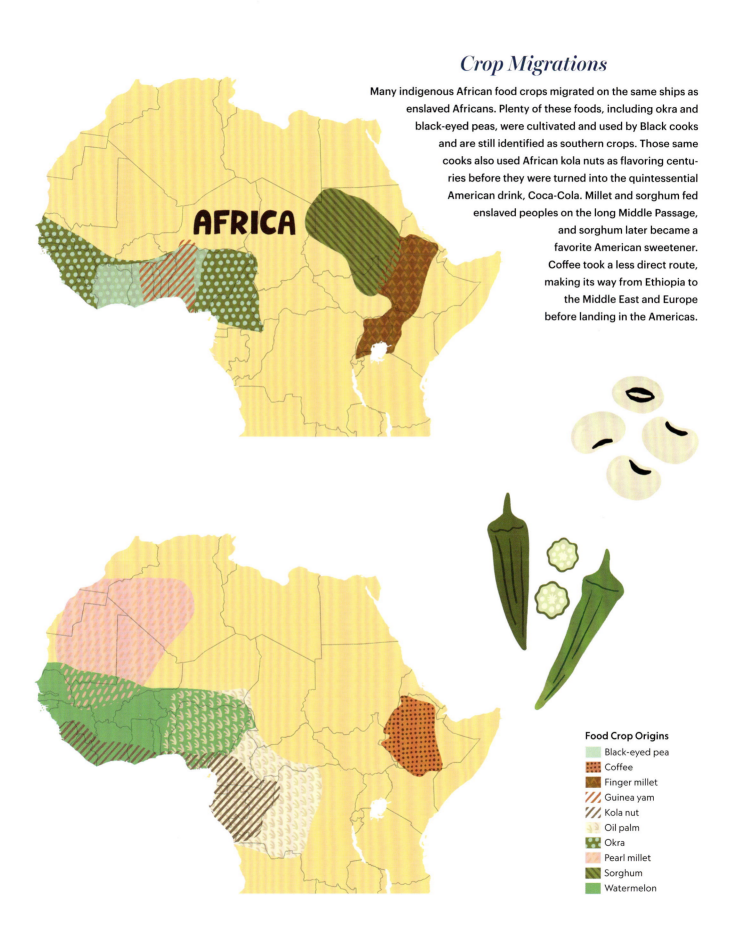

Food Crop Origins
- Black-eyed pea
- Coffee
- Finger millet
- Guinea yam
- Kola nut
- Oil palm
- Okra
- Pearl millet
- Sorghum
- Watermelon

THE BUILDING BLOCKS OF SOUTHERN CUISINE

> "Southern whites, threatened by blacks' newfound freedom, responded by making the fruit a symbol of black people's perceived uncleanliness, laziness, childishness, and unwanted public presence."
> —WILLIAM R. BLACK, "HOW WATERMELONS BECAME A RACIST TROPE," THE ATLANTIC

OPPOSITE: Watermelon is indigenous to Africa; despite centuries of stereotypical tropes, the fruit is widely eaten today.

Catfish

West Africans utilized a species of catfish native to the region in a variety of ways. Black peoples continued this tradition in the colonies and the United States. Some whites refused to eat catfish, as it was so strongly associated with Black peoples that it was considered dirty and inappropriate for white consumption. But Mary Randolph's 1824 *The Virginia Housewife* has a recipe for catfish soup, which notes that it is "an excellent dish for those who have not imbibed a needless prejudice against those delicious fish"—possibly hinting at this stigma.

Today, the fish has largely outgrown its reputation as solely a Black dish common at fish fries and soul food restaurants. Catfish is now widely eaten and served on menus as a southern staple. This mirrors the progression of southern cuisine in which the "wall of culinary segregation gradually disintegrated over the centuries as signature ingredients of the African diaspora stealthily made their way into white kitchens and onto white tables," as Judith A. Carney and Richard Nicholas Rosomoff discuss in *In the Shadow of Slavery*.

Watermelon

Watermelon is indigenous to Africa and believed to have arrived in America with the slave trade. Enslaved peoples grew and cultivated watermelons in their gardens. After emancipation, Black folks continued to grow watermelon, often selling it and using it as a tool for economic advancement. "Southern whites, threatened by blacks' newfound freedom, responded by making the fruit a symbol of black people's perceived uncleanliness, laziness, childishness, and unwanted public presence," notes William R. Black in the *Atlantic* article "How Watermelons Became a Racist Trope."

After the Great Migration, Black vendors in Harlem and other northern American cities continued to incorporate watermelon into their entrepreneurship, selling pickled watermelon rinds (see recipe on p. 136) among other southern foods. Today, despite persistent stigma associated with the Black community, watermelon remains widely eaten in the South and beyond.

Beyond African Foodways

Black peoples helped set the culinary standards of early southern cuisine, whether those touchstones were rooted in Black traditions or not. Black cooks on plantations, as well as free Black bakers and caterers in the South, created a name for themselves perfecting dishes ranging from okra stews to extravagant cakes and recipes rooted in European traditions.

A Domestic Cook Book: Containing a Careful Selection of Useful Receipts for the Kitchen, published in 1866 by Malinda Russell, a free Black woman, draws on her

Nat Fuller, Eliza Lee, and other chefs shopped at the public market in Charleston in the 1800s, as depicted in "Section Old Market."

experiences in the American South before migrating to Michigan. Russell's cookbook incorporates techniques and influences from a variety of traditions. It contains numerous recipes for delicacies including sponge cake, shortcake, and cream puffs (all from European culinary traditions), as well as savory dishes and methods for salves, ointments, and other household items. Russell's work, the first cookbook published in the United States by a Black woman, demonstrates her breadth of culinary experience from her career as a lady's companion and running a boardinghouse. It's also a reflection of the labors and services of Black cooks, predominantly women, that helped define southern cuisine and hospitality.

Charleston, South Carolina, offers plenty of examples of the breadth of Black culinary expertise and contributions in the antebellum South. South Carolina's enslaved population outnumbered whites through the 18th century while Charleston served as one of the nation's largest slave-trading hubs. In the late 1700s and early 1800s, many of Charleston's caterers, renowned food service providers, and entrepreneurs were Black. Sally Seymour, a formerly enslaved woman, ran a pastry shop where she also trained an enslaved workforce. After her death, her daughter Eliza continued the family business with her husband, John Lee. At a time when pastry cooks were some of the most valuable enslaved laborers, they trained and traded in skilled enslaved cooks, influencing Charleston's cuisine for generations. "It could be argued that the Seymour-Lee family did more than any other persons in the antebellum era to improve the quality of cooking available in Charleston, influencing elite domestic consumption through the pastry cooks they trained to expertise, as well as the public fare available in [the] city," writes David S. Shields in *Southern Provisions: The Creation and Revival of a Cuisine.*

Focus On: Hot Sauce

According to market research company Circana (formerly the NPD Group), hot sauce is on hand in more than 50 percent of kitchens in America. While many communities, including Indigenous peoples in the United States, have a long history of using spicy peppers and pepper sauces, hot sauce's modern usage has ties to the Black experience.

West Africans used a range of chilies, spices, and peppers to season foods, as well as for medicine to treat stomach illnesses, rheumatism, and dysentery. Chilies, though not indigenous to Africa, had been introduced by traders in the 1500s. They subsequently became provisions on slave-trading ships, an important staple for the Middle Passage. In the colonies, chilies continued to be used as medicine. Spicy chilies such as habanero and cayenne were grown in the colonies as early as the 17th century, and records show that enslaved peoples grew them in their gardens. Some of the earliest North American cookbooks include chili-vinegar preparations that align with records of how enslaved and Indigenous peoples used chilies in the British colony of Jamaica.

Eventually, chili vinegar, a precursor to what we now think of as Louisiana-style hot sauce, evolved from a medicine into a condiment. Enslaved peoples were essential in that shift. In the 1850s, Louisiana planter Maunsel White began producing a chili-vinegar concoction using the Tabasco chili, which his family began selling under the name Maunsel White's Concentrated Essence of Tabasco Peppers. A New Orleans paper noted that White's concoction was useful for combating cholera deaths, of particular importance to enslavers concerned about the loss of laborers and to locals who had been afflicted with a cholera epidemic a decade prior.

Eventually, White's sauce became widely used in New Orleans eateries and was often served alongside seafood, particularly oysters. "Any commercial success Colonel White earned from his pepper sauce depended on enslaved laborers," writes Adrian Miller in *Soul Food: The Surprising Story of an American Cuisine, One Plate at a Time.* "African Americans farmed and harvested acres of Tabasco chillis. White's Parisian-trained, Big House kitchen slaves were most likely executing White's early experiments in concocting a pepper sauce."

Though White's hot sauce empire eventually faded, the tradition of spicy, vinegar-based chili sauces lived on. Almost 20 years after White began growing Tabasco chilies, McIlhenny began producing its Tabasco sauce, now sold around the world. Today, hot sauces of all kinds are popular American condiments that remain strongly associated with the Black community. The oldest known Tabasco sauce bottle—more than 135 years old—was found during an excavation of a Black-owned saloon in Virginia City, Nevada. From spicy Black barbecue to Nashville hot chicken, spicy dishes and hot sauce are still recognizable strains in Black food culture in America that tie back to West African foodways.

> A discomfort with the painful history of enslavement drove popular narratives to deemphasize the lives and roles of the enslaved.

During that same period, household cooks for elite families in Charleston were largely African American, and often trained by free Black pastry cooks. They used local ingredients, French techniques, and their own unique inflection to set the standards of local cuisine. In the 1860s, Nat Fuller, a Black man who had a gas stove and oven (cutting-edge technology for that time), was the city's most popular caterer. Fuller hosted a mixed-race dinner party to celebrate the end of slavery in the United States, a feat in a society where racial caste lines were strictly observed. One of Fuller's trainees, Thomas R. Tully, also became a renowned Charleston chef and caterer. Tully served a menu at a society dinner in 1866 that included six courses ranging from fish to game, and a final pastry course that included multiple types of cakes, pies, and ice cream. It featured French-style sauces alongside dishes associated with local cooking and Black food traditions, such as pigs' feet with tomatoes.

Charleston's market vendors were also largely Black, from butchers and game hunters to vegetable sellers. The market was a vital part of the city's food sector, the primary source for foodstuffs until the 20th century, when grocers beat out the Charleston Market in the food trade. Historical records note the bounty and splendor of the market, fueled by Black hands, Black labor, and Black buying decisions, whether on their own behalf or conducting business for their enslavers.

While much of their history has been lost—eroded by time, a lack of written records, and outright racism—Black peoples in the region were deeply connected to all parts of the food system. And they imparted their knowledge and preferences, often tied to African traditions, to their communities for generations.

Lack of Recognition

Black peoples are seldom credited for their contributions to southern cuisine. A discomfort with the painful history of enslavement drove popular narratives to deemphasize the lives and roles of the enslaved. As a result, much of Black history in the South has been obscured. In addition, limited firsthand accounts exist from early Black populations who primarily passed on their histories and knowledge systems through oral tradition. Stereotypical and overly simplified narratives have further minimized the impact of Black cooks, who have often been portrayed as "born cooks" or "mammies." This implies they relied solely on instinct or needed the guiding hand of a white mistress to craft true culinary magic. The truth was very different.

Instead, it was often a Black presence, a Black hand, which drew on British and other European culinary techniques, knowledge gained from Indigenous peoples, and African foodways to craft southern cuisine.

OPPOSITE: The 1872 painting "Charleston Square" shows the city's main market, where African American artisans and vendors sold food and gifts.

Beyond the South

Black peoples played an important role in the development of early American cuisine in other parts of the nation, too. Yes, the most visible and traceable impact of early Black participation in the American economy and food system was in the South. Yet the expertise of Black peoples, as caterers, culinary tastemakers, cooks, and culinary laborers, made its mark elsewhere as well.

The North

Black populations were far less concentrated in the North, especially after those states voted to abolish slavery in 1804 and the domestic slave trade shifted to meet labor demands in the South. However, Black peoples in the North still impacted the landscape of cuisine. Most notably, many of the great early American caterers in northern cities were Black. They built lavish operations and acted as tastemakers and culinary trendsetters in places such as New York, New Jersey, Pennsylvania, and Washington, D.C., during the antebellum period.

Look to the example of Joshua B. Smith, a free Black caterer who hosted events for 1,600 people and for Boston's Harvard College in the mid-1800s. Smith eventually served on the state legislature. In Philadelphia, a center of Black catering expertise, James Prosser operated multiple restaurants (including one considered the best in the city), catered large society banquets, and sold wholesale turtles and oysters (popular foods during that time). Prosser died in 1861 with a sizable fortune from his numerous food businesses. Also in Philadelphia, James Augustin inherited a prominent restaurant from his father and continued the family tradition, serving as chef, steward, caterer, and provisioner throughout his lifetime. Augustin and a partner catered a banquet for the secretary of the U.S. Navy in 1877. In addition, prominent Black culinarians in Chicago, Baltimore,

An old oyster jar from the Thomas Downing Oyster House

Oyster farming became a key enterprise for Black populations along the mid-Atlantic.

Washington, D.C., and beyond made their mark on the American fine-dining scene before emancipation.

One well-known example is Thomas Downing, of New York oyster fame. Downing was the freeborn son of enslaved parents, and over his lifetime he became a famed Black restaurateur, caterer, and abolitionist. Oyster cellars were a culinary phenomenon common in cities such as Baltimore and New York in the antebellum period. They typically served oysters, fish, turtle, and other seafood-centric cuisine, and "African Americans were particularly significant in developing the cookery associated with these spaces," writes David Shields in *The Culinarians: Lives and Careers From the First Age of American Fine Dining*.

Downing helped establish a new standard for oyster cellars during his lifetime, creating a fine-dining atmosphere and building a reputation for sourcing and serving top-quality oysters, first through his own fishing efforts and later via negotiated relationships with oyster captains. The Thomas Downing Oyster House became a fixture among New York's elite society, popular among politicians, writers, and merchants, as well as ladies and families—a departure from the rough atmosphere common at other oyster houses of the time, which were predominantly men's spaces. Queen Victoria is counted among Downing's customers, and he catered the famed multimillion-dollar banquet held at

Delmonico's Restaurant to welcome Charles Dickens to New York for his second visit in 1868. The banquet was attended by approximately 3,000 people.

Downing also worked for the benefit of all African Americans. His oyster house was a stop on the Underground Railroad, and he funded African American schools, helped found an organization that worked to prevent Black peoples from being kidnapped and sold back into slavery, and engaged in multiple legal battles centered on segregation in public spaces. Sadly, African Americans couldn't dine in his restaurant because of segregation.

Shields notes, "He died the patriarch of a dynasty of politically active and aesthetically refined caterers. The Downing name inspired respect and reverence in New York, Newport, Rhode Island, and Washington, D.C., well into the twentieth century."

The Early American West

Though the idea of the early American West evokes images of white cowboys in scuffed boots, that's an incomplete picture of history. As America expanded westward, so did populations of Black peoples. Black peoples were forcibly marched westward on the Trail of Tears, some alongside their Indigenous enslavers. Black migrants (both free and enslaved) also moved to California and Colorado during the gold rush as homesteaders made their way into the region. Additionally, Black railroad workers helped expand the nation's newest transportation system, and Black soldiers joined the Buffalo Soldiers Black cavalry regiment, which was charged with protecting new western settlements and pioneers, as well as building roads and infrastructure. The history of the early American West includes many famed Black figures, including cowboys Bill Pickett and George Hooker, as well as Bass Reeves, a formerly enslaved deputy U.S. marshal who captured more than 3,000 people during his tenure in Oklahoma.

Along with the nation's land expansion, the livestock industry grew rapidly. In Arizona, California, Colorado, Montana, Nebraska, Oklahoma, South Dakota, Texas, Wyoming, and even in Canada, Black peoples made their mark on the livestock industry. It's estimated that Black peoples made up one-quarter of the cowboys working on cattle drives and ranches. Enslaved peoples from Senegambia, the historical name for the West African region between the Senegal and Gambia Rivers, were particularly prized for their experience raising cattle in Africa. Many were enslaved as livestock farmers in North America and, following emancipation, put those skills to use on cattle operations in the American West. Primarily Black men but also some women worked wrangling horses or as cooks and cattlemen—some even became ranch owners.

It's estimated that Black peoples made up one-quarter of the cowboys working on cattle drives and ranches.

OPPOSITE: Barrel racer Esperanza Tervalon, seen with her horse JaxieBaby, carries on a tradition of Black equestrians, cowboys, and rodeo performers.

Though racism and discrimination were still present—Black cowboys were often assigned the toughest and most dangerous jobs—some overcame those barriers to become trusted confidants and even full partners on cattle operations. Black cowboys also created their own rodeo circuits, as even rodeos were segregated. The Soul Circuit, a Black rodeo in Texas, still operates to this day—a living, breathing demonstration of how a significant Black cowboy population created a social and cultural activity for their community. Black rodeos typically continue to operate on the weekends to accommodate people who cannot take time off during the workweek, and they serve foods associated with Black culture like fried fish and barbecue.

Black cowboys also made their presence felt in the cook pots of trail drives and ranch fires, fueling laborers in one of America's most important new industries. "What is certain is that from the molasses that seasoned the bread puddings, to

"Sunday Afternoon on Claiborne Ave.," by Akasha Rabut, was featured in a Denver museum exhibit that explored the unique history of cowboy culture in America.

the barbecuing of antelope ribs, to the ineffable spicing of the dishes, black cowboy cooks brought an African culinary hand to the pots of the West," writes Jessica B. Harris in *High on the Hog: A Culinary Journey From Africa to America*.

Matthew Hooks was one such cowboy. Born in 1867 to formerly enslaved parents, he spent most of his career in the Texas Panhandle breaking horses and working on trail drives. He eventually used his influence and finances to help found two Black communities in Texas: Clarendon and the North Heights area of Amarillo. Hooks was also known for his skills as a range cook. That his reputation lives on is significant, as so little is known about the lives of Black cowboys. Most accounts and records simply mention names, where they were from, and where they worked. For historical records to mention Hooks's cooking means that his food made a significant impact on those around him, as did his philanthropy and skill breaking horses.

Beyond the ranching industry, Black residents had limited job prospects in the towns and cities that sprang up during western expansion. Being a cook, one of the service positions open to Black residents, was a common job. Though Black women are often left out of historical narratives of the American West, they were vital to western expansion, laboring alongside men as cooks, gardeners, and physical laborers, and tending children.

Mary Fields was a former slave, convent groundskeeper, and sharpshooter who also worked as a café owner and cook in the early American West. She also became the first Black woman "star route" mail carrier in the United States (these were private-contract mail delivery service routes, called "highway contract routes" today). Her life in Montana after emancipation is the stuff of legend, and illustrative of the varied roles women filled in the American West. Lucretia "Aunt Lou" Marshbanks was another legendary figure: Born in slavery in Tennessee and trained as a cook and housekeeper, she traveled West after emancipation and ended up working as kitchen manager at the Grand Central Hotel in Deadwood, South Dakota. She eventually purchased her own property, the Rustic Hotel, in Sawpit Gulch, which included a popular restaurant under her direction. Eventually, Marshbanks sold the hotel and retired to Wyoming, where she purchased a ranch and raised horses and cattle. Other Black women caterers and professional cooks made their mark on the region, too, among them Abby Fisher, who published *What Mrs. Fisher Knows About Old Southern Cooking* in

Roper and steer wrestler Willie B. Pink and a young cowboy behind him at the Diamond L Pro Rodeo in 1978

In 1955, Robert Gwathmey painted a man picking cotton in "Sunup."

1881 after migrating to California, and Mary Ellen Pleasant, an extremely successful cook, business owner, and abolitionist in California during the gold rush.

Just as they were in the American South, Black peoples were part of a long process of culinary transformation through which numerous cultures and identities negotiated the boundaries of local cuisine.

Wealth & American Cuisine

Much has been said about the impact of wealthy white men on American cuisine. Some of the Founding Fathers have even been called "founding foodies." Yet the advancements in cuisine credited to these figures were likely impossible without the system of enslavement that underpinned the era's economy. Black contributions to American cuisine go far beyond physical labor and shared knowledge. The immense wealth generated by enslavement and Black labor also made an indelible mark on American cuisine—and though that impact is at times harder to trace, it still reverberates today.

A Slave Economy

In the late 1700s, the American economy began to shift with the growth of cotton, which helped fuel American industrialization. The invention of the cotton gin in the 1790s—and the expansion to new territories in the South and West—drove surging demand for labor. As a result, enslavement marched south and west in what Edward E. Baptist calls an "interlinked expansion of both slavery and financial capitalism" in *The Half Has Never Been Told: Slavery and the Making of American Capitalism*.

The importation of enslaved peoples was barred in the early 1800s, pushing the domestic slavery market to fulfill the demands of the expanding industry. Merchants specialized in trafficking enslaved peoples from northern regions to the Deep South for sale. During this period, termed the Second Middle Passage, more than one million enslaved peoples were forcibly transported to the Deep South, taken from their homes, sold away from their families, and marched on foot and transported by boat and later by train. Even some free Black peoples were kidnapped and sold in the South during this era. Historical accounts tell of a widespread sense of fear among Black peoples, enslaved and free.

"The commodification and suffering and forced labor of African Americans is what made the United States powerful and rich," emphasizes Baptist. By 1840 cotton production—and its dependency on enslaved labor, the commodification of Black bodies, and violence and monitoring—made up two-thirds of all American exports. And by 1865, the American South produced the majority of the world's cotton supply.

Interconnected industries and systems developed around cotton and other slave-produced goods (including tobacco and rice), leaving no part of the economy untouched. The wealthy were able to secure loans based on commodities produced by enslaved peoples. Those same enslaved laborers were also used as collateral in this international system of lending and credit. Their bodies, abilities, and lives could be seized if someone defaulted on a loan. Enslaved peoples were considered financial investments, their "value" subject to market fluctuations.

Slavery's impact on the economy was not just confined to the South. Even after slavery was abolished in the North in the 19th century, industries related to the business of enslavement and slave-produced goods persisted, including northern textile factories, cotton brokers, axe-making companies, hat and shoe producers, insurance brokers, and shipping suppliers. America's rapid shift toward urbanization and industrialization was interlinked with enslavement across the country, and the immense wealth it generated.

> "The commodification and suffering and forced labor of African Americans is what made the United States powerful and rich."
>
> —EDWARD E. BAPTIST, *THE HALF HAS NEVER BEEN TOLD: SLAVERY AND THE MAKING OF AMERICAN CAPITALISM*

Culinary Trendsetters

So how did all that wealth, generated by and at the expense of Black enslaved peoples, impact cuisine? The most glaring answer: It enabled wealthy enslavers to build reputations as some of the nation's earliest culinary trendsetters, experimenters, and tastemakers. • Wealthy members of the plantocracy class, from sugar planter François-Gabriel "Valcour" Aime in Louisiana to rice planter and South Carolina governor Robert Francis Withers Allston, made their fortunes on the backs of enslaved Black laborers. Enslaved labor financed, in whole or in part, the agricultural and culinary experiments made in their gardens and kitchens, the training of chefs and staff, and the importation of expensive ingredients.

We can only wonder how much the slave-generated wealth and labors of Black culinarians impacted their dining choices and practices. What fineries and imported foodstuffs that graced their tables were financed and prepared by enslaved Black peoples?

Hercules Posey & Ice-Cold Treats

The country's first president, George Washington, maintained icehouses that offer a clear example of slave labor's impact on the food space. Washington was one of America's wealthiest presidents: He owned an 8,000-acre estate maintained by hundreds of enslaved Black peoples. The wealth they generated helped fund his lifestyle and the culinary largesse that he enjoyed and bestowed on his guests.

An icehouse from the 1700s—an insulated and specially built structure considered advanced refrigeration technology at the time—has been unearthed at Mount Vernon, the site of Washington's former residence and plantation. To care for the icehouse, enslaved laborers had to venture out in the coldest weather for the dangerous job of cutting and hauling blocks of ice from the Potomac River. Those blocks were then preserved in the icehouse

The dining room at George Washington's Mount Vernon estate in Virginia

during the summer months, allowing cold treats like ice cream to be served at Washington's dinners and events.

Additionally, Washington's enslaved chef, Hercules Posey, was one of America's first celebrity chefs. Posey served as Washington's chef at Mount Vernon and in the presidential residence, located in Philadelphia at that time. Posey became enslaved by Washington because of an unpaid debt by his previous enslaver. In cruder terms, he was considered property and forfeited to pay a debt. Posey was renowned for his culinary prowess and earned income for himself by selling extra food from the president's kitchen. He was known to like fine clothing and also as a stern and detail-oriented leader in the kitchen. He was responsible for managing and producing an array of feasts and meals, serving the finest cuisine of the day to impress guests, officials, and others with dishes and drinks such as puddings, roasted meats, wine, punches, and, of course, iced treats and delicacies such as ice cream. Posey is also famous for his escape to New York during Washington's lifetime; records indicate he was working as a cook and laborer in New York City in the early 1800s after

> **Without a doubt, America's love of macaroni and cheese is part of James Hemings's legacy.**

his escape. He lives on as an almost larger-than-life figure in the American culinary canon.

James Hemings & an Iconic Dish

Macaroni and cheese's prevalence in the United States offers another example of the interplay between Black labor, wealth, and culinary trends in America. Thomas Jefferson, the third president of the United States, is often credited with popularizing macaroni and cheese, and French cuisine in general, in the country. However, it was actually enslaved chef James Hemings, who, through his skills and labor, enabled Jefferson to serve fine French cuisine, including macaroni and cheese, to his guests.

Hemings's culinary legacy began in the 1700s as an enslaved laborer at Monticello, Jefferson's Virginia plantation. Hemings was a carriage driver and house servant who eventually accompanied Jefferson to France in the 1780s, when the future president was appointed to help negotiate treaties in Europe. In France, Hemings began three years of culinary training. He apprenticed under a pastry maker and restaurant keeper, and even trained—at great cost to Jefferson—in the household of a member of the royal family. During his time in France, Hemings became conversational in French and ultimately took on the role of chef de cuisine at Jefferson's Paris residence.

Hemings could have become emancipated under French law, but—for heavily debated reasons—he remained enslaved by Jefferson. When Jefferson's time in France ended, Hemings returned to the United States with him in 1789. Given his culinary expertise and training, "Hemings was probably the best trained chef in America of his time, and essentially one of the first to blend the best of French technique with American ingredients and flavors," emphasizes David Shields in *The Culinarians*.

Without a doubt, America's love of macaroni and cheese is part of James Hemings's legacy. Cheesy baked macaroni was a well-known dish in Paris at the time Hemings trained there, and after his return to the United States, he helped popularize it at home. Based on historical records, macaroni and cheese was a frequent meal served at Monticello; Jefferson imported dozens of pounds of macaroni between the 1790s and his death in 1826.

By the early 1800s the legacy of Jefferson's largely Black enslaved chefs and culinary staff had permeated into larger society, as had Jefferson's tastes for dishes such as macaroni and cheese. Initially, the trend spread slowly, likely from chef to apprentice, from kitchen to kitchen, passed among free and enslaved Black cooks. Then, macaroni and cheese made its way into early American cookbooks like *The Carolina Housewife* (1847), written by Sarah

Rutledge, an enslaver whose likely Black kitchen staff worked to prepare the recipes included in the tome.

Black labor was instrumental in fueling Thomas Jefferson's lifestyle beyond his culinary needs. While macaroni and cheese, at the time, was associated with wealth and the European upper crust, in reality Jefferson was in debt for most of his adult life. The costs of his fancy lifestyle—imported ingredients, travel, and the training of Hemings and other enslaved Black chefs—was likely financed by loans. And the Black peoples enslaved by Jefferson served as collateral for those loans, and were often sold to settle debts and recoup income when needed.

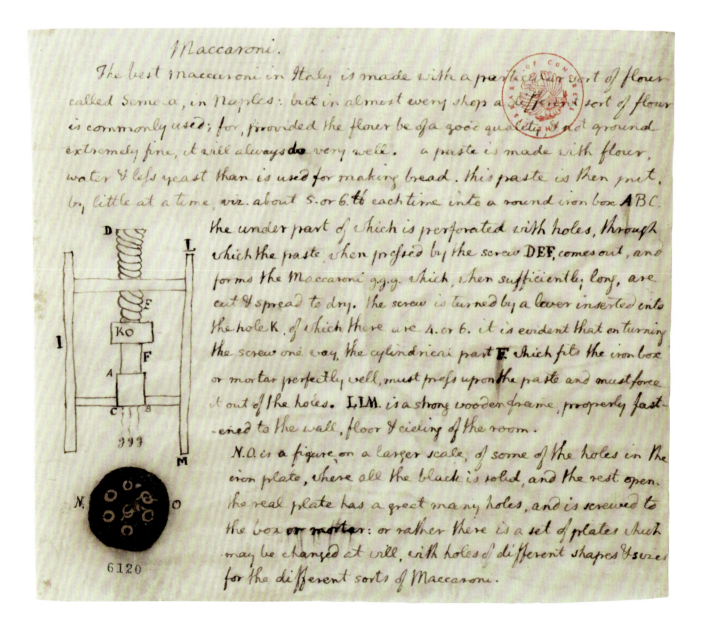

A handwritten card detailing the use of a macaroni press is preserved at Thomas Jefferson's Monticello estate.

Food for Thought

The Owens-Thomas House & Slave Quarters

It's a gorgeous, breezy spring day in Savannah, Georgia, in 2023. I walk into the courtyard of the stately historic property in the heart of the city that makes up the Owens-Thomas House & Slave Quarters. I don't know much about the site beyond what I read on the property's website. "The Owens-Thomas House & Slave Quarters allows visitors to explore the complicated relationships between the most and least powerful people in the city of Savannah in the early 19th century."

After a few minutes of waiting, the tour begins. First, we are taken through the slave quarters, which occupy part of a building that also used to house horses and carriages. There, up to 14 enslaved peoples once lived. As we take in the sparse and cramped quarters, we hear about the likely labor they undertook. In an urban environment such as Savannah, much of the needed labor for elite families was domestic in nature, often the role of enslaved women. That held true at the Owens-Thomas House, where an enslaved staff of primarily women and teenage girls cooked, cleaned, laundered, and helped raise their enslavers' children.

We cross the manicured courtyard to the mansion. The property was purchased in 1830 by wealthy landowner and enslaver George Welshman Owens. Owens, his family, and the people they enslaved lived together on the property. The house stayed in the family for 121 years, until it was given to the Telfair Academy of Arts and Sciences in 1951.

Though I don't know much about architecture or design, it's impossible to miss the grandeur of the mansion, which has been restored to showcase intricate molding, a grand staircase, a library, and more. From the carpentry to the formal dining areas, the wealth on display is omnipresent in the upper floors of the mansion.

We take in that splendor and then our tour ends in the basement. There our guide departs and we are left to read the signage throughout the space and take in the stark contrast from the floors above. The space, which has bare stone floors and none of the opulence or comfort of the floors above, has been preserved so that the site can offer a more complex historical narrative.

TOP: The exterior of the former home of a wealthy landowner who relied on enslaved laborers for his fortune. BOTTOM LEFT: Visitors walk through the courtyard and slave quarters of Savannah's Owens-Thomas House museum to understand the stark disparities among the living quarters. BOTTOM RIGHT: A harp inside the main home exemplifies the extreme riches of the family.

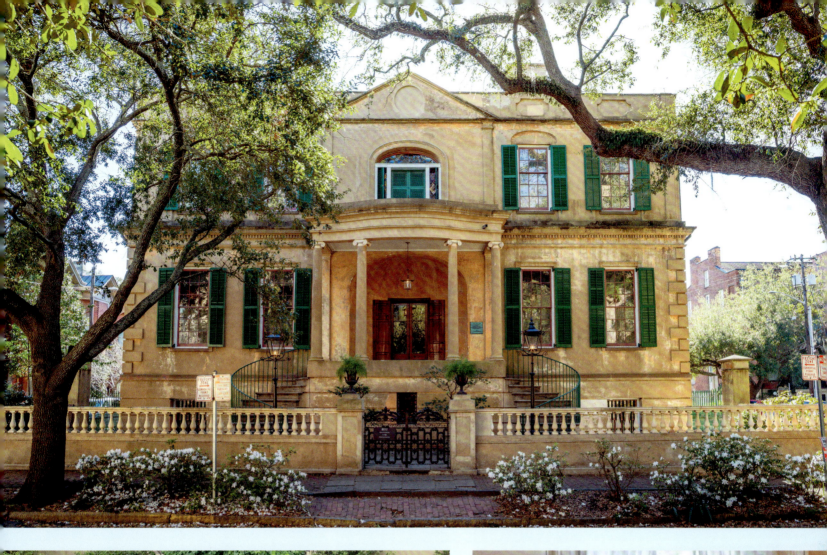

ABOVE: A wall displays the names of enslaved peoples who labored at the Owens-Thomas House. OPPOSITE: Enslaved peoples—primarily women and teenage girls—cooked meals and worked in the basement of the main home.

There, I learn about how the mansion had indoor plumbing, incredibly advanced technology in the early 1800s. To keep it operating, the Owens family's enslaved staff acted as the city's first plumbers, managing a system that no one else in Savannah had expertise to operate.

It's in that basement where I see the ice chamber, a reminder of how wealthy the Owens family had to be to have a private storage area to preserve ice. Outside the chamber a sign notes how enslaved laborers often oversaw the delivery of ice blocks to the home, ensuring that cold drinks and ice cream would be available to other elites invited to dine there.

In the kitchen I learn about Diane, an enslaved cook who labored in that space, making food for 12 to 22 people daily. "Diane began her day before the sun came up and worked until well after dark," the sign reads. She likely slept in the basement because of her workload. She was responsible for crafting the elaborate meals and spreads served when the family entertained guests. The household also had two imported ranges, new technology that Diane "needed to learn to use and maintain … without access to written manuals or formal training." Diane and other enslaved laborers (likely women) who assisted her in the kitchen had to manage that technology, oversee and utilize the ice stored below, reply to the service bell that connected the work areas to the mansion, and so much more.

I'm left with questions that apply to most wealthy white households from the antebellum United States. What culinary treats did enslaved culinarians like Diane serve to guests in the 1800s that caused other socialites and elites to insist they should have the same in their own homes? What culinary trends did they set or emulate and make their own? And how much of the lifestyle and culinary largesse of their enslavers would have been possible without the labor and wealth created by Black hands?

Sugar

Worldwide, processed sugar is a standard part of everyday diets. In 2018, more than 172 million tons of sugar were consumed around the world. Added sugars permeate processed foods, desserts, drinks, breads, and even dressings and marinades. For millions of people, sugar (in one form or another) is an essential part of their daily routines, melded in coffees, teas, and other beverages. On holidays and special occasions, sugar has a special place in the form of desserts, which vary from tradition to tradition, place to place. And as with cotton, the rise of sugar as a global industrial powerhouse relied on Black labor and expertise to generate profit.

Though average sugar consumption has declined in the United States since its peak in the late 1990s, sugar remains a significant part of the American diet—in apple pie, funnel cake, sweet potato pie, shortcake, doughnuts, ice cream, and pudding.

It is also dangerous. Sugar has been linked to a number of serious health problems, including diabetes and some cancers. Those diseases are more likely to affect and kill Black peoples than white residents in America, a direct reflection of ongoing food apartheid, discrimination, and other factors.

Sugar's Expansion in the Colonial Era

The process of refining sugarcane and producing sugar was developed in India about 3,000 years ago. Because it was labor intensive to produce, sugar was consumed only by the wealthy for hundreds of years and generally unavailable to working people, who instead used sweeteners like honey. The wealthy, including royalty, used sugar to make centerpieces and treats that were both dessert and artwork, spinning sugar and caramel to form animals, buildings, fanciful figures, and other imagery for royal banquets. Sugar was also used as medicine. It was thought to have a purifying and strengthening effect and was added to sweeten bitter remedies.

William Clark drew enslaved peoples cutting sugarcane as part of his "Ten Views in the Island of Antigua" series from 1823.

The shift in sugar consumption began with Portuguese colonial explorations in the 15th century. The Portuguese colonized the island of Madeira, where they began growing and refining sugar, and then expanded production to the colony of São Tomé. The Spanish began producing sugar on the Canary Islands during the same period. In these colonies, Indigenous peoples, and later enslaved Africans, were tasked with the hard labor. Sugar plantations remade local landscapes and radically changed ecologies, shifts that had lasting impacts on the Atlantic islands and later on sugar-producing areas in the Americas.

It wasn't until sugar production expanded beyond islands in the Atlantic that sugar morphed from a luxury commodity to a commonplace ingredient. As colonial economies sought profitable agricultural products and exports, sugar became one of the staple crops, and plantations were established throughout

SUGAR • 87

the Americas and the Caribbean. Consumption of sugar and its by-products increased rapidly. In just a few hundred years sugar went from a finery reserved for the wealthy to a commonplace ingredient available to the working-class family. By the mid-17th century Boston had coffee shops. By the late 18th century, Parisian coffee shops were serving ultrasweet coffee, which was available even to the poor from street peddlers. In Britain, tea drinking—with sweetened cups—proliferated. Throughout Europe, tea and coffee shops emerged as social spaces and arenas to conduct business and political affairs. In the North American colonies, coffee became a preferred drink.

It's safe to say that by the 18th century, sugar was a major factor fueling the Transatlantic Slave Trade. Sugar was not only a primary export to Europe but was also an important product of global trade connecting Africa, the Americas, the Caribbean, and Europe. Caribbean sugar-producing economies exported sugar as well as molasses to North America. In New England, sugar-related industries developed, such as processing facilities to turn molasses into rum. Food and lumber, vital to feed enslaved laborers on sugar plantations and to fuel sugar mills, were shipped in turn from New England to the Caribbean. Rum from the Caribbean was also shipped to Africa, where it was used as currency to purchase more enslaved peoples and transport them back to the Americas. There, they were often sold for labor on plantations in exchange for currency and goods such as sugar and molasses. Thus, with the arrival of new African enslaved laborers, the sugar cycle could begin again and connect economies across oceans.

In a span of about 400 years, sugar, sugar by-products, and the plantation economy shifted global diets. Sugar became an important factor in international politics and policy, sparking conflict between nations seeking to protect

The United States Food Administration promoted information about sugar rationing in 1918.

sugar supplies and producers. Though slavery was eventually abolished in the sugar-producing Americas, in many places indentured servitude took its place as the primary system of production for sugar, bringing more migrants and peoples into contact with the sugar trade. But the trade of African slaves was the linchpin that allowed sugar to transform from a rare luxury to a much more affordable commodity and a widely consumed and utilized good.

Sugar, the Plantation Economy & Culinary Impacts

Though we often talk about the horrors of cotton plantations, little is mentioned about the connection between Black history and sugar in the United States. In the late 1700s, sugar processing began in Louisiana, where a domestic sugar trade deeply reliant on enslaved labor took root. There are only a few climates in which sugarcane grows successfully, so sugar plantations in the United States were limited. However, Louisiana's rich soil and the labor of enslaved peoples allowed sugar plantations to flourish. The state ultimately produced one-quarter of the world's sugar supply by the early 1800s. And sugar slavery in Louisiana developed on a similar trajectory to that of the cotton plantation industry in other parts of the South. A growing demand for enslaved laborers coalesced with upgraded machinery and a brutal system of labor management to facilitate a mass transfer of enslaved peoples to the South as part of the Second Middle Passage. In Louisiana sugar parishes, the enslaved population

> By the mid-1800s, more than 100,000 Black enslaved laborers toiled without pay in Louisiana.

Focus On: The Pecan

The interplay of plantation-generated wealth, Indigenous ingredients, and Black labor and expertise is evident in the history of the pecan. Pecans are indigenous to North America and were long eaten and utilized by Native Americans before colonial contact. After numerous failed experiments by plantation owners and botanists to produce commercially viable pecans, it was a skilled enslaved gardener named Antoine who first successfully domesticated the tree nut in the 1840s.

Antoine was enslaved at Oak Alley Plantation, a Louisiana sugar plantation outside New Orleans. The plantation included sugarcane fields, a sugar mill, and, on average, 110 to 120 enslaved laborers. There, Jacques Telesphore Roman, Antoine's enslaver, recognized his skill with plants and prior experience grafting trees. Antoine was tasked with grafting pecan twigs from a tree that was producing nuts appropriate for consumption onto other trees. Antoine's experiment, which drew on his unique skill set, was successful, and eventually nuts from Antoine's trees were awarded a prize at the 1876 Centennial Exhibition in Philadelphia. Antoine's pecan variety was given the name Centennial, and over time, his methods became the foundation of the modern commercial pecan industry. Pecans began to be consumed broadly and appeared in recipes in the United States beginning in the late 1800s. By 1936, 20 million pounds of pecans were produced in Georgia alone.

increased more than fourfold between 1827 and 1850. As it did in the cotton belt, in sugar parishes the Black population outnumbered the white population.

By the mid-1800s, more than 100,000 Black enslaved laborers toiled without pay in Louisiana. Adults and children conducted extremely dangerous work on sugar plantations and in processing factories. Sugar production was more mechanized than other sectors, and factories operated round the clock. Historical accounts note that enslaved peoples were at times tortured if they were unable to keep up production, and there were numerous maimings and deaths in the production work. In fact, the sugar plantation system was known for work regimes so deadly that the enslaved population couldn't replenish itself.

In the heyday of American plantation sugar production, Black enslaved labor made Louisiana the nation's second wealthiest state. There, sugar made its way from Black hands at harvest to Black hands again at preparation, when Black labor and culinary expertise helped shepherd in the taste for sugary sweetness that overtook the North American colonies as it did the world. Black cooks and bakers turned sugar into cakes, pies, and other foodstuffs for sale and for their enslavers.

The Sugar Legacy

Today, critics note that sugar production in the United States continues to reflect the system of exploitation that underpinned its founding. Prison labor is still used in Louisiana to grow sugarcane. FBI reports have documented forced labor in Louisiana sugar production well into modern times. In the 1980s, there was a congressional investigation into exploitation of West Indian sugar workers. In addition, accusations of land theft persist. In Wallace, Louisiana, an area once home to many sugar plantations, the Whitney Plantation Museum explores this long history, describing itself as "the only museum in Louisiana with an exclusive focus on the lives of enslaved people."

We may never be able to trace each and every culinary development that occurred in the gardens, kitchens, and homes of sugar plantations or was funded by the profits of slave-produced sugar. However, the ubiquity of sugar in the American diet is a direct result of this system of exploitation that underpinned the foundation of American capitalism at the expense of Black peoples. In many ways, much of the dominance of corporate food monopolies and worker exploitation that some food writers and critics have pointed to as less savory hallmarks of American cuisine are also a result of the brutality of American capitalism and how foundational it is in settler colonialism and enslavement.

> We may never be able to trace each and every culinary development that occurred in the gardens, kitchens, and homes of sugar plantations or was funded by the profits of slave-produced sugar.

OPPOSITE: Enslaved peoples once tended the grandiose grounds of Oak Alley Plantation in Vacherie, Louisiana.

Food for Thought

Sugar, the Caribbean & the Diaspora

While sugar plantations in the United States were largely limited to Louisiana, sugar had a far more expansive footprint in the Caribbean. More than 90 percent of the nearly 11 million enslaved Africans who survived the Middle Passage were brought to Central and South America and the Caribbean. Today, many peoples in the Caribbean have African ancestry, a legacy of the slave trade and the dominance of sugar plantations in Caribbean economies for multiple centuries.

The impacts of the slave trade are also felt in the foodways of the region. In many parts of the Caribbean, sorghum became the staple ration, as it could grow in soils depleted of minerals by sugarcane production. Sorghum, an African cereal closely related to millet, is mentioned in planter records as a crop introduced by enslaved peoples and found in slave cultivation plots in Jamaica and Brazil. In Curaçao it became a staple crop, used to feed the swelling population of enslaved laborers. There, enslaved peoples could gain their freedom if they produced more than 300 bushels of sorghum. This demonstrates just how important African grains were to the food supply there.

Throughout the Caribbean this pattern played out. Black enslaved laborers replaced African yams with indigenous cassava, utilizing knowledge from Indigenous peoples regarding its preparation to make new food traditions. Black peoples, often women tasked with food preparation for the plantation, took imported ingredients like plantains, grown to feed enslaved laborers, and turned them into staples of local cuisine. Consider ackee, a fruit related to lychee commonly eaten in curries or cooked with fish. Ackee is native to West Africa and was brought to Jamaica during the slave trade. Saltfish was imported from North America during the colonial era and became a staple of enslaved laborers' diets in Jamaica. Today, ackee served with saltfish is the national dish.

The impacts of the African diaspora link communities across borders and oceans. The composed rice dishes of Senegal and other West African countries are the culinary cousins of dishes such as red rice and hoppin' John found in the United States, and also dishes such as rice and peas, commonly associated with Jamaica, as well as Cuban congrí. Throughout the Caribbean, various forms of callaloo, a thick stew made with taro leaves (a West African crop), are commonly consumed. In the United States, diaspora communities often substitute collards and other greens for taro in their versions of callaloo.

OPPOSITE: Jean-Baptiste Debret illustrated two workers operating a sugar mill in his 1835 lithograph titled "Voyage Pittoresque et Historique au Brésil."

Sweet Potato Biscuits

Cook time: 13 minutes, plus 1 hour chilling time | Makes 8 to 10 biscuits

2 cups all-purpose flour, plus more for dusting

2 tablespoons packed light brown sugar

1 tablespoon baking powder

1 teaspoon ground cinnamon

1 teaspoon salt

½ teaspoon baking soda

1 heaping cup cooked sweet potato (from about 1 large sweet potato)

⅓ cup buttermilk

10 tablespoons (1 whole stick plus 2 tablespoons) very cold or frozen butter

1 tablespoon butter

¼ cup pure maple syrup or honey

Preheat oven to 475°F. In a large bowl, whisk together flour, brown sugar, baking powder, cinnamon, salt, and baking soda. Refrigerate dry ingredients until cold, about 30 minutes.

In a small bowl, using an electric mixer or fork, mash sweet potato and buttermilk until almost smooth (small pieces of sweet potato are OK). Cover and refrigerate until cold, about 30 minutes.

Dump dry ingredients onto a work surface. Using large holes of a box grater, grate cold/frozen butter into flour, tossing the butter in the flour to coat. Work quickly to keep butter from melting.

Using your hands, gently mix sweet potato mixture into flour mixture until just combined and no dry flour spots remain. Press dough into an 8-by-5-inch rectangle about 2 inches thick. Fold into thirds, like folding a letter. Repeat the folding—rectangle, then into thirds—two times, dusting with a little flour if too sticky.

Press dough out into a 1-inch-thick circle. Using a 2½-inch biscuit cutter or glass, cut out circles. Dip cutter in flour between biscuits to prevent sticking. Gather dough scraps, roll into 1-inch-thick circle, and cut out more biscuits. Place biscuits close together in a 12-inch cast-iron skillet or on a baking sheet lined with parchment. Bake biscuits for about 13 minutes.

Meanwhile, in a small skillet, melt 1 tablespoon butter with maple syrup or honey over medium heat. Brush tops of biscuits with flavored butter. Serve warm.

Macaroni & Cheese

Cook time: 45 minutes | Makes 8 servings

- 1 pound elbow macaroni
- 4 tablespoons unsalted butter, divided
- 3 tablespoons all-purpose flour
- 1½ teaspoons garlic powder
- 1 teaspoon mustard powder
- 1 teaspoon onion powder
- 1 teaspoon smoked paprika
- 1 teaspoon freshly ground black pepper
- Pinch of nutmeg
- 3 cups whole milk
- 1 (12-ounce) can evaporated milk
- 6 ounces smoked Gouda, shredded
- 8 ounces extra-sharp cheddar, shredded
- 8 ounces Gruyère, shredded

Preheat oven to 400°F. Coat a 3½-quart casserole dish with cooking spray.

In a large pot, cook macaroni in boiling salted water until al dente, according to package instructions. Drain macaroni and return noodles to pot. Add 1 tablespoon butter and stir until melted.

Meanwhile, in a large saucepan, melt remaining 3 tablespoons butter over medium heat. Add flour and stir until well incorporated, 2 to 4 minutes. Add garlic powder, mustard powder, onion powder, smoked paprika, pepper, and nutmeg and stir until fragrant, about 1 minute. Whisk in whole and evaporated milks and bring to a simmer. Cook, stirring often, until thickened, 3 to 5 minutes.

In a medium bowl, toss Gouda, cheddar, and Gruyère. Measure ⅔ cup of cheese mixture and set aside. Add remaining cheese to the saucepan and stir until melted, 2 to 3 minutes. Stir macaroni into the cheese sauce, then transfer to the prepared casserole dish.

Top everything with the reserved ⅔ cup of cheese. Bake until the edges are bubbly and the top is golden brown, 20 to 30 minutes.

Baked Eggplant, p. 100

Baked Eggplant

Cook time: 45 minutes, plus at least 3 hours chilling time | Makes 6 servings

- 3 medium eggplants, halved lengthwise
- 1½ to 2 tablespoons salt
- 8 ounces bacon, finely chopped
- 1 small onion, finely chopped
- 1 medium carrot, peeled and finely chopped
- 1 celery stalk, finely chopped
- 1 green bell pepper, seeded and finely chopped
- 3 cloves garlic, finely chopped
- 4 tablespoons finely chopped parsley, divided
- 1 tablespoon finely chopped fresh thyme
- 2 teaspoons finely chopped fresh rosemary
- 1 (14.5-ounce) can diced tomatoes
- 1 (14.5-ounce) can white beans, drained and rinsed
- 1 cup panko breadcrumbs
- ½ teaspoon freshly ground black pepper
- 1 teaspoon garlic powder
- ½ teaspoon onion powder
- 1 cup grated Parmesan cheese, divided

Line a bowl with 4 layers of paper towels. Set a baking or cooling rack inside a rimmed baking sheet.

Using a spoon or melon baller, scoop out the flesh from each eggplant half, leaving a ¼-inch border around all edges. Transfer flesh to the prepared bowl. Lightly salt the eggplant flesh, tossing to evenly incorporate. Lightly salt the inside of eggplant shells and place upside down on the prepared rack. Cover and refrigerate shells and flesh for 3 hours to overnight.

Preheat oven to 400°F.

In a large skillet, cook bacon over medium heat, stirring often, until crispy, about 8 minutes. Using a slotted spoon, transfer bacon to a paper towel–lined plate to drain.

Add onion, carrot, celery, and bell pepper to pot and cook, stirring often, until just beginning to soften, about 5 minutes. Stir in garlic, 2 tablespoons parsley, thyme, and rosemary; cook, stirring constantly, until aromatic, about 1 minute. Add tomatoes and cook, stirring often, until liquid is slightly reduced, about 2 minutes. Remove from heat.

Transfer ¼ cup bacon to a small bowl and set aside. Add remaining bacon to pot, along with eggplant flesh and beans; stir to incorporate.

Wash and dry baking sheet used for eggplant shells; place shells, skin-side down, on baking sheet. Stuff each shell with tomato-and-bean mixture. Sprinkle ½ cup Parmesan cheese evenly over each eggplant half.

In a medium bowl, toss together panko, black pepper, garlic powder, onion powder, reserved bacon, and remaining ½ cup Parmesan cheese. Top eggplants with panko mixture.

Bake until eggplant is cooked through and breadcrumbs are golden brown, 20 to 30 minutes.

Garnish with remaining 2 tablespoons parsley before serving.

Son of a Gun Stew

Cook time: 1 hour 30 minutes | *Makes 6 servings*

2 tablespoons vegetable oil, divided

1 pound stew beef, cut into 1-inch cubes

1½ teaspoons salt, divided

1½ teaspoons freshly ground black pepper, divided

½ cup chopped onion

¼ cup chopped carrot

¼ cup chopped celery

¼ cup chopped fresh herbs (such as oregano, marjoram, thyme, parsley, dill, and/or rosemary)

1 (6-ounce) can tomato paste

7 cups beef, chicken, or vegetable stock

4 cups mixed root vegetables (such as sweet potato, turnip, rutabaga, carrot, parsnip, winter squash), peeled and cut into ¾-inch cubes

3 tablespoons pearled barley

3 tablespoons Worcestershire sauce

1 (15-ounce) can beans (such as black, pinto, black-eyed peas, navy, lima, or kidney), drained and rinsed

Cornbread, for serving (see pages 36 & 37)

In a large heavy-bottom pot, heat 1 tablespoon oil over medium-high. Season beef with ½ teaspoon salt and ½ teaspoon pepper. Working in batches, add beef to the pot and cook, turning occasionally, until well browned, 5 to 6 minutes per batch. Transfer meat to a bowl.

Reduce heat to medium and add remaining 1 tablespoon of oil to pot. Add onion, carrot, celery, and herbs; season with remaining 1 teaspoon salt and pepper and cook, stirring often, until vegetables begin to soften, 3 to 5 minutes. Add tomato paste and stir until slightly darker in color, about 1 minute. Add stock, root vegetables, barley, Worcestershire sauce, and beef with any accumulated juices. Bring to a boil, then reduce heat to medium-low. Simmer uncovered, stirring occasionally, until beef and vegetables are tender, 45 minutes to 1 hour.

Stir in beans and simmer until heated through, about 5 minutes longer. Adjust seasoning to taste. Serve with cornbread.

Bread Pudding

Bake time: 1 hour 10 minutes | Makes 8 servings

- 3 large eggs
- ¾ cup packed dark brown sugar
- 3 cups whole milk
- 1 cup heavy cream
- 4 tablespoons butter, melted and cooled
- 2 teaspoons vanilla extract
- 1½ teaspoons ground cinnamon
- ¼ teaspoon salt
- Pinch ground or grated nutmeg
- 10 cups cubed (about 1-inch cubes) soft bread, such as brioche
- 1 tablespoon coarse (raw) sugar, optional
- Whipped cream, vanilla ice cream, or sweetened condensed milk, for topping

Preheat oven to 400°F. Spray a 13-by-9-inch baking dish with cooking spray.

In the bowl of a stand mixer or in a large bowl using an electric hand mixer, beat eggs and brown sugar on high until thick ribbons form, about 4 minutes. Add milk, heavy cream, butter, vanilla, cinnamon, salt, and nutmeg. Beat on low speed, then gradually increase speed to medium and beat until just well blended, about 1½ minutes.

Place bread in the prepared baking dish, then gently pour egg mixture on top. Let stand for 10 minutes, then sprinkle with coarse sugar, if using.

Place a large roasting pan on an oven rack, then set baking dish with bread pudding into the roasting pan. Gently pour enough hot water into the roasting pan to come halfway up the sides of the baking dish. Carefully push the rack into the oven.

Bake bread pudding until custard is set in the center, about 1 hour 10 minutes.

Leave the dish in the oven. Switch oven to broil and cook until top is browned, 30 to 60 seconds.

Remove the baking dish from the water bath and let it stand for 5 minutes. Serve with whipped cream, ice cream, or sweetened condensed milk.

CHAPTER THREE

Nationalizing Black Cuisine

The Post-Emancipation Era

By the beginning of the Civil War, Black foodways and a combination of Indigenous and new traditions had helped create the foundation of southern cuisine. Few racial differences remained in the region when it came to food consumption. Rather, most differences in culinary practice were based on socioeconomic class. • In the 100 years following the end of chattel slavery, Black migration, Black innovation, and

Black struggles for equality coalesced to spark profound social and culinary changes in the United States. The years between emancipation and the changes brought about by the Great Migration and the civil rights movement were rife with conflict. Despite facing limited opportunities for employment and persistent discrimination, Black peoples in the United States continued to make their mark on the American food system.

In some ways, segregation ensured that Black peoples would remain integral to the American food space. Limited employment and advancement opportunities often relegated Black peoples to agricultural, food service, and domestic worker positions, which meant Black peoples continued to shape the culinary tastes of the country.

During the Great Migration, an influx of Black southern migrants to other parts of the United States spread awareness of and appreciation for southern cuisine. Restaurants, stores, and social venues catering to southern Black tastes proliferated throughout the country, and dishes like southern-style fried chicken, gumbo, and chitlins spread along with them. Black peoples made their mark in the food space, acting as culinary tastemakers, caterers, chefs, cooks on trail drives, and food service workers throughout the country. The impact reverberated throughout the nation's economy, helping to build and reshape social systems, including the food system. But the impact of Black food went far beyond cuisine. Black food spaces served as vital political and cultural centers, nurturing Black leaders, artists, and even the civil rights movement.

OPPOSITE: **Ellis Wilson's "Field Worker," painted between 1948 and 1951, depicts a family walking through a tobacco field.**
PAGES 104-105: **Founded in 1962, Sylvia's Restaurant is a community favorite for authentic soul food in Harlem, New York.**

Black Tastemaking During Jim Crow

Though many have claimed that other issues caused the Civil War, the truth is that the right to own, trade, and control enslaved bodies was central to the conflict. Declaration documents from several states including Mississippi, Texas, South Carolina, and Georgia explicitly noted defending the right to continue enslaving Black peoples. The political histories of Florida, Alabama, Louisiana, and Virginia also reveal how pro-slavery sentiments helped fuel secession. Driven by the issue of slavery, the Union and Confederate Armies entered five long years of war.

Following the Civil War, the nation grappled with integrating the 11 Confederate States, rebuilding, and establishing a new legal and social order for millions of newly freed Black peoples, who accounted for approximately 12 percent of the total population. Ultimately, segregationist and repressive policies persisted, enacted after only a short period of favorable legal and social programs that supported newly freed Black peoples, known as Radical or Congressional Reconstruction.

In the South, the Jim Crow era began, a period of an imposed racialized caste system that lasted until the civil rights movement of the 1960s. Under Jim Crow, Black peoples were second-class citizens. Strictly segregated social spaces were created for white and Black use, and the now-infamous "Whites Only" and "Colored" signs were used to designate and enforce the social order. While it's common to focus on Jim Crow and racist violence in the South, white supremacy also reigned in other parts of the United States. The vast majority of communities and public spaces, including restaurants, remained segregated. Black peoples were subject to racist violence and were even lynched in the North as

A wooden sign used for racial segregation

Painted in 1977, "The Sharecroppers' Day of Reckoning" by Alice Moseley illustrates sharecropping in the American Southeast.

well. Job opportunities for Black peoples remained limited, and white communities throughout the United States systematically excluded Black peoples through violence, custom, and law.

Though segregation and discrimination persisted, emancipation did force systems previously dependent on enslaved laborers to evolve. In urban areas, Black residents sought employment as cooks, caterers, street vendors, and domestic workers, as well as at inns and wherever else their skills permitted. In agricultural areas, the sharecropping system took hold, where Black (and poor white) farmers labored on plots of land they did not own. This system was often exploitative, saddling tenant farmers with debts they couldn't pay, and allowing wealthy landowners to reestablish a labor force lost to emancipation.

Emancipation and sharecropping brought limited changes to the food traditions of the South. Corn and pork remained staples of southern foodways, and socioeconomic class served as the primary line of division between Black and white populations. However, the sharecropping system did limit the ability of many Black Southerners to grow gardens for cash crops.

Culinary Tastemaking

Continuing a trend that began before emancipation, many Black peoples in the North and in urban areas found work in taverns, cookshops, and inns and as

caterers, street vendors, and grocers. Though the urban poor often struggled, some free Black peoples in the North achieved fortune and fame through their work in the food space following the Civil War. These Black culinarians owned catering empires that defined fine dining at the time; opened taverns, alehouses, and oyster bars; and acted as tastemakers in their cities and regions. "They set culinary standards and were powerful arbiters of style, with enough clout to launch modes and fads," writes Jessica B. Harris in *High on the Hog: A Culinary Journey From Africa to America*.

Throughout the nation in the late 19th century, Black food folks built thriving businesses and served as the preeminent culinary trendsetters in their cities. Take, for example, James Augustin, a second-generation Black culinarian in Philadelphia who crafted and catered some of the most important events of the 1860s and 1870s, including dinner parties for high-society families in New York, Massachusetts, and Maryland, as well as a feast for the U.S. Navy secretary in 1877. Farther south, Frozine Madrid opened a well-known French Creole restaurant in the 1860s in Mobile, Alabama, famous for its fish dishes and caramel custard. Meanwhile, Lexius Henson ran a saloon and restaurant in Augusta, Georgia, in the 1870s. As the city's only fine-dining establishment, it was outfitted with an oyster bar, cigar stand, and ladies' restaurant served by an all-female staff.

In Baltimore, Benjamin Franklin Simms built a thriving catering and provisioning businesses after being mentored by famed caterer and cook Henry Jakes. A menu from one of Simms's events in 1892 includes oysters half shell, canvasback duck, and roast turkey—dishes that we still associate with community gatherings and fine dining even today. In Chicago, Charles Henry Smiley's catering business made him one of the city's most successful Black businessmen. His headquarters, built in 1894, were estimated to be worth $100,000, and he was known as one of the foremost employers of Black staff members in the Midwest, maintaining relationships with wealthy clients, politicians, and society elites. In the 1890s in New Orleans, formerly enslaved Nellie Murray was the city's most celebrated and sought-after caterer. Descended from multiple generations of enslaved cooks, Murray traveled to Europe as a personal chef, catered for events such as the 1903 National American Woman Suffrage Convention, and was renowned for her Creole cooking.

Along with defining fine dining and professional food service, a post-emancipation Black female labor force continued to make its hand felt in the stewpots and kitchens of America's middle class. It was common in the late 1800s for middle-class households to have domestic help. Live-in maids or day workers handled cleaning, childcare, laundry, and meal preparation. Following emancipation, these domestic positions were one of the few avenues for employment for

> Black culinarians owned catering empires that defined fine dining at the time; opened taverns, alehouses, and oyster bars; and acted as tastemakers in their cities and regions.

OPPOSITE: The staff of Sylvia's gathers outside the legendary soul food restaurant in Harlem, New York.

> ### *Focus On:* The Mammy Stereotype & Aunt Jemima
>
> Award-winning author and journalist Toni Tipton-Martin calls the use of racist imagery of Black peoples in food advertising, designed to simultaneously sell goods and reinforce a racial hierarchy, the "Jemima code." One of the most common tropes used in this code is that of the mammy, commonly represented as a fat Black woman who caters to the white family she works for, her grin and cheerful affect used as evidence she is "happy" with her servitude or is a loyal and faithful servant who does not mind unequal treatment and limited rights.
>
> You're probably familiar with this trope in one of its most popular forms, that of Aunt Jemima pancake mix and syrups. In 1875, a slave field song turned minstrel tune, "Old Aunt Jemima," featured a Black female mammy and quickly gained popularity. That imagery was used to market the self-rising pancake mix. Nancy Green, a formerly enslaved Black woman, portrayed the Aunt Jemima character at the 1893 World's Columbian Exposition in Chicago to represent the company. When Quaker Oats purchased the Aunt Jemima brand in 1925, it kept the image and name until controversy regarding the logo bubbled over in 2020. Aunt Jemima was then rebranded as Pearl Milling Company. However, a marketing representative for the brand told *Fortune* in 2021 that the company intends to keep the Aunt Jemima brand alive to maintain its trademark.
>
> The imagery of the mammy, like that of Aunt Jemima, has been used in the United States to mark authenticity and deliciousness. Simultaneously, the mammy degrades Black women's culinary contributions, framing them as the result of an almost mythical element rather than a product of true expertise and skill. The mammy and other similar tropes have served to render Black cooks almost invisible in culinary history.

Black women. In the early 1900s, it's estimated that two-thirds of Black women were domestic servants or launderers. Consider these roles when you look at community cookbooks featuring recipes supposedly from wealthy or middle-class white housewives: *The Creole Cookery Book,* published in 1885, features recipes from housekeepers, for instance. Though we can never know for certain how many of those domestic workers were Black women, many surely were in late 1800s New Orleans. Their culinary knowledge and techniques became the preference of their employers and made their way into their employers' cookbooks. Many of the cookbooks of the era may not explicitly credit Black women, but these books act as a recorded memory of Black cuisine and culinary expertise.

Black labor marked American culinary practices beyond food service. In Charleston, Charles C. Leslie owned and operated a large fishing operation, directing and employing a primarily Black workforce in the late 1800s. Leslie's enterprise made Charleston the richest market for local seafood in the United States at the time. He became a food purveyor throughout South Carolina and supplied the scientific community with expertise and samples that led to initiatives such as America's first nursery for soft-shell crabs and protection measures for fish populations under stress. Leslie was ahead of his time in promoting seafood sustainability.

Emancipation coincided with another important institution: the passenger railroad. The Pullman Company emerged as a railway giant in the golden era of American rail travel, and by the end of the 19th century Pullman cars carried passengers from Mexico to Canada and throughout the United States. The Pullman Company hired Black men, many formerly enslaved, to act as porters catering to white customers for little pay. Porters served as valets, entertainers, cooks, waiters, and more for passengers. Working with limited ingredients in tight quarters, porters turned out dishes such as roast lamb, chicken croquettes, roast beef, and various ice creams. The Pullman Company eventually became the nation's largest employer of Black workers.

The life and work of Rufus Estes offers an example of the caliber of service expected of Pullman porters. Estes was born enslaved in Tennessee in 1857, worked as a cook's assistant in Nashville as a teenager, and in the 1880s secured a job as chief line cook at a celebrated French restaurant in Chicago. At 26, Estes joined the Pullman Company as a porter.

Estes preserved a basic outline of his life and knowledge in his book, originally titled *Good Things to Eat, as Suggested by Rufus: A Collection of Practical Recipes for Preparing Meats, Game, Fowl, Fish, Puddings, Pastries, Etc.*, which he published in 1911. The cookbook contains nearly 600 recipes, many associated with Black culinary traditions such as gumbo and pigs' feet, in addition to macaroni and cheese, lobster bisque, puddings and meringues, an entire section on soufflés, and decadent dishes such as truffle-chestnut stuffing. *Good Things to Eat* also describes his time as a porter for the Pullman Company, where he served notables such as President Grover Cleveland, President Benjamin Harrison, and opera singer Adelina Patti.

Pullman porters remained exclusively Black until the mid-1900s. Rufus Estes and the more than 10,000 other porters like him made up a Black middle class during a time of transition in the United States. Though they worked long hours, faced much discrimination, and were largely reliant on tips, Pullman porters also had a modicum of privilege due to their positions. They were able to support their families and children's education and act as cultural conduits, bringing home Black newspapers along with social trends from their journeys.

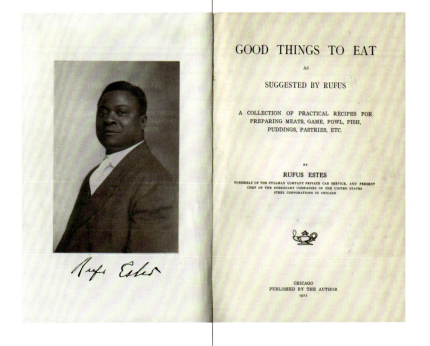

The title page of Rufus Estes's *Good Things to Eat*, the first cookbook written and published by an African American

The Great Migration Takes Black Culinary Traditions National

After the end of the Civil War and the brief period of hope brought by Radical Reconstruction, life in the South grew more difficult for Black peoples. Jim Crow laws, named after a character in a minstrel show, were imposed to legalize racial segregation in the South. White supremacist organizations proliferated, and many of the gains of the early reconstruction period were rolled back. Black peoples who defied these racialized codes faced arrest and violence, and sometimes risked death. Thousands of Black peoples were lynched by white mobs, without due process, in acts of racialized terror between the late 1880s and the 1940s. Most, but not all, of these lynchings were perpetrated in the South. The return of African American soldiers from World War I inflamed white Americans. There was a wave of violence and terrorism targeting Black Americans and servicemen, who were met with lynchings, degradation, murder, and more. During the summer of 1919, white supremacist violence and riots spread across more than 25 cities in what is known as the Red Summer. Though the violence did not begin or end that summer, scholars estimate that at least 250 Black Americans were killed over a 10-month period.

Degradation, violence, and segregation directed toward Black peoples in America in the early 1900s coincided with little economic opportunity for Black residents in the South. Educational opportunities were also limited. In rural communities, Black students were not allowed in schools after primary grades. Meanwhile, up north, wages for Black professionals were considerably higher, and news of this spread through Black newspapers and traveling Black professionals like Pullman porters.

A letter from Sam Hayes seeking help in employment from Olivet Baptist Church dated April 1917

114 • AMERICAN SOUL

"The Migration Series, Panel No. 1" by Jacob Lawrence portrays the Great Migration of African Americans.

Responding to push-and-pull factors, a mass migration of Black peoples began in the early 1900s. During this Great Migration families built and rebuilt homes across networks in the North, Midwest, and West while in search of better lives. Between 1916 and 1970 an estimated six million Black peoples left the South, previously home to 90 percent of the nation's Black population. By the end of the Great Migration in 1970, only an estimated 50 percent of Black Americans remained in the South.

Primarily driven by hope for a better life, millions of Black peoples moved from the South to cities such as Chicago, New York, Philadelphia, Detroit, St. Louis, San Francisco, Oakland, Pasadena, and beyond. In total, nearly half the Black population of the United States resettled in a period of about 60 years, profoundly reshaping American foodways.

Black southern migrants held on to their food traditions whenever possible in their new homes. Food served as comfort, drew on important memories, reified identity, and expressed culture. Responding to new southern customs emerging in northern areas, the grocery stores, street vendors, and restaurants catering to burgeoning Black communities began to showcase southern foods: Local shops stocked more pork products, greens, peanuts, and other southern staples; neighborhood garden plots cropped up where there was adequate space. When garden space was unavailable, which was often, canned or dried vegetables replaced the fresh varietals that Black Southerners were used to. Hot sauce, fried fish and chicken, cornbread, and grits proliferated from urban street carts, in homes, and at an array of restaurants appealing to Black Southerners' tastes.

For most Black migrants, the boiled and fried foods of the rural South remained staples out of necessity and nostalgia. Many housing tenements, hastily adapted to meet surging demand, lacked adequate cooking facilities and kitchen storage, or charged extra for kitchen privileges. Foods that could be fried or prepared in one pot were simple to cook and demanded less energy. Fried chicken, for example, traveled well (it was often eaten cold during journeys north or westward), could be prepared quickly in kitchens with limited supplies, and was readily available for purchase from street vendors and restaurants. Meanwhile, Black entrepreneurs making their way in new cities and towns catered to clientele longing for a taste of home with dishes such as hoppin' John and pigs' feet. "Often their fortunes were made by selling dishes that amply demonstrated cultural resilience of some iconic black foods. Inadvertently, they also aided the northward movement of traditional African American foodways from the South," writes Jessica B. Harris in *High on the Hog*.

A group of migrants from Florida travel to Cranberry, New Jersey, in search of work picking potatoes.

The influx of southern migrants didn't come without controversies in Black communities. Initially, urban middle-class and elite Black residents frowned on the food traditions of southern migrants. Communal campaigns and Black newspapers extolled the virtues of "proper" housekeeping and behavior, in which food played a role. Greens, pork chops, and fried chicken were characterized by some as undesirable or unmentionable foods. This focus on respectability was a direct result of generations of stereotyping Black peoples and their foodways in the United States. However, throughout the decades of the Great Migration those views began to shift.

By the end of the multiple waves of Black migration and resettlement that took place between 1916 and 1970, a new racial consciousness was sweeping through the United States. A growing sense of Black pride and the Black Power and civil rights movements coalesced to blur dining lines in Black communities. By the end of the Great Migration, class-based fissures and stigmas that had prevented some wealthier Black urban populations in the North from embracing southern food habits had been washed away. Black peoples of all classes and backgrounds had grown to embrace southern homestyle cooking.

The impact of Black migrants on American cuisine and American diners was felt far and wide, beyond the confines of Black communities. In New York, white customers got a taste of Black cooking and southern cuisine in Harlem by frequenting its clubs, restaurants, and street vendors. On the opposite coast, the Great Migration brought barbecue to Los Angeles. Today, southern Black roots still impact the city's barbecue scene; some family barbecue businesses can trace their roots to the South and follow them through waves of Black migration westward. "As a direct result, the heart of LA's barbecue scene has been proudly Black and tacitly southern for generations," writes Farley Elliott, senior editor at Eater LA, in "Witness the Renaissance of LA's Black Barbecue Scene." Ultimately, Black migrants from the South helped shape the dining practices of communities and cities far and wide.

The Harlem Renaissance

During the period of the Great Migration, a "Negro Renaissance" (as it was termed by writer and activist Langston Hughes) bloomed. Throughout the nation, cities became focal points for Black art and expression, drawing poets, painters, musicians, and other performers throughout the 1920s and '30s. This era marked the rise of modern Black literary and cultural greats: Zora Neale Hurston, Duke Ellington, W. E. B. Du Bois, Booker T. Washington, Louis Armstrong, and others helped popularize Black arts such as jazz music and redefine Black culture and global culture.

By the 1920s, more than 200,000 Black residents lived in the previously predominantly white neighborhood of Harlem. The area emerged as a center for Black cultural creation and art, as well as a locus for Black food adaptation and entrepreneurship. In Harlem, pigs' feet collided with cultural criticism as Black communities throughout the United States were reshaped. As a result, Harlem became the namesake and symbolic center of a national phenomenon, now commonly called the Harlem Renaissance.

Harlem was a mecca of Black churches, eateries, clubs, and social events. Housing was expensive and often crowded, with limited facilities, forcing new residents to get creative to make ends meet. Black women often set up catering operations from their apartments, and street vendors proliferated. One such entrepreneur, Patsy Randolph, collected cast-off watermelon rinds from restaurants and other vendors, pickled

> Harlem became a microcosm for the culinary experimentation happening throughout the United States. The neighborhood was a destination for Caribbean, South American, and African migrants.

them, and sold them. Her profit margin on the pickled rinds was reportedly more than 95 percent. Another woman, Lillian Harris Dean, a Black migrant from Mississippi, made her fortune in New York selling southern staples such as pigs' feet. "Pig Foot Mary," as she was called, was able to purchase property and retire in California after she smartly leveraged her expertise in southern cuisine with astute investments.

To cope with rent gouging and the high cost of living in Harlem, people often threw rent parties in their apartments, advertising a fun time for a modest fee for local Black residents who were not permitted in segregated clubs. Many rent parties included a spread of gumbo, hoppin' John, potato salad, chitlins, and other specialties. With the furniture cleared out, lights turned down low, and music going, rent parties were a means of survival and creating community for Black peoples in their new homes.

When rents skyrocketed in Harlem in the 1920s and '30s, residents threw parties with entry fees.

In the 1920s, Prohibition created a vibrant underground nightlife in Harlem, with famous spots like the Cotton Club catering to an exclusively white clientele, served by a kitchen staff that was entirely Black and entertained by light-skinned faux-exotic dancers and performers. Adventurous white patrons would venture to Harlem to test out the thriving street-food scene or to dine at local clubs. Though club cuisine typically drew on a mix of culinary traditions, it also offered dishes that drew on southern and Black foodways, such as the chicken okra soup offered at the Cotton Club.

Harlem became a microcosm for the culinary experimentation happening throughout the United States. The neighborhood was a destination for Caribbean, South American, and African migrants, and their foodways intermingled with each other. You could find African yams, sweet potatoes, sugarcane, bananas, plantains, cassava, and other plants from the Caribbean at markets. Vendors sold everything from *arroz con pollo* to Jamaican curry and barbecue. Records from the Federal Writers' Project, part of the Works Progress Administration, show that Black Americans, Latin Americans, and West Indians patronized the same Harlem restaurants and jazz venues, resulting in what Frederick Douglass Opie characterizes as the "blending and sharing of black and Hispanic music and food" in *Southern Food and Civil Rights: Feeding the Revolution*.

This was also one of the most important historical periods for Black literature and cultural expression, and the works of luminaries such as Du Bois, Claude McKay, and others illustrate some of the changes the Great Migration wrought on foodways during that period. Their works touch on issues of race, class, and gender as they related to food politics, including explorations of respectability and status as well as food stereotypes associated with Black peoples, such as gluttony, mammies, and more. Black foodways offered avenues for cultural criticism in the prominent works of this era, and foods like fried chicken were used to discuss the role of women in society and relationships, memory and culture, and the economic struggles of Black peoples.

The stock market crash of 1929 and the Great Depression dampened the glory days of the Harlem Renaissance, though Black creativity did not end with it. However, Black economic progress almost entirely disappeared during the Great Depression. The 1935 riot in Harlem marked the end of the renaissance era, a symbol of a transition that gave way to persistent discrimination, violence, and limited economic opportunities that would mark Black American life for the next few decades.

During the Harlem Renaissance, artists like Canada Lee (center), Hilda Simms (center back), and Langston Hughes (front right) threw lively gatherings like this party in 1944.

Soul Food: Stigma & Beyond

Toward the end of the Great Migration, the Black Power and civil rights movements gave the nation a new name for the Black and southern foods that had made their way throughout the nation—soul food. The nostalgic, often celebratory foods of Black southerners, soul food became the culinary symbol of a new Black consciousness. • From the advent of the term in the 1960s during the rise of the Black pride movement, definitions within the Black community have varied regarding what constitutes soul food. Is it just spicier southern food? Is it a tradition separate from southern cuisine entirely? Some say soul food is southern food with more seasoning. Others say there are minute difference between soul food and southern cuisines and the real distinction comes from who is doing the cooking (Black versus white). Despite ongoing debate, the name became widely utilized, and soul food is one of the most prominent symbols of Black cuisine today.

The Nation of Islam Versus Soul Food

Debate surrounding soul food started just as soon as the term began to be used. Some activists and groups rejected soul food as harmful to the Black community and unworthy of celebration or veneration.

The Nation of Islam (NOI), founded in 1930, remains one of the most recognizable Black organizations in America. As a religious and political group, the NOI has an explicitly Black nationalist ideology that draws on some elements of the Islamic religion. Though NOI teachings emphasize Black independence and uplift, its leadership has also espoused openly antisemitic, anti-LGBTQ, and racist rhetoric. The Southern Poverty Law Center has designated the NOI as a hate group.

The Nation of Islam operated a network of commercial farms—including egg producer Muslim Farms—during the 1960s and '70s.

In 1963, Malcolm X (center) dined at Temple 7, a halal restaurant frequented by Black Muslims in Harlem.

In part buoyed by charismatic and famous members like Muhammad Ali and Malcolm X, the NOI experienced a boom in membership and political power during the civil rights movement. An explicit part of the NOI's platform is a rejection of unhealthy foods—specifically soul food. Leader Elijah Muhammad harshly critiqued soul food and the dietary practices of southern Black peoples, characterizing them as part of a "slave diet" and urging followers to turn away from them in favor of healthier alternatives. The NOI encouraged its supporters to eschew pork and alcohol, eat healthy foods, and regain financial independence by practicing economic unity, pooling resources, and supporting Black-owned businesses. The organization's entrepreneurial ventures focused heavily on food service and food cultivation as a means to achieve financial security and communal health. In the mid-1960s the NOI owned 10,000 acres of farmland, cultivated crops, and raised farm animals. It operated grocery stores, restaurants, bakeries, and a slaughterhouse. Today, the NOI still owns and operates farmland in multiple states, and the organization's influence can still be seen in the dietary habits of Black Americans; though exact numbers are hard to come by, a significant portion of Black Americans do not eat pork, many in part because of the NOI's influence.

Southern Versus Soul Food

Though many characterize the entirety of southern food as unhealthy, soul food has become a particular target for vitriol and critique from within the Black community and those outside it. This view ignores the interwoven histories of southern and soul food. The separation of the two cuisines has ultimately allowed for stereotypes to be applied to soul food and not the foods of white Southerners. Namely, it's been said that soul food is unhealthy, greasy, and always fried; that it came from the masters' scraps; that it encompasses the worst, most undesirable parts of the animal; and that it's unsophisticated.

This reductive view of soul food ignores American culinary history and obscures Black expertise and ingenuity. Narratives about "undesirable" foods such as chitlins and possum offer an example of how the discourse around soul food and Black foodways has been racialized. Possum was used in minstrel shows to caricature Black food as unhealthy and less than. Yet possum was a popular dish—one also consumed by whites—in southern cuisine in the 1800s, so much so that it was served at boardinghouses and even at the University of North Carolina. Chitlins, pigs' feet, hog jowls, and other pig parts deemed less popular on modern plates have a similar history. The common narrative that only Black peoples consumed these foods, and only in the form of scraps left to them by enslavers, is a farce. The taste for them was widespread across racial lines, including among enslavers. Even Mark Twain noted chitlins were one of his favorite foods.

Pork chitterlings (chitlins)—pork belly and intestine pieces—at a supermarket in Texas

122 • AMERICAN SOUL

Narratives about these foods as leftovers, white man's scraps, and undesirable parts don't reflect historical reality and simply add stigma to Black foodways. Chef Jennifer Hill Booker said it best in an op-ed for the James Beard Foundation: "It seems that in order for Soul Food to be fully embraced, to be considered healthy and elegant, it must become Southern food, with the original black hands in the pot replaced by white ones."

Other food writers and historians similarly point out that the popular definition of soul food ignores much of Black southern history. The American South is a region with long growing seasons that produces an incredible amount of produce, a region with rivers and coastlines abundant with fish. *That* was the natural environment underpinning southern cuisine and the development of Black foodways.

Gardens & Plant-Based Traditions

The mischaracterizations of soul food ignore long-standing garden traditions and the role of popular nutritional powerhouses, such as collard greens, in Black foodways. It obscures long-standing traditions in the Black community that link food to broader social justice issues and animal welfare. Black gardening traditions that emphasized growing food for sustenance and to fill nutritional gaps, particularly in the South, are a well-established historical fact. Adding to that, historically, many Black activists were vegans or vegetarians, and those dietary practices spread throughout Black communities during the civil rights movement. For many Black vegans, food was yet another avenue for activism and a means to reject the effects of capitalism and chattel slavery on the health of Black peoples. Mischaracterizations of soul food also obscure the many Black contributions to the modern farm-to-table movement, which is viewed as healthy and "clean," and in fact ties back to Black and Indigenous knowledge systems, labor, and traditions.

West and Central African societies traditionally ate largely plant-based diets. It wasn't until enslavement and colonization that African (and many Indigenous) diets began to incorporate more animal products. Before the expansion of colonization, the slave trade, and the advent of the modern industrialized food system, Black culinary practices relied primarily on vegetables, legumes, grains, and herbs. Enslaved communities often had limited rations or depended on food they could source themselves from gardens, foraging, and fishing. Meat was often used as seasoning or was consumed only at celebratory meals and not as an everyday main. Black peoples in the United States often maintained gardens as well, from the subsistence gardens of enslaved peoples to the personal gardens of sharecroppers to southern Black garden traditions that persist today.

> Toward the end of the Great Migration, the Black Power and civil rights movements gave the nation a new name for the Black and southern foods that had made their way throughout the nation—soul food.

Black Food Enters the Political Conversation

The phrase "food is political" has been hotly debated in recent years. Some dismiss it as lazy shorthand for an understanding of how food connects to history, culture, representation, and power. Others prefer to view cuisine as simply the sum of ingredients and techniques divorced from history altogether. However, for Black peoples, as for many marginalized groups, food often occupies both a cultural and political space, and it is deeply connected to issues of self-determination, identity, justice, and more.

Remembrance, honoring heritage, nurturing community, sharing culture—all are vital elements of Black food spaces in the United States. Black food spaces—those restaurants, bars, clubs, inns, eateries, and other spots owned by, operated by, or catering to Black peoples—took on cultural and political significance in part because of segregation and persecution. For a significant portion of American history, dining remained segregated, and anti-Black discrimination persists in many forms today. Unfriendly and downright dangerous environments—from enslavement to Jim Crow, to segregation and lynching, to stereotyping and police brutality—have forced Black peoples to seek and create safe spaces. And many of those spaces have centered on food and beverage.

By example, juke joints were rural southern venues that evolved out of Black gathering spaces during enslavement. They became centers for Black music, entertainment, food, and gambling. Later, the web of clubs, juke joints, and theaters spanning the United States from North to South—known as the Chitlin Circuit—offered spaces for Black peoples to drink, listen to music, dance, eat, blow off steam, and congregate. The circuit was

A rock-and-roll concert poster from 1956

Legendary musician Aretha Franklin sings at Chicago's Park West Auditorium in 1992.

named after the soul food the establishments sold, with dishes such as barbecued pork, grits, pigs' feet, and, of course, chitlins gracing the menus.

"The menus represented a continuum of the cookery that came from the slave quarters and special-occasion meals during the antebellum period," notes Frederick Douglass Opie in *Southern Food and Civil Rights*. It was in those gathering places that blues music was born, which in turn influenced rock-and-roll, jazz, R&B, and country music. In those venues, Black entertainers and jazz greats like Ray Charles, B. B. King, Aretha Franklin, and Louis Armstrong honed their craft and gained broader commercial acceptance performing for largely Black diners and audiences, gathered over plates of food connected to Black history.

The Civil Rights Movement

As the Great Depression struck, the country entered a period of frustrated dreams. Black peoples were hit hardest and bore the brunt of competing for jobs formerly considered too lowly for white workers. Many turned to food-related ventures to get by, catching and selling fish, street vending, and cooking. Black women, excluded from other jobs, continued to play outsize roles as domestic laborers.

Beginning in the late 1920s and coinciding with the Great Depression, Black peoples and activists in the United States began protesting limited job opportunities. They pressured businesses to change hiring practices. Through boycotting and picketing, often targeting food markets and convenience stores such as Piggly Wiggly, they pressured companies to hire Black employees. Initially, these campaigns targeted stores in Black communities or with a predominantly Black clientele. The tactic spread from Chicago to Harlem and beyond as Black Americans united around various direct-action campaigns urging boycotts of businesses that refused to hire Black workers.

These nonviolent direct-action campaigns continued, gaining traction and fueling a new sense of civic engagement in the Black community. Ultimately, this led to the civil rights movement of the mid-1950s. Of course, Black food helped fuel the movement. Black culinarians raised funds to support protest efforts and created safe spaces for organizers, activists, protesters, and leaders to build community and plan for continued direct action, often over meals of traditional Black southern foods.

The Montgomery bus boycott of the 1950s offers an example. Aimed at ending segregation on city buses in Montgomery, Alabama, the boycott hinged on Black riders abstaining from using city buses. Of course, food played a central role in the success of the boycott. Georgia Gilmore, a Black woman known for her cooking, was fired for supporting the boycott. To make ends meet, she founded a catering business and restaurant out of her house, a move encouraged by Martin Luther King, Jr., who lived nearby. Gilmore's restaurant served as a safe meeting space for movement leaders, offering a chance to enjoy a meal and strategize. It was also one of numerous Black eateries where whites also dined despite Jim Crow laws. Guests included Robert F. Kennedy and Lyndon B. Johnson.

Gilmore and other Black women organized the Club From Nowhere, which sold baked goods and meals of dishes like fried fish, stewed greens, and pound cake to help fund the boycott. The Club From Nowhere helped support the carpool system of more than 300 cars that boycotters relied on while abstaining from the city bus system. The women also fed boycott participants whose extended commutes left little time for cooking by offering take-home plates at reasonable prices.

The Montgomery bus boycott ended on December 21, 1956, after 381 days. The Supreme Court ruled that segregation on public buses was unconstitutional. The boycott served as a model for direct-action campaigns to follow during the civil rights era. And Gilmore's activism continued long after the end of the boycott.

In Atlanta, there's another example: Paschal's, a small lunch spot with 30 seats that grew into a restaurant, motel, and nightclub in the 1940s. One of the only

Remembrance, honoring heritage, nurturing community, sharing culture—all are vital elements of Black food spaces in the United States.

OPPOSITE: Celebrities and luminaries, including 11-year-old David Robinson (center) and (right from center) Jackie Robinson, Rachel Robinson, Rosa Parks, and Rev. Fred Shuttlesworth, walk in the 1963 March on Washington for Jobs and Freedom.

places that offered a white-tablecloth setting for Black diners, Paschal's also served as a stop on the famed Chitlin Circuit. Despite its being designated for "coloreds only," white diners also frequented Paschal's.

At the restaurant, a meeting room was set aside for Martin Luther King, Jr., and other civil rights activists who frequently met there. The 1963 March on Washington for Jobs and Freedom was in part planned at Paschal's. The restaurant also sponsored and hosted activist luncheons and provided food and bail money for jailed student protesters. And it served as a meeting place for those who were arrested to reunite with their families. Paschal's literally fueled civil rights activists and leaders, while providing an important meeting and planning space to help further the movement.

Ben's Chili Bowl, a Lasting Example

Located in Washington, D.C., Ben's Chili Bowl is a modern reminder of the legacy of Black food spaces as both cultural and political centers. Opened by Ben Ali and his then fiancée Virginia on August 22, 1958, the restaurant still operates out of its original location on U Street. Virginia Ali describes Ben's Chili Bowl as a "proudly African American–owned business." The U Street area was known as Black Broadway when the restaurant opened, renowned for its musical venues where greats such as Duke Ellington and Nat King Cole would perform. At that time, D.C. was still a segregated city, and Ben's served as a safe space for students from the nearby historically Black Howard University, as well as performers and revelers, to dine.

Martin Luther King, Jr., dined at Ben's Chili Bowl. And in August 1963 the restaurant donated food to the March on Washington. In April 1968, during the D.C. riots following the assassination of King, Ben's was given permission from the city to stay open past curfew and given passes for its night-team members to come to work. The riots decimated many businesses and U Street, an area that was struck again by rising drug use in the 1970s and '80s. Ben's was one of only three businesses to survive three decades of turmoil, at times reducing its staff to just one employee.

In 2004, Ben's was awarded a James Beard Foundation Gallo of Sonoma America's Classics award for its status as one of America's "down-home eateries that have carved out a special place on the American culinary landscape." In October 2009, cofounder Ben Ali passed away at the age of 82.

Today, Ben's Chili Bowl's Original Chili Half Smoke is considered by many Washingtonians to be the city's signature dish. The half-smoked pork-and-beef

Representative John Lewis, a member of Atlanta's Concerned Black Clergy, speaks at Paschal's Restaurant in 1988.

Feeding the Civil Rights Movement

① Ben's Chili Bowl, Washington, D.C., fed protesters at the 1963 March on Washington. ② Big Apple Inn, Jackson, Miss., provided meeting rooms for Black activists, including Freedom Riders Fannie Lou Hamer and Medgar Evers. ③ Brenda's Bar-B-Que Pit, Montgomery, Ala., fed and aided organizers of the Montgomery Bus Boycott of 1955–56. ④ Dooky Chase's, New Orleans, La., offered meeting spaces for civil rights strategists, including Thurgood Marshall and Martin Luther King, Jr. ⑤ Florida Avenue Grill, Washington, D.C., provided a gathering place for civil rights leaders planning the 1963 march. ⑥ The Four Way Restaurant, Memphis, Tenn., provided a meeting spot, and food, for planning the 1968 "I Am a Man" protest. ⑦ Lannie's Bar-B-Q Spot, Selma, Ala., fed and supported voting rights activists. ⑧ Lassis Inn, Little Rock, Ark., protected Black community organizers during the integration of Little Rock High School in 1957. ⑨ Paschal's Restaurant, Atlanta, Ga., fed and supported civil rights organizers and student protesters. ⑩ Woolworth's lunch counter, Greensboro, N.C., desegregated after a 1960 student sit-in that sparked a national movement.

sausage is served on a grilled bun with mustard, onions, and house-made spicy chili. Ben's also continues to be active in the local community, feeding essential workers during the COVID-19 shutdown and protesters who took to the streets of D.C. during the Black Lives Matter rallies. While Ben's now has multiple locations around the broader D.C. area, the business is still a family affair. Ben and Virginia's three sons and two daughters-in-law help run its operation, marketing, and branding.

In the Words of Virginia Ali

Though Virginia Ali has retired from running Ben's Chili Bowl, she still visits almost every day. Ali is proud of how much of Ben's history is interconnected with the historically Black community surrounding its original location in Shaw. When Ali came to Washington, D.C., the city was still segregated. "I couldn't go downtown to dinner, couldn't go to the theater," she says. She couldn't even try on clothes in the big department stores. "But we had everything we needed in our Shaw community, with Howard right there," she adds. "When we opened the Chili Bowl, we found everyone we needed in our community, all locally owned African American businesses, from the plumber to the cabinetmaker. They stayed with us until they retired."

The Alis worked hard to make Ben's Chili Bowl into a vibrant center where students could gather, locals could go on dates or grab late-night food, and Black peoples could feel welcome. "We spent 10 years working without a whole week's vacation together," she remembers. "We had to take separate vacations if we wanted to take a week or two. But we wanted to make sure that our guests are treated well. I want them to feel like they're coming into my home."

It's clear that the Alis' focus on providing a space for the community was felt and appreciated. The community has acted to preserve the Chili Bowl when necessary. During the riots following the assassination of Martin Luther King, Jr., Ben's Chili Bowl not only remained open but also was undamaged in part because of community action. "When the uprising began, there were these young folks who thought that Ben's Chili Bowl was their home away from home," she says. "These young people would hang out front and tell everyone during the uprising, 'No, no, don't touch Ben's.'"

In 2009, President Barack Obama visited Ben's Chili Bowl on his welcome-to-the-city tour. His visit was a testament to Ben's status as a celebrated space in the Black community and an exciting surprise for Virginia Ali. "We never believed [having a Black president] was possible. Someone my age, we went to segregated schools. We were so excited."

In 2020, after a news report claimed Ben's Chili Bowl was "on the brink" of closure, the community once again demonstrated its support. Ali says, "We got letters from all over the country, and the response that we got from across the country was heartwarming." People far and wide sent notes of what Ben's meant to them, along with donations. With that support, Ben's Chili Bowl continued what it had always done: serving the community in times of need. "We were able to take the dollars and well-wishes they sent us and prepare boxed lunches for Howard Medical Center, teachers, the fire department, and protesters."

> *"I couldn't go downtown to dinner, couldn't go to the theater... But we had everything we needed in our Shaw community, with Howard right there."*
>
> —VIRGINIA ALI, CO-FOUNDER OF BEN'S CHILI BOWL

OPPOSITE: Virginia Ali (pictured here in 2023) and her husband, Ben, donated food from their restaurant, Ben's Chili Bowl, during the March on Washington in 1963.

Food for Thought
The Black Panther Party & Food Activism

The Black Panther Party, founded in 1966 by Huey P. Newton and Bobby Seale, also used food as a tool for activism in the 1960s and '70s. • The Panthers launched the Free Breakfast for Children Program to feed hungry and underprivileged children in 1969, one of the first of its kind in the nation. It was part of an intersectional approach linking a variety of social programs,

including free medical clinics and legal clinics, to broader issues of social justice and Black uplift. At its height, the Black Panther Party's free breakfast program served thousands of children daily in more than 45 areas, offering some students their very first experience eating breakfast before school. Donations were solicited from local grocery stores and churches. Party members and volunteers prepared meals and served them in community spaces. Teachers, principals, and other school professionals noted the results, telling newspapers that their students were more attentive, less tired, and didn't complain of hunger pangs.

After the assassinations of Robert F. Kennedy and Martin Luther King, Jr., the Black Panther Party stepped into the limelight with a message of self-determination and Black Power. This message was thrilling for some, but others viewed it as a threat. The Panthers were often vilified in media, portrayed as angry, violent, and a danger to the nation. The breakfast program drew the attention and ire of then FBI chief J. Edgar Hoover, who singled out the program as a threat to the bureau's efforts to destroy the Black Panther Party.

The Panthers and the Free Breakfast for Children Program were regularly targeted by officials, and the efforts against the program were not subtle. FBI agents went to extremes to publicly bash the program, including telling parents it was used to teach racism or that the food served to the children was contaminated with diseases. In cities such as Oakland, California, and Baltimore, Maryland, party members were harassed in front of participating children.

In 1982, the Black Panther Party officially ceased operations. However, the effects of the Panthers' Free Breakfast for Children Program are still felt today. It helped put pressure on the federal government to expand its own free breakfast pilot program. In 2019, the federal School Breakfast Program fed almost 15 million children in the United States; in 2023, it provided 2.4 billion free and reduced-cost breakfasts.

OPPOSITE: **Members of the Black Panther Party serve a free breakfast to children at Sacred Heart Church in San Francisco.**

Pepper Pot

Cook time: 1 hour 30 minutes, plus 1 hour (or overnight) marinating time | Makes 6 to 8 servings

For the meat
- 3 tablespoons jerk seasoning blend
- 1 tablespoon crushed red pepper
- 2 teaspoons dark brown sugar
- 2 teaspoons dried thyme
- 2 teaspoons garlic powder
- 2 teaspoons ground ginger
- 2 teaspoons kosher salt
- 2 teaspoons onion powder
- 1½ pounds beef stew meat, trimmed and cut into 1-inch cubes
- 1 pound boneless pork roast, trimmed and cut into 1-inch cubes
- 6 tablespoons vegetable oil, divided
- Zest and juice of 2 lemons

For pepper pot
- 1 pound cassava root, peeled and cut into 1½-inch pieces
- 1 pound yellow potatoes, scrubbed and cut into 1½-inch pieces
- 1 large sweet potato, peeled and cut into 1½-inch pieces
- 1 onion, finely chopped
- 2 large carrots, peeled and cut into 1½-inch pieces
- 1 red bell pepper, seeded and cut into 1½-inch pieces
- 1 green bell pepper, seeded and cut into 1½-inch pieces
- 1 yellow bell pepper, seeded and cut into 1½-inch pieces
- 5 cloves garlic, chopped
- 2 tablespoons finely chopped fresh parsley
- 2 tablespoons chopped fresh thyme
- 2 bay leaves
- 3 to 7 chilies of your choice (habanero, serrano, jalapeño, Scotch bonnet, Fresno), finely chopped
- 7 cups beef bone broth
- 2 pounds lacinato (Tuscan) kale, ribs removed, roughly chopped

In a medium bowl, mix jerk seasoning with crushed red pepper, brown sugar, thyme, garlic powder, ground ginger, salt, and onion powder. Add beef, pork, 3 tablespoons of oil, and lemon zest and juice to the bowl. Stir to coat meat. Set aside and let marinate at room temperature for 1 hour, or cover and refrigerate overnight.

After meat has marinated, heat remaining 3 tablespoons of oil in a large Dutch oven over medium-high heat. Working in batches, cook meat until browned in spots, about 4 minutes per batch. Transfer meat to a bowl.

Add cassava, yellow and sweet potatoes, onion, carrots, and bell peppers to the pot. Sweat the vegetables until fragrant, about 3 minutes. Add garlic, parsley, thyme, and bay leaves. Cook, stirring often, until fragrant, about 2 minutes. Add chilies and cook about 2 minutes. Add bone broth and bring to a boil. Add meat and any juices to the pot. Reduce heat to maintain a rapid simmer.

Let stew simmer uncovered until meat is tender, stirring occasionally, 45 to 60 minutes. Stir in kale and let simmer until wilted, about 3 minutes. Adjust seasoning with salt, additional jerk seasoning, and crushed red pepper to taste before serving.

Pickled Watermelon Rinds

Make time: 2 days | Makes about 1 quart

½ cup kosher salt

5 cups watermelon rinds, cut into 1-inch pieces

¾ cup apple cider vinegar

¾ cup white vinegar

¾ cup sugar

¼ cup pickling spices

2 tablespoons dried mint or 2 large sprigs fresh mint (optional)

1 (2-inch) knob fresh ginger, peeled and sliced

¼ cup maraschino cherries

In a large pot, stir salt into 6 cups water until dissolved. Add watermelon rinds. Cover and let stand at room temperature overnight.

Scoop out ½ cup of salt water and reserve, then drain watermelon rinds. Return rinds and reserved salted water to pot and stir in 2½ cups cold water. Bring to boil over high heat, then reduce heat to medium-low and simmer for 10 minutes.

Meanwhile, in a small saucepan, add apple cider vinegar, white vinegar, sugar, pickling spices, mint (if using), and ginger and bring to a boil, stirring until sugar is dissolved.

Add vinegar mixture to the rinds, simmer on medium-low heat for 20 minutes. Add cherries and simmer until watermelon rinds are tender, about 10 minutes more. Remove from heat and let cool for 30 minutes.

Divide rinds and liquid into two 16-ounce glass jars. Let cool uncovered for 2 hours. Seal jars and refrigerate overnight. Eat within a month.

Buttermilk Biscuits

Bake time: 20 minutes | Makes 12 biscuits

- 4½ cups all-purpose flour, plus more for work surface
- 1½ tablespoons baking powder
- ¾ teaspoon baking soda
- 4 teaspoons kosher salt
- 1 cup (2 sticks) plus 2 tablespoons butter, frozen
- 6 tablespoons Crisco, frozen
- 1¾ cups buttermilk
- 1½ tablespoons honey
- 6 tablespoons melted butter, for finishing

In a large bowl, whisk flour, baking powder, baking soda, and salt. Place in the refrigerator until cold, about 30 minutes.

Preheat oven to 475°F. Line a 13-by-9-inch baking dish with parchment paper.

Use the large holes on a box grater to grate frozen butter and Crisco into dry ingredients; toss to evenly incorporate. Pour buttermilk and honey into dry ingredients; stir with your hands or a spatula just until dough comes together—it should be shaggy.

Dump dough onto a floured work surface. Press into a 13-by-8-inch rectangle, and fold the short ends over the middle, like folding a letter, dusting with flour as needed. Repeat, pressing into a rectangle and folding one more time, being careful to not overwork the dough.

Use a rolling pin to gently roll out the dough into a rectangle almost the size of the 13-by-9-inch baking dish. It should be about 3 to 4 inches thick. Place the dough in the baking dish and gently press out into the corners of the dish. Then cut the dough into 12 squares.

Bake biscuits until golden, about 17 to 20 minutes. Brush tops with melted butter before serving.

Chicken Croquettes

Cook time: 3 hours 30 minutes, including freezing and chilling time | Makes 18 croquettes

For the croquettes

1 cup buttermilk

¾ cup chicken stock

¾ cup heavy cream

2 tablespoons Dijon mustard

3 tablespoons butter

1 small onion, grated

1 celery stalk, finely chopped

¼ cup finely chopped fresh herbs (such as parsley, dill, marjoram, oregano, thyme, and/or rosemary)

3 tablespoons all-purpose flour

3 cloves garlic, grated

2 teaspoons poultry seasoning

1 teaspoon salt

1 teaspoon white pepper

2 egg yolks

1 rotisserie chicken, meat finely shredded (5½ to 6 cups), skin and bones discarded

½ cup grated Parmesan cheese

For the breading

⅔ cup all-purpose flour

4 eggs

1 cup heavy cream

½ teaspoon salt

½ teaspoon ground white pepper

2½ cups plain dry breadcrumbs

5 cups vegetable oil, for frying

To make the chicken: In a medium bowl, whisk together buttermilk, chicken stock, ¾ cup heavy cream, and mustard. Set aside.

In a Dutch oven, melt butter over medium-high heat. Add onion and celery and cook, stirring often, until celery begins to soften, about 5 minutes. Add herbs, flour, and garlic; cook, stirring often, until garlic is fragrant and flour is well combined, about 2 minutes. Stir in poultry seasoning, salt, and white pepper.

Gradually whisk buttermilk mixture into Dutch oven. Bring to a gentle boil, whisking often, for about 7 minutes. Reduce heat to low.

In a medium bowl, whisk the egg yolks. Gradually whisk in 3 ladlefuls of hot buttermilk-and-vegetable mixture into egg yolks, whisking constantly. Pour egg mixture into Dutch oven and increase heat to medium to bring back to a gentle boil, stirring often, for about 5 minutes. Add chicken to pot, one handful at a time. Turn off heat and stir in Parmesan.

Transfer chicken mixture to a large bowl and refrigerate, uncovered, until cool enough to handle, about 1 hour.

Spray a baking sheet with cooking spray. Spoon 3 tablespoons of chicken mixture onto baking sheet, forming a mound. Repeat with remaining chicken mixture. Refrigerate for 30 minutes.

To bread the croquettes: Add flour to a medium bowl. Working with a few mounds of chicken at a time, keeping the remaining croquettes in the refrigerator, shape the mounds into oblong ovals. Roll the ovals in flour, shaking off any excess, and place on a plate. Repeat until all croquettes have been rolled in flour and place plate(s) in freezer for 30 minutes. Croquettes will not be frozen solid, just cold enough to handle.

In another medium bowl, whisk together eggs, 1 cup heavy cream, salt, and white pepper. Pour the breadcrumbs into a shallow bowl or pie plate.

Dredge the floured croquettes in the egg mixture, one at a time, then in the breadcrumbs, turning to coat and pressing to adhere; return to plate and place in freezer. (If croquettes are difficult to work with, freeze for 20 minutes more.) Repeat dredging in egg and breadcrumbs, adding a second coating to each croquette. Freeze croquettes for 45 minutes.

In a medium saucepan, heat oil over medium-high until a deep-fry thermometer registers 365°F. To test if oil is hot enough, sprinkle a few breadcrumbs into it. If they bubble furiously, oil is ready.

Working in batches, fry croquettes in oil, turning after 1 minute, until golden brown, about 3 minutes per batch. Be sure to return oil to 365°F between batches. Use a slotted spoon to transfer croquettes to paper towel–lined plates to drain. Serve hot.

Lemon Cream Pie

Make time: 30 minutes, plus 4 to 6 hours chilling time | Makes 8 servings

For the filling
1 cup milk or half-and-half

¾ cup sugar

⅓ cup cornstarch

½ cup fresh lemon juice (from 2 to 4 lemons)

3 large egg yolks

2 tablespoons butter

1 teaspoon vanilla or lemon extract

1 tablespoon lemon zest

1 (9-inch) deep-dish pie crust, fully baked according to package instructions and cooled

For the Swiss meringue topping (optional)
3 large egg whites

⅔ cup granulated sugar (superfine, if available)

¼ teaspoon vanilla extract

Pinch of salt

For the filling: In a medium saucepan, whisk together milk, 1 cup water, sugar, cornstarch, and lemon juice. Bring to boil over medium heat, whisking constantly.

Whisk egg yolks in the top of a double boiler or in a medium-size heatproof bowl. Gradually whisk about 1 cup of the hot milk mixture into egg yolks, then add egg yolk mixture back into saucepan. Whisk over low heat until thickened, about 2 minutes. Add butter, extract, and lemon zest and stir until butter melts.

Pour filling into cooled crust. Cover with parchment or wax paper to prevent the top from hardening. Refrigerate until cold, 4 to 6 hours.

For the Swiss meringue topping (if using): When the pie filling is fully cooled, turn on broiler, with oven rack about 8 inches from heat source.

In the bowl of a stand mixer, stir egg whites and sugar on low just to blend.

Fill the bottom of the double boiler or a large saucepan with 3 inches of water, and bring it to a simmer. Place top pan with egg white mixture over bottom pan. Cook, whisking often, until egg whites are warm to the touch and sugar has dissolved, 1 to 2 minutes.

Fit a stand mixer with whisk attachment. Beat egg whites on medium-high until stiff peaks form, about 7 to 10 minutes. Add vanilla and salt and beat to blend.

Spoon meringue on top of pie, forming decorative swirls, making sure to spread all the way to the crust. Broil until the meringue is browned in spots, 30 to 60 seconds.

Alternatively, decorate the top of the pie with whipped cream.

CHAPTER FOUR

Looking Ahead

The Future of Black Food

American cuisine continues to evolve: what's popular, what's considered healthy, what's common, and what's trendy change rapidly. Just as Black peoples have long been culture makers in a variety of other spaces, from music to comedy, so, too, do they continue to impact the dynamic modern food landscape in the United States. There is no way to predict how American foodways will evolve in the next 100 years, but as we consider the future, movements in the Black food space are undoubtedly worth paying attention to.

Today's culinary tastemakers—from executive chefs in Michelin-starred restaurants to historians featured in streaming documentaries to content creators on social media—are defining the future of Black and American cuisine in myriad ways. What remains the same is a sense of pride, history, and hope.

While honoring the past, we are embracing and honoring these new trends around the world more than we ever have before. There is no American cuisine or American food landscape as we know it today without Black food and beverage traditions, professionals, and businesses. The numerous Black food and beverage festivals now in the United States serve as spaces to celebrate, explore, and acknowledge those contributions. I'm lucky to have attended many of these events, where I've soaked up spaces that center on joy, innovation, and the contributions of Black culinarians.

And content creators like me share deeper stories with creative freedom not always found on traditional media. These communities, like my own platform Feed The Malik, promote Black-centric culinary stories, small businesses, and culinarians near and far to audiences hungry for this information. Creators are breaking norms and reaching new audiences whose own tastes and cultures have not been served by traditional media.

It's an exciting time of unpredictability as we step into a future that embraces more diverse cultures—the histories, flavors, and foods that have made American cuisine what it is today and what it will become.

OPPOSITE: **Okra is a staple ingredient that has become the focus of vegan menus across the country.**
PAGES 144–145: **The Gullah Express food truck brings Gullah Geechee food to diners around St. Helena, South Carolina.**

Black Veganism

When you say "Black food in the United States," many immediately think of dishes such as pork chops, fried chicken, fried fish, and barbecue—all used as a catchall for Black American cuisine. The reality is something different. In fact, there is a long-standing thread of plant-centric dining traditions in Black communities.

• West African diets relied largely on plants. Meat was typically used as a seasoning rather than the main course. A similar dietary pattern persisted among enslaved Black peoples in the United Sates. In the South, a region with a long growing season, the Black population of enslaved peoples often lived with limited rations and little meat, except at celebratory occasions like harvest holidays or when they could source it themselves. Everyday cooking among enslaved peoples featured small amounts of animal products. Though it's stereotypically known for barbecue and fried fish and chicken, southern cuisine actually features robust plant sources such as rice, black-eyed peas, okra, sweet potatoes, and greens. It wasn't until the Great Migration, an emerging sense of Black identification around soul food, and the impacts of the industrialized food system that Black eating habits began to be more firmly linked to meat-centric consumption.

Many Black activists, including Angela Davis and Dick Gregory, have embraced veganism or vegetarianism. Those dietary practices became particularly resonant during the civil rights movement, when food was viewed as yet another avenue for activism and a means to reject the effects of capitalism and chattel slavery on the health of Black peoples. Such groups have long eschewed or altered the pork- and other animal-centric dishes associated with soul food and drawn connections between animal rights and human rights.

Other currents in the Black community have advocated for a plant-centric diet. In the Rastafarian tradition, a vegetarian diet is seen as beneficial for health and an improved connection with nature.

Tassili's Raw Reality Café is a Black-owned vegan restaurant in Atlanta, Georgia.

Most Rastafarians are not strictly vegan, but vegetarianism is widely embraced within the community. Black celebrities like will.i.am and members of the Wu-Tang Clan are vegan, and even Beyoncé and Jay-Z have advocated for the benefits of a vegan diet. New media spaces also reflect the growing vegan preferences of Black communities, with bloggers like Jenné Claiborne of Sweet Potato Soul and platforms such as Black Vegans Rock connecting Black vegans and providing them with resources and recipes.

Today, Black Americans are almost three times as likely as white Americans to identify as vegan and are cutting meat out of their diets at a higher rate than other populations. Black vegan restaurants are flourishing throughout the country, offering everything from raw foods to vegan versions of southern and

soul food classics like macaroni and cheese or greens seasoned with liquid smoke rather than ham or turkey.

An Advocate for the Masses

In the 1960s, Dick Gregory became one of the first Black comedians to gain recognition from a broad national audience. His 1961 *Tonight Show* appearance was groundbreaking for a Black performer at the time. Gregory was also active during the civil rights movement and outspoken about racial justice issues and politics in the United States. He attended the 1963 March on Washington, protested police brutality, spoke at colleges and rallies, and went on a number of hunger strikes.

Gregory also extended his nonviolent practice to animals and adopted a vegetarian diet in 1965. He became an outspoken advocate for a healthy lifestyle for Black communities, linking food to civil rights. In 1974 he published *Dick Gregory's Natural Diet for Folks Who Eat: Cookin' With Mother Nature*, a health-centric guide featuring recipes, natural remedies, meal plans, and nutritional information. Gregory's book acknowledged the barriers many Black peoples face in accessing healthy food and aimed to empower through education. His work took an intersectional approach that tied food and nutrition to social justice and political issues, in particular Black liberation and civil rights. His legacy continues to impact Black vegans and vegetarians, as well as food justice advocates working to remedy issues of food apartheid within Black and marginalized communities. Activists such as Rosa Parks, Angela Davis, and Colin Kaepernick also adopted vegan or vegetarian diets.

The Next Generation

Today, a growing cadre of Black chefs, restaurateurs, bakers, bloggers, and influencers are changing how we view veganism. Tabitha Brown has racked up millions of followers on social media by sharing her tips on wellness and plant-based eating. Chef, author, and publisher Bryant Terry has spent much of his career telling diverse and nuanced stories about plant-based eating, centering Black stories in his cookbooks and in his programming as the chef in residence at the Museum of the African Diaspora in San Francisco. Haile Thomas promotes wellness and plant-forward eating through her work, particularly as the co-founder of the nonprofit HAPPY (Healthy, Active, Positive, Purposeful, Youth). Many others, including Charity Morgan (a private chef who provides vegan meals to NFL players) and Pinky Cole, known for her restaurant chain Slutty Vegan, demonstrate how Black food and foodways encompass and lead innovation in plant-based culinary traditions.

> Today, Black Americans are almost three times as likely as white Americans to identify as vegan and are cutting meat out of their diets at a higher rate than other populations.

OPPOSITE: A traditional southern New Year's Day meal of cornbread and a stew of black-eyed peas and collard greens

Black Food Sovereignty

It's estimated that more than 23 million people in the United States, about 7 percent of the total population, live in food deserts—areas where access to affordable and nutritious (and often culturally appropriate) food is limited. Some scholars believe that number is actually higher. Numerous factors are linked to food deserts, including lack of public transportation, poverty, and few nearby retailers providing fresh food.

People living in food deserts are at higher risk for diseases such as diabetes and high blood pressure, and are more likely to suffer from certain chronic diseases as well.

Though "food desert" is the term used by the United States Department of Agriculture, the term "food apartheid" has gained currency in recent years. Many critics note that "food desert" implies that afflicted communities are empty and devoid of life, taking on the barren connotation of desert environments. "Food apartheid," on the other hand, better encompasses the active policies of disinvestment, redlining, and discrimination that have created these food-scarce areas.

Black communities in the United States are disproportionately located in food deserts, even when studies control for poverty levels. It's estimated that Black Americans are three times more likely to face food insecurity than whites. People living in communities afflicted by food apartheid are often more reliant on processed and fast foods and may find it difficult to obtain culturally appropriate food. Their access to the food system is restricted and their dietary practices affected: Fast food, carryout, prepared beverages, and prepackaged foods likely make up a larger portion of their diets than among those who have access to more food options. And their perception and understanding of American cuisine is filtered through these experiences and factors.

Ron Finley's community garden in South Central Los Angeles, a predominantly Black and Latino community

To help, Black food folks have spearheaded communal initiatives to improve food access, drawing on historical threads that link legacies of Black entrepreneurship, activism, and collaboration.

During enslavement, Black peoples, faced with limited autonomy over their diets and meager rations, engaged in activities such as gardening, fishing, hunting, and foraging to diversify their food and fill nutritional gaps. These traditions continued after emancipation in many Black communities in the United States, though they were often impeded by industrialization, segregation, and redlining. Today, many Black activists and food folks, particularly in urban environments, have again turned toward gardening and food cultivation as a means to restore sovereignty in communities afflicted by food apartheid. Urban agriculture projects have proliferated in many cities, from D.C. to Los Angeles.

By example, Ron Finley, known by many as the Gangsta Gardener, has turned a local garden project in predominantly Black and brown South Central Los Angeles into a growing organization that combats what he calls "food prisons" by teaching urban communities how to grow their own foods. Finley now has a gardening class on the platform MasterClass, extending his reach to audiences far and wide through on-demand video lessons.

In Detroit, chef Ederique Goudia, a Louisiana native, leverages her skills as a chef and business owner to tackle food waste and food insecurity and connect Black and other marginalized communities to resources. Goudia, who describes herself primarily as a "connector," co-founded Taste the Diaspora Detroit in 2021, a mutual-aid organization that convenes Black chefs, farmers, and makers for events featuring foods of the African diaspora. These events assist Black-owned businesses and help feed food-insecure communities in Detroit, as well as support other local social justice causes. In 2021, Goudia, along with Taste the Diaspora co-founders Raphael Wright and Jermond Booze, also organized an effort to raise funds for Wallace, Louisiana, after it was hit hard by Hurricane Ida. Wallace is a predominantly Black town and the site of the Whitney Plantation, which is dedicated to telling the stories of enslaved peoples.

Goudia's work is emblematic of the efforts of Black food folks around the United States to tackle food sovereignty and support their communities in a variety of ways, be it through initiatives to help Black food professionals build wealth or to feed the urban poor. However hyperlocal, these initiatives are making real impacts on communities and reshaping how they interact with the food system and with cuisine.

The work of Black culinarians to improve access to food ties back to a long history of culinary and social activism within the United States. Food has long served as an avenue for advancement for Black peoples—a means to improve lives, support communities, and demonstrate expertise. That in itself can be viewed as a revolutionary act in a society where Black peoples have long been discriminated against, shut out of opportunities, and portrayed as unskilled.

Today, that legacy continues, carried on by Black chefs, cooks, home bakers, and community members. Throughout the nation, Black peoples are working to improve self-sufficiency and food sovereignty for communities in need. With a nod to the historical ties between Black food and social change, these organizations continue to deliver access to healthy food, support the unhoused, provide resources for community gardens, and fill food access gaps caused by economic and social disruption.

> Black food folks have spearheaded communal initiatives to improve food access, drawing on historical threads that link legacies of Black entrepreneurship, activism, and collaboration.

OPPOSITE: Ron Finley—the Gangsta Gardener—brings food sovereignty to South Central Los Angeles.

Expanding Narratives

After generations of building, refining, and expanding the canon of American cuisine, Black contributions are now more widely recognized in the American food space. On restaurant menus, at public events, in the origin stories and branding of food products, and in media coverage, Black labor, expertise, and knowledge are finally getting their fair due. This shift toward deeper, more nuanced narratives of Black foodways comes after hundreds of years of food award systems and media coverage that obscured or excluded Black narratives.

Changing Media Landscape

Media plays a key role in shaping our perception of and interactions with food. Its coverage can help cement a food or beverage trend, spread knowledge of new culinary techniques, and determine what constitutes "good" food or who is considered an expert. Food media has evolved rapidly in recent decades, and the rise of new media platforms (from TikTok to blogs) has broadened the perspectives shared with consumers today.

When we think of traditional media, we think radio, television, newspapers, and magazines, which are often owned by conglomerates with large budgets and resources. For instance, Eater is a product of Vox Media, which is in turn owned by Comcast. Historically speaking, Black-owned businesses, Black culture and food, and Black peoples have often been excluded from traditional media narratives—unless those narratives focused on racial tensions, revolts of enslaved peoples, or coverage of an exceptionally famous Black person such as Ray Charles or Beyoncé. But, haltingly, some positive changes have been made in traditional media in recent years. The staff at major media organizations has diversified, as have the stories they cover in food and beyond. A host of cookbooks and other books on Black food and foodways have been published

A medallion for the James Beard Foundation Award for Excellence

James Beard Award–winning chef Mashama Bailey writes notes while working the line at her restaurant, The Grey, in Savannah, Georgia.

(though white authors still produce an estimated 95 percent of books from major publishing houses).

Representation of Black foodways on television has also improved. Black contestants have participated and emerged as winners on shows such as *Top Chef*, *Chopped,* and *Hell's Kitchen*. Stand-alone Black food shows have also begun to make waves. The popular *High on the Hog*, named after historian Jessica B. Harris's book on Black American foodways, debuted in 2021 on Netflix. After a popular first season, the show was renewed for a second. Other food narratives have been on the screen, too, such as Mashama Bailey's episode of *Chef's Table* and *Fresh, Fried and Crispy,* hosted by food media personality Daym Drops. Black food is slowly becoming more than an often-ignored part of American food culture on television.

Shifts in the media landscape have also accelerated changes in food storytelling. Beginning in the early 2000s, the internet brought a dramatic transformation to the media space. Podcasts, social media platforms, digital newsletters, and blogs emerged as new media spaces where people could find information about anything from relationships to food. These new media outlets have been transformative in representations of Black food history in popular culture. The ability to reach a wide audience without the backing of a legacy media institution has somewhat democratized the way consumers access information.

This shift toward media decentralization has had positive and negative impacts on society. On one hand, it has allowed conspiracy theories to spread, and social media platforms have struggled to contain hate speech and misinformation. But on the other hand, it has shifted power away from traditional media organizations and toward a more diverse array of voices. No longer does it require a job at the *New York Times*—and the degree, multiple interviews, and a demonstrated track record to get there—for someone to reach a massive audience. Instead, with the right combination of luck and skill, and the addition of a few apps on a phone, an independent voice has the potential to reach millions.

KJ Kearney, a Gullah Geechee influencer and community organizer who founded the platform Black Food Fridays, offers an example of how new media spaces can be leveraged to reach large audiences. After founding Black Food Fridays in 2020 to encourage people to support Black-owned food businesses, Kearney expanded his work to encompass Black food history. He started a TikTok series called Black Food Facts and in a few short weeks, using just an iPhone, created 20 videos viewed more than 3.8 million times—all focused on Black food history. Black Food

Family and friends join hands to say grace before their meal.

Facts educates viewers about topics ranging from Abby Fisher's 1881 cookbook to how enslaved distiller Nathan "Nearest" Green taught the founder of Jack Daniel's to make whiskey. "Even Black people are surprised" when he shares the diversity of Black foodways in the United States, says Kearney. He won a James Beard Award in 2024 for his work on Black Food Fridays.

In 2016, Anthony and Janique Edwards didn't have a refrigerator or stove in their Brooklyn apartment. Limited in making food at home, they were inspired to create EatOkra, an app that connects diners to Black-owned restaurants, filling a gap in food reporting that often leaves Black-owned food and beverage businesses off directories and best-of lists. Today, the app connects approximately 400,000 users to businesses in their communities. EatOkra has partnered with Uber Eats on initiatives to support Black-owned restaurants and provide them with resources, and it was named one of Apple's 15 App Store award winners in 2021. Looking to the future, co-founder Janique Edwards says, "Now we are trying to figure out what does advocacy look like outside of directing people to patronize Black-owned businesses. It's one thing to love the industry and another thing to understand the needs of restaurant operators."

It's not just content creators and app developers leveraging new media to expand on Black and American foodways. Consider Memphis-based Cxffeeblack, described by co-founder Bartholomew Jones as "a multimedia company with a consumable curriculum" that utilizes social media to "present information in a way that is culturally congruent" and make coffee relevant to Black peoples and their lives today.

Jones, a former teacher and independent artist, founded Cxffeeblack in 2018 with his wife, Renata Henderson. What started out as a merchandise company has now grown to encompass events, a coffee club, a roastery, and programming aimed at coffee education. Cxffeeblack draws on a long legacy of Black artistry and entrepreneurship, especially in the American South, emphasizes Jones, as it seeks to reclaim coffee, a good stolen from African producers, grown by enslaved peoples, traded as part of the Transatlantic Slave Trade, and now the foundation of a vast multibillion-dollar global industry. Cxffeeblack works to "make coffee Black again," as Jones says, sharing knowledge and using social platforms to raise funds for a documentary focusing on a trip to Africa to meet suppliers and for a barista exchange program.

Black creatives and culinarians are leveraging new media to expand their reach, honor history, and change conversations in the United States about

KJ Kearney, pictured here at Gillie's Seafood in Charleston, South Carolina, founded Black Food Fridays, a social media initiative to support Black-owned restaurants, in April 2020.

EXPANDING NARRATIVES • 159

> *No longer does it require a job at the New York Times—and the degree, multiple interviews, and a demonstrated track record to get there—for someone to reach a massive audience. Instead, with the right combination of luck and skill, and the addition of a few apps on a phone, an independent voice has the potential to reach millions.*

cuisine and culture. But despite new media opportunities, challenges persist. Black creatives and influencers face a racial pay gap reported to be as high as 35 percent when compared with the earnings of their white peers, as inequities in the workplace are being replicated in the new media environment. Black makers and founders also face inequities in funding for culinary projects, digital or otherwise, and studies report a consistent gap between funding and capital available for Black business owners and for other groups. On new media platforms, allegations of algorithmic bias and censorship of Black and marginalized voices persist, especially those calling attention to social justice issues. Despite these issues, community by community, subscriber by subscriber, a changing media landscape is driving a cultural shift in which the diversity of Black foodways and the talent of Black food folks are more broadly recognized and explored.

Black Social Movements & Food Media

Just as the soul food moniker came about during a time of social and political change in the United States, so has food media shifted in the wake of modern Black social movements. In 2020, the United States was rocked by a series of high-profile killings of Black civilians at the hands of police. Social media—and the ability to share shocking and gut-wrenching video footage—acted as a catalyst, fueling what the *New York Times* reported as potentially the "largest movement in the country's history." An estimated half a million people participated in June 6, 2020, Black Lives Matter protests in the United States.

In the midst of a deluge of corporate support for Black Lives Matter and other Black-centric causes and organizations, food media also shifted. Allegations were raised against major food media organizations and outlets of appropriation, a failure to give due credit, and a consistent framing of Black and similarly marginalized cultures as "other." *Bon Appétit* offers one of the most prominent examples of this era of reckoning. The magazine faced a rash of condemnation and high-profile resignations following allegations of discriminatory behavior against Black and other marginalized staff and contributors.

Likewise, the James Beard Foundation, which hosts the most prestigious awards in American food, canceled the 2020 and 2021 James Beard Awards and audited the awards system to address bias and diversity. The foundation's revised mission statement emphasizes a commitment to diversity, equity, and sustainability, and entrants must now describe how their work aligns with that mission and adhere to a code of ethics.

In 2023, Best Chef in the South finalist Timothy Hontzas of Johnny's Restaurant in Homewood, Alabama, was disqualified from the James Beard Awards after the ethics committee found it "more likely than not" that he had violated the code of

ethics for allegedly yelling at staff and customers. The decision to disqualify Hontzas prompted conversation around multiple issues in U.S. food media, including whether yelling qualifies as abuse, consideration of the unequal power dynamics between managers and subordinates in kitchens and restaurants, and the transparency (or lack thereof) in food award systems. Some former James Beard Award winners, also chefs, then took to Instagram to share their displeasure with Hontzas's disqualification. Chef John Currence of Oxford, Mississippi, posted a photo of his James Beard Award smashed by what appeared to be a brick. In his post, Currence denounced the decision to disqualify Hontzas, noting that women and minorities are "over-performing industry averages in award recognition," and accused the James Beard Foundation of "fake virtue-signaling."

Why does this controversy matter? It demonstrates that food awards and food media, systems that shape our perceptions of food culture, are still hotly contested arenas when it comes to issues of representation and equity. Questions of who is included, who belongs, who is recognized, and even who is allowed to misbehave speak to unequal power structures that underpin the foundation of American cuisine and American capitalism. In food, we are beginning to see a shift where contributions by Black and other marginalized peoples—including women, who for so long have labored unrecognized in U.S. kitchens—are being acknowledged. However, that shift will likely be challenged for years to come as new ideas of what is—and isn't—American food, what is trending, and what constitutes the "best" in American cooking continue to evolve.

Protest art and signs hang on the fence surrounding Lafayette Square at Black Lives Matter Plaza in Washington, D.C., following the murder of George Floyd.

EXPANDING NARRATIVES • 161

Diasporic Culinary Exchange

Foodways connected to the African diaspora impacted American cuisine across many generations. Travel, migration, and trade brought Black-inflected ingredients and foodways to the United States through the slave trade and throughout the more than 150 years since emancipation. Increasing globalization and travel have furthered those bonds between the American culinary landscape and diasporic influences as well.

The way Americans define Blackness as an identity has also expanded far beyond the confines of peoples descended from Africans with ties to the southern United States. Black, as a moniker, has grown to encompass all peoples of African descent, conveying a growing understanding of how globalized diaspora communities have become. Reflected in this shift is an expansion of what is considered Black cuisine in the United States, which can now encompass soul food, West African cuisine, Caribbean dishes, and much more.

Colonial Impacts

Colonial North America offers many examples of how diasporic foodways impacted the development of early American cuisine. Consider Philadelphia, the original capital of the United States, which was established in the late 1600s on Lenape land. The colony utilized enslaved labor early on, and the city became a trading hub as it grew. Black peoples were present from the very early days of the city's founding and contributed to the development of its foodways. In addition, Philadelphia had extensive trading ties with the Caribbean. Most enslaved peoples brought into the area were trafficked from the Caribbean rather than directly from Africa, brought to North America only after having lived and worked in the Caribbean. In addition to laborers, Philadelphia also imported a variety of goods from

A painting by John Lewis Krimmel from 1811 portrays a woman serving pepper pot to customers in the Philadelphia Market.

the Caribbean, including sugar, rum, molasses, pineapples, coconuts, and coffee.

This connection with the Caribbean directly impacted Philadelphia's culinary scene. Pepper pot, a thick stew with hot peppers, meat, and vegetables, is one prominent example. Pepper pot was brought to Philadelphia by enslaved peoples and popularized there by Black women hawkers who would make and sell servings of the steaming-hot stew as a street food in the early days of the city. Initial interpretations of pepper pot in Philadelphia included ingredients tied to the slave trade and Caribbean foodways, such as cassava and plantains.

Over time, pepper pot became known as a culinary symbol of the city. Campbell's even made a canned version for more than a century, though it was discontinued in 2010.

Modern-Day Impacts

More recent immigration has also changed the foodways within the United States. Caribbean cuisine offers one prominent example. In New Orleans, chef Nina Compton heads Compère Lapin, a restaurant named for a Creole and Caribbean folk character. In 2016, Compton was named one of 16 Black chefs changing food in America by the *New York Times* and is also a James Beard Award winner. At Compère Lapin, she infuses flavors of St. Lucia, where most locals descend from enslaved Africans, with New Orleans, which has a local cuisine heavily steeped in Black history. Another celebrated chef, Kwame Onwuachi, known for his book *Notes From a Young Black Chef* and numerous restaurants, often incorporates both Caribbean and African influences in his culinary projects. Then there's Paola Velez, a James Beard Award nominee who cofounded the decentralized bake sale Bakers Against Racism, which raised nearly two million dollars for social justice in 2020. Velez, who is Afro-Dominican, grew up in New York and in the Dominican Republic, a heritage she brings to her acclaimed desserts. Many of Velez's recipes draw on ingredients and flavors common in the Caribbean or her history growing up in the Bronx, an area in the United States heavily impacted by migrants from the African diaspora.

More recent immigration from Africa and among diasporic populations has also changed the foodways in the United States. Between 2000 and 2016, African migrants made up the fastest-growing population group in Philadelphia. Today, an estimated 50,000 Africans reside in the City of Brotherly Love, with large populations from Ethiopia, Nigeria, Ghana, and Liberia. Washington, D.C., and surrounding areas in Northern Virginia and Maryland are home to the largest population of Ethiopians outside the conti-

Top Chef star and author, chef Kwame Onwuachi perfects a plate of uni escovitch at his former restaurant Kith/Kin in Washington, D.C.

nent of Africa. The migration to D.C. began in the 1950s and '60s, as students came to study at local universities, and continued for decades following revolution and unrest in Ethiopia. In both Philadelphia and D.C., African migrants have created waves in the culinary space, opening restaurants and local markets offering familiar goods. In Philadelphia, a growing number of West African restaurants showcase everything from Senegalese to Liberian cuisines. In D.C., Ethiopian restaurants have long been local favorites and award winners, and newer projects have even blended Ethiopian ingredients and flavors with U.S. cuisine, such as soul food.

Ethiopian cuisine has made its way into modern food trends. In the midst of growing interest in vegan, vegetarian, and plant-centric dining, home cooks throughout the United States are experimenting with the numerous vegetarian stews typical of Ethiopian cuisine. The *Washington Post* food section featured recipes for an Ethiopian lentil-based stew, misir wot, touting its "meatless" status, as well as a roasted carrot recipe with a spicy sauce dubbed "Ethiopia's sriracha." These recipes, based on African foods, specifically Ethiopian, also relate directly to modern American dining trends.

As American plates shift toward whole foods, "superfoods," and sustainability, traditional West African ingredients and dishes are emerging at the forefront of cuisine. Look to fonio, for example. Fonio is a grain native to West Africa, considered one of the continent's oldest cultivated cereals. It is commonly eaten in parts of Nigeria, Senegal, Mali, Guinea, and Burkina Faso. In 2021, the food media went wild for fonio. Yahoo News, the *Washington Post*, and the *Today Show* compared it to quinoa as the next possible trending grain. Media reports emphasized that fonio is adapted for a changing climate and flourishes in drought conditions and nutrient-deficient soils, is nutrient dense and gluten free, and cooks quickly, all aligned with American trends and desires for easy, nutritious, and planet-friendly foods. The most prominent fonio in the United States is distributed by Yolélé Foods, founded by chef and author Pierre Thiam from Senegal. Thiam is well known for his African fine-dining restaurant concepts and has become a prominent proponent for fonio's potential. His TED Talk on fonio has been viewed more than 1.2 million times, and his work with Yolélé has been featured in a variety of major U.S. food media outlets.

Black communities within the United States are reckoning with growing recognition of food practices, traditions, and ingredients in various ways. Oxtail, in particular, illustrates how this process is playing out. Oxtail, a common ingredient in Caribbean cooking, is eaten throughout the world and has recently gained major media attention in the United States. Recipes for Caribbean preparations of oxtail are now being enjoyed by more people throughout the

> Who's to say the next sriracha, chai latte, boba, or even matcha goody to hit it big on menus and gain wider adoption throughout American cuisine won't be a food deeply rooted in Black or diasporic culture and history?

> ### *Focus On:* Black Food Festivals
>
> Growing recognition of Black foodways and Black contributions to American cuisine have also been reflected in a recent outgrowth of Black food and beverage festivals in the United States. Long-standing events like Taste of Soul in Los Angeles—a street festival celebration of all things "soulful," from musical performances to food, that was founded in 2006—have been joined by a host of newer fêtes. Day Bracey founded the nation's first Black beer festival in Pittsburgh in 2018, now known as Barrel & Flow, which has grown to draw thousands of attendees. In 2021, chef Kwame Onwuachi, in partnership with *Food & Wine* and Salamander Collection (a luxury hotel company), launched the Family Reunion, a Black food and wine festival. The Bay-Haven Food and Wine Festival, another multiday celebration of Black food and beverage, launched in Charlotte, North Carolina, in the same year. In 2023, chef Marcus Samuelsson and Fawn Weaver, CEO of whiskey brand Uncle Nearest, collaborated to curate Honeyland Festival in Sugar Land, Texas, which features food, music, and beverages that celebrate Black culture.
>
> I consider myself lucky to have attended some of these festivals while researching this book and for my platform as an influencer. During these experiences, I heard over and over from other attendees (usually overwhelmingly Black) about the importance of these festivals. Attendees emphasized that these events were safe spaces to dance, joke, make connections, and admire the work of Black food and beverage professionals, without needing to code-switch or explain why centering Black stories and talent is important. From the talent who made the festivals possible—the chefs, bakers, mixologists, panelists, and others—I heard similar sentiments. Many noted that they felt free to make soul food or a French-inflected dish or anything in between. They considered these events their time to collaborate and do what they do best, without having to explain why they were or were not conforming to stereotypical expectations of their talents.

United States than ever before. In response to the growing appreciation for oxtail, many Black peoples have begun joking that rising oxtail prices are a result of non-Black peoples "discovering" how good oxtails taste. As a tongue-in-cheek response, many Black peoples will purposefully comment on social media content and recipes featuring oxtails, saying negative things such as that they taste really bad or have exaggeratedly negative health impacts. This response jokingly seeks to decrease oxtail's popularity among non-Black populations to lower its price.

We have already seen the widespread adoption of ingredients rooted in Black and African experiences. Caribbean cuisine was named a top global culinary trend in the "What's Hot 2023 Culinary Forecast" by the National Restaurant Association. In the fast-food arena, fried chicken has experienced a multiyear heyday, making it the focus of new menu items and restaurant expansions as sales have grown. Grocery chain Trader Joe's recently debuted a ready-made boxed version of the West African dish jollof rice. Despite criticism that the Trader Joe's version lacked flavor and could be considered appropriative, its appearance on the shelves of one of America's largest grocery stores signifies how Americans are gaining a broader awareness of, and desire for, African foods. It also signifies the decline of a monolithic representation of Blackness and Black cultures. As more foods and culinary practices rooted in Black and African foodways gain recognition and acceptance in the United States, they open doors for new conversations about what is desirable, trendy, and healthy in American dining. Who's to say the next sriracha, chai latte, boba, or even matcha goody to hit it big on menus and gain wider adoption throughout American cuisine won't be a food deeply rooted in Black or diasporic culture and history?

Chef Erick Williams served a dish of grilled chicken thighs, Egyptian grains, benne and sesame seeds, and chicken jus at the 2021 Family Reunion, an annual Black food festival.

DIASPORIC CULINARY EXCHANGE • 167

Washington, D.C., a Case Study

Washington, D.C., once known as Chocolate City for its majority Black population, has a long history of Black contributions and leadership in food and beverage. Black peoples in the city, both free and enslaved, have historically worked for wealthy families and the nation's elite in a variety of roles. They have been at the forefront of some of the city's best restaurants and bars and contributed to D.C.'s growing reputation as a foodie city.

Through waves of successive migration, African diaspora communities in the area have driven innovation in the food space. Though some politicians have lambasted the city's dining options, local residents often view these criticisms as more political strategy than actual fact. In 2017, Zagat ranked D.C. as one of the country's most exciting food cities. In 2019, the *New York Times* called the District a "great restaurant city" and Bloomberg named it "Most Exciting Food City in America." And as of 2024, the District boasts 24 Michelin-starred restaurants.

D.C.'s Black History

Washington, D.C., was founded in 1791 to serve as the capital for the new nation. The District serves as the seat for the federal government and draws more than 20 million visitors a year. And it has long been home to Black peoples, who helped build the District into what it is today. About a third of the city's residents in 1800 were Black, mostly enslaved peoples. In the mid-19th century nearly every D.C. family of wealth had Black service staff and cooks. "Black hands—enslaved and free—wove the fabric of social life in the nation's capital, and Black peoples, widely considered by whites as inherently bred for servitude, were integral to cementing a white family's social status as an elite household," writes Adrian Miller in *The President's Kitchen Cabinet: The Story of*

A trumpet owned by influential jazz musician Louis Armstrong

Before it was demolished, the Republic Theatre was a popular movie house on U Street.

the African Americans Who Have Fed Our First Families, From the Washingtons to the Obamas.

Enslaved Black cooks labored in the White House and beyond. The city's history is full of figures like Alethia Tanner, who purchased her and her family's freedom through income made from her garden plot. Tanner also eventually helped found local Black churches.

Following emancipation in the 1860s, freed Black peoples moved to Washington, D.C., as part of the Great Migration. The District was host to a burgeoning Black middle and professional class, it had Black schools and churches, and there were government jobs available to Black peoples. The city developed thriving Black economic and cultural centers in the Shaw and U Street Corridor neighborhoods. In fact, until the middle of the 20th century, the U Street Corridor was often referred to as Black Broadway, as its entertainment venues attracted legendary Black performers such as Billie Holiday, Duke Ellington, and Aretha Franklin.

Despite its long history as a home for Black peoples and center of Black culture, the District has experienced many race-related challenges. The city remained segregated until the civil rights movement. Historians point to anti-Black racism

and D.C.'s large Black population as a reason it hasn't been given statehood. And D.C. continues to struggle with segregation and gentrification. The District's Black population has contracted since its peak in the 1970s. Today, D.C. is no longer a Black-majority city, and a 2021 study by the University of California, Berkeley, named the D.C. region as the 15th most racially segregated in the nation.

Food & Beverage in the District

Black culinary excellence in D.C. includes *and* extends far beyond foodways connected to the diaspora. Multiple Ethiopian restaurants are featured in the Michelin Guide for the District, as well as numerous Caribbean restaurants. Black chefs also lead some of D.C.'s most prominent restaurants, with concepts focused on a variety of cuisines. Dōgon, a fine-dining Afro-Caribbean concept by celebrated chef Kwame Onwuachi, is named in honor of Benjamin Banneker, a free Black man who assisted with the original survey that established the boundaries of Washington, D.C., in the 1790s. Dōgon was named one of the best new restaurants in America in 2024 by *Esquire* magazine, and its staff includes an array of Black talent, including chef de cuisine Martel Stone.

At Anju, a celebrated Korean restaurant near Dupont Circle, Angel Barreto serves as executive chef and partner. Barreto's work serves as a reminder that though Black culinary professionals have often been pigeonholed into cooking soul food or stereotypically "Black foods," like any culinary professional, they have the ability to excel working with a broad array of cuisines and influences.

Barreto knows all too well that Black chefs often face that stigma. Barreto, who is Black and Puerto Rican, originally intended to work in politics but ultimately opted to go to culinary school and pursue a career in food. At the time of his decision, his family was hesitant. Over generations, they had worked hard to get away from the service industry. "My family grew up in the South," he explains. "My grandmother was a sharecropper—she picked cotton. At that time, you had a job taking care of someone's house or had very limited income opportunities as a Black person. They wanted their kids to have a better life than they did." Barreto had to grapple with that history when he chose cooking as a career.

Barreto has also had to contend with people who doubt his ability to cook Korean food in his position as executive chef and partner at Anju. Barreto considers himself a student of the cuisine, seeking to honor it and learn as much about it as he can. At Anju, his food is the extension of a lifelong love for Korean food that was kindled by his experiences living in Korea as a child. "People always ask, 'How can cook you Korean food?' as if it's so bizarre," he says. "In reality, we are capable of doing anything we put our minds to. We are not bound by our diaspora and history."

Inflected by generations of migration, D.C.'s food scene reflects the growing diversity of Black foodways in the United States.

OPPOSITE: A tableful of jerk chicken wings and doubles, fry bread topped with cumin-flavored channa, from Peter Prime's Cane restaurant in Washington, D.C.

"I'm optimistic," Barreto says. "Things are getting more diverse, and people are breaking out of traditional barriers. It helps to see more chefs who are Black who are doing well. It goes to show that there's no boundaries. That's been the history of Black peoples since the inception of this country, and we have constantly proven that we are so much more. I think D.C. will continue to prove that."

Barreto was a James Beard Award nominee for Rising Star Chef of the Year in 2020, named one of Food & Wine's Best New Chefs in 2021, and selected as 2024 Chef of the Year at the Restaurant Association of Metropolitan Washington Awards.

D.C.'s long history of Black excellence also extends into the beverage space. In the late 1800s and early 1900s, an elite group of Black bartenders in D.C., the Mixologist Club, were celebrated members of the professional service class. The club hosted galas and mixologist competitions and tended bar at political events. Members were profiled in local media and even weighed in on local politics.

Artist Archibald Motley, Jr., painted a bustling restaurant scene in his 1935 work "Saturday Night."

Black-centric venues, arts and cultural events, and organizations like the Mixologist Club developed in part as a result of the District's segregation. They nurtured collaboration among Black professionals and within D.C.'s large Black community. The legacy of the Mixologist Club and the high standards it set for Black bar professionals in D.C. is evident today.

In 2018, D.C. bartender Kapri Robinson founded Chocolate City's Best, an organization for bar professionals of color, after noting the lack of Black and brown representation at major cocktail competitions. Chocolate City's Best hosts a cocktail competition and provides mentoring and education for participants. In 2020, Robinson also co-founded Empowering the Diner, a D.C. event series that creates more inclusive experiences for people of color in bars and restaurants.

Robinson characterizes her efforts as working to "make sure that people who look like me, Black folks, people of color, have a stage to be on, have a place to say and be themselves without microaggressions weighing them down." She emphasizes that much of the increasing recognition and achievement among Black food and beverage professionals has come about because Black organizations and leaders are building new opportunities. "So many organizations are coming about that we are finally writing a history for ourselves in this industry," she says. Robinson has been named Bartender of the Year numerous times, including in 2023 by the Liquor Awards and in 2024 by Tales of the Cocktail Foundation.

Looking to the Future

Inflected by generations of migration, D.C.'s food scene reflects the growing diversity of Black foodways in the United States. The labor and expertise of Black chefs, bakers, cooks, servers, bartenders, restaurateurs, and others have helped define the city and turn it into a prominent player in the national culinary arena. In addition, Black leadership extends far beyond the confines of traditionally Black culinary and beverage spaces, demonstrating a continuation of the breadth of experience and deep knowledge that long ago helped build Black people's reputations as "born cooks." Whether it be preparing French food in the White House, Ethiopian-inspired burgers downtown, or collaborative cocktail experiences that fuel social causes, Black food and beverage professionals in D.C. continue to make waves.

Bartender and star of *Drink Masters* on Netflix, Kapri Robinson co-hosts *Soul Palate Podcast*, a platform to "normalize the Black and Brown palate."

Rice Waffles

Cook time: 4 to 6 minutes per waffle | Makes 8 to 10 waffles, depending on iron size

¾ cup all-purpose flour

¼ cup cornstarch

1 tablespoon dark brown sugar

2 teaspoons baking powder

1 teaspoon kosher salt

1 cup buttermilk

4 tablespoons butter, melted and cooled

2 large eggs, yolks and whites separated

1 cup cooked rice, cooled

In a medium bowl, whisk together flour, cornstarch, brown sugar, baking powder, and salt.

In a small bowl, whisk together buttermilk, butter, and egg yolks. Gently stir the wet ingredients into the dry ingredients.

In a stand mixer fitted with the whisk attachment, whisk egg whites to stiff peaks, but not dry.

Fold rice into waffle batter, then fold in the egg whites.

Bake in a waffle iron according to the manufacturer's instructions.

Peach & Peppa Chutney

Cook time: 1 hour | Makes about 2 quarts

6 large fresh peaches, pitted, cut into 1-inch chunks

1 green bell pepper, seeded and chopped

⅔ cup packed light brown sugar

½ cup honey

¼ cup apple cider vinegar

1 teaspoon kosher salt

¼ teaspoon allspice

1 (3-inch) knob fresh ginger, peeled and sliced

1 stick cinnamon

1 bunch scallions, white and light green parts only, chopped

1 large carrot, peeled and chopped into chunks

Zest and juice of 3 limes

10 Scotch bonnet peppers, stems removed

3 cloves garlic, chopped

2 jalapeños, stems removed

In a large saucepan, add peaches, bell pepper, brown sugar, honey, apple cider vinegar, salt, allspice, ginger, cinnamon stick, and ⅔ cup water. Bring to a boil, then reduce heat to low and let simmer, stirring occasionally, until liquid is thickened, about 1 hour. Remove cinnamon stick and ginger. Let cool to room temperature.

Pulse scallions, carrot, lime zest and juice, Scotch bonnet peppers, garlic, and jalapeños in a food processor until finely chopped. Stir into cooled peach chutney mixture. Transfer everything to quart, pint, or half-pint mason jars. Cover and refrigerate for up to a month.

Boiled Turnips & Greens With Smoked Turkey

Cook time: 2 hours | Makes 6 to 8 servings

- 1 pound smoked turkey necks, tails, or wings
- 1 chicken bouillon cube
- 2 tablespoons vegetable oil
- 3 medium turnips, trimmed, cut into ½-inch cubes
- 1 large onion, thinly sliced
- 3 cloves garlic, chopped
- 1 tablespoon ground cumin
- 1 tablespoon yellow mustard seeds
- 1½ tablespoons salt
- 2 teaspoons freshly ground black pepper
- ½ cup apple cider vinegar
- 2 tablespoons sugar
- 2 pounds turnip greens, chopped
- Hot sauce (optional)

In a large pot, add turkey, bouillon cube, and 6 cups water. Bring to a boil, stirring to dissolve bouillon. Once dissolved, reduce heat to medium-low; simmer for 1 hour.

Meanwhile, in a large skillet, heat oil over medium-high. Add turnips, onion, and garlic and cook, stirring often, until onion begins to soften, about 3 minutes. Add cumin, mustard seeds, salt, and pepper. Cook, stirring often, until fragrant, about 3 minutes more.

Add turnip mixture to pot with turkey. Stir in apple cider vinegar and sugar and bring to a boil. Add turnip greens, one handful at time, stirring to wilt between additions. Simmer uncovered, stirring occasionally, until turnips are tender, 45 minutes to 1 hour.

Season to taste with salt and hot sauce (if using) before serving.

Vegan Chili

Cook time: 55 minutes | Makes 6 servings

- 2 tablespoons vegetable oil
- 1 pound plant-based ground meat or 1 pound finely chopped portobello mushrooms
- 1 large onion, chopped
- 1 large sweet potato, peeled and cut into ½-inch cubes
- 2 bell peppers (any color), chopped
- 2 carrots, peeled and chopped
- 2 stalks celery, chopped
- 2 tablespoons chili powder
- 2 tablespoons ground cumin
- 2 tablespoons tomato paste
- 4 cloves garlic, chopped
- 1 tablespoon mustard powder
- 2 teaspoons fresh thyme leaves
- 2 teaspoons freshly ground black pepper, plus more for seasoning
- 2 teaspoons salt, plus more for seasoning
- 2 teaspoons smoked paprika
- 1½ teaspoons chopped fresh oregano
- ½ teaspoon ground or grated nutmeg
- 3 tablespoons soy or Worcestershire sauce
- 1 cup vegetable stock
- 1 (14.5-ounce) can diced tomatoes
- 1 (15-ounce) can beans (such as kidney, pinto, black, or black-eyed peas), drained and rinsed

In a large pot, heat oil over medium-high. Add plant-based meat or mushrooms and cook, stirring often, until starting to brown, 5 to 7 minutes. If using plant-based meat, use a slotted spoon to transfer it to a bowl; if using mushrooms, leave in pot.

Add onion, sweet potato, bell peppers, carrots, and celery and cook, stirring often, until vegetables are crisp-tender, 5 to 6 minutes. Add chili powder, cumin, tomato paste, garlic, mustard powder, thyme, black pepper, salt, smoked paprika, oregano, and nutmeg. Cook, stirring often, until fragrant, 1 to 2 minutes. Stir in soy or Worcestershire sauce, then vegetable stock and tomatoes. If using plant-based meat, return to pot.

Bring to a boil, then reduce heat to medium-low and simmer uncovered, stirring often, until thickened and vegetables are soft, about 30 minutes. Stir in beans and simmer until heated through, about 10 minutes more.

Season to taste with salt and pepper before serving.

Pound Cake

Bake time: 1 hour 15 minutes, plus 1 hour cooling time | *Makes 10 to 12 servings*

1¾ cups unsalted butter (3½ sticks), at room temperature, plus more for greasing pan

2½ cups granulated sugar

1 teaspoon baking powder

¾ teaspoon kosher salt

5 large eggs, at room temperature

2 large egg yolks, at room temperature

¾ cup cream cheese, at room temperature

⅓ cup buttermilk, at room temperature

2 teaspoons vanilla extract

3 cups all-purpose flour, plus more for dusting pan

Preheat oven to 375°F. Grease a 10-cup Bundt pan with butter. Lightly flour pan, then knock out any excess flour.

In the bowl of a stand mixer fitted with paddle attachment, beat butter, sugar, baking powder, and salt on high speed until fluffy and pale yellow, scraping down sides and bottom of bowl halfway through, about 8 minutes in total. Scrape down sides and bottom of bowl.

On medium speed, add eggs and egg yolks one at a time, beating to blend and stopping occasionally to scrape down sides and bottom of bowl. Continue beating on medium-high until creamy and fluffy, about 2 minutes. (If ingredients were cold when added, batter may look broken. Let warm to room temperature, then continue beating until creamy and fluffy.) Scrape down sides and bottom of bowl.

Add half the cream cheese, half the buttermilk, and the vanilla extract and beat on medium-low until smooth and well incorporated, about 1 minute. Scrape down sides and bottom of bowl. Add half the flour. Mix on low until just incorporated, about 30 seconds. Scrape down sides and bottom of bowl. Repeat with remaining cream cheese, buttermilk, then flour.

Pour batter into prepared pan. Tap pan on counter several times to release excess air, then smooth the top. Bake until a tester inserted into the center of cake comes out clean, rotating pan halfway through baking, about 1 hour 15 minutes. (Tent cake with foil if browning too quickly.)

Let cake cool in pan for 30 minutes. Invert cake onto a wire rack and let cool at least 30 minutes longer.

CHAPTER FIVE

A Celebratory Feast

Honoring Black Foodways

No exploration of Black food is complete without a celebratory feast. The pages ahead highlight just a small sliver of the richness of Black contributions to American cuisine. From greens to historic barbecue traditions to baked goods to cocktails, this feast draws on more than 400 years of Black history in the United States. The recipes are gathered from a variety of sources, some modern and others

developed from historical records. Others have been provided by Black food folks in the United States today, including the culinary luminaries interviewed for this book—such as Cheryl Day and Benjamin "BJ" Dennis. All represent a taste of the deep and enduring impacts of Black peoples on the way Americans dine, celebrate, and understand food. Each honors the richness of the Black diaspora and the foods that have been long-standing staples of American—and Black—cuisine.

With these recipes, you'll taste the flavors of the United States and explore the foods that have been passed down for generations in Black communities. The flavors and ingredients, in large part, were brought to this country from across the Atlantic and developed by the expertise of Black cooks enslaved in white American kitchens, or by trendsetters and tastemakers as the Great Migration established these dishes and these ingredients as an essential part of the national cuisine. There is history in these dishes, there is a depth of tradition and memory, and, most of all, there is celebration.

This final feast contains profiles of some of the most celebrated voices in Black food today, folks who have expanded what it means to create and understand cuisine in America. As in other sections, these vignettes offer starting-point sources to explore alongside recipes that are exquisite examples of modern American cooking. The lives and work of the culinary leaders contained within remind us of our history. They also encourage us to celebrate our rich cultural heritage. Through these profiles, recipes, and reflections, we can begin to paint a fuller picture of the dynamic and evolving canon that is American cuisine.

OPPOSITE: **A homemade salad of watermelon, potatoes, radishes, and tomato**
PAGES 182–183: **From left:** Dancer Chanel "Tootie" Williams; entertainer Freddie Ross, Jr., aka Big Freedia; visual artist Devon Hurst; and producer BlaqNmilD have a dinner party with home-cooked soul food at Ross's home in Little Woods, New Orleans.

Rice

Utilized broadly in an array of cuisines worldwide, rice is a common thread among many culinary traditions. In the United States, its development is inextricably linked with the Transatlantic Slave Trade. As Black peoples were trafficked from Africa to the North American colonies, they transmitted complex agricultural knowledge systems that established rice as a thriving plantation crop. Their knowledge helped create incredible wealth in rice-growing regions and transmit rice-cooking preferences that underpin regional cuisines in America today.

Complex Agricultural Legacies

Narratives about the Transatlantic Slave Trade often frame enslaved peoples as almost blank slates, disembodied of all the knowledge, preferences, and cultures that they were connected to before being trafficked to the colonies for labor. This framing ignores their agency, skills, and humanity. It also allows enslaved peoples to be written out of history, excluded from stories of nation building and cultural creation. Inherently, it assumes a Eurocentric viewpoint that proposes only European cultures are "advanced," with knowledge worth transmitting to others.

Early scholarship surrounding rice and its legacy in the United States followed this pattern and proposed that planters must have created the agricultural system that developed around rice cultivation in North America. All rice species were assumed to be from Asia, and the Portuguese were initially credited with introducing irrigated rice systems to West Africa despite evidence that those systems predated Portuguese exploration in the region. It wasn't until the late 1800s that scientists began to consider that some rice found in Africa may be a distinct, indigenous varietal.

Rice in many West African societies is central to religious and daily rituals as well as to cultural identity. Records from Islamic explorers note rice cultivation

A rice fanner basket made by an enslaved person on South Carolina's coast prior to 1863

In South Carolina, rice plantations relied on the unpaid labor of enslaved peoples.

and production in the region prior to the 10th century. Beginning in the mid-1400s, historical accounts from European navigators and traders indicate that irrigated-rice agriculture existed in West Africa. Agricultural systems varied in West African rice-growing societies, encompassing lowland and upland crops, transplanting, and the use of specialized tools. Complex land-use strategies were employed to adapt rice to various microclimates, water availability, and rainfall variances. Sluices, dikes, canals, and embankments were also utilized to control water flow and to grow rice in tidal zones affected by salt water, known as the mangrove system. In West African agricultural systems, rice processing and cooking were exclusively female domains. Seed selection was also a task typically performed by women, who had to account for a variety of factors, such as predators, the local environment, taste, and milling ability. These intricate rice-management systems and cultures were the result of hundreds of years of local experimentation and labor encompassing both indigenous and imported rice varietals.

The region extending from the Gambia River to Liberia became known as the Rice Coast by Europeans, reflecting local rice expertise. Scientists had previously proposed that all African rice crops were of the *Oryza sativa* varietal, the species indigenous to Asia. Eventually they identified a second varietal, *Oryza glaberrima,* as indigenous to Africa. Both species of rice were grown in West Africa, and eventually used to provision slave ships and brought on the Middle Passage to the Americas. Once in colonial North America, enslaved peoples played a key role in establishing and developing rice on the continent.

Transfer of Knowledge Systems

Rice was integral to the economy and agricultural systems of the Carolina colony. What is now coastal South Carolina produced more rice than any other region during the colonial period, generating immense wealth from the work and expertise of enslaved laborers. By the 1770s, South Carolina exported more than 60 million pounds of rice per year, making Charleston one of the world's wealthiest cities.

In the late 1600s, Black peoples with knowledge of wet-rice agriculture were vital to the crop's success in North America. Records show that planters relied on and acknowledged Black expertise regarding rice growing and had documented preferences for enslaved peoples from rice-growing regions. Some planters even entered into business agreements in order to import enslaved laborers directly from those regions in West Africa, illustrating that planters knew of and valued enslaved expertise in rice agriculture.

Complex rice-growing techniques and systems that had been used for hundreds of years in West Africa were replicated in the Carolina colony and in parts of Georgia, including rotational land use during the early rain-fed rice production system, controlled flooding to desalinate fields, and the use of sluices and other irrigation control techniques. Beyond transferring rice-growing knowledge systems to the colonies, enslaved laborers also performed the immense physical labor to prepare and transform the land for rice production. The embankments and water-control mechanisms implemented there required moving earth the volume of the largest pyramids multiple times over, clearing woodlands, and maintaining canals, all by hand.

Bags of Carolina Gold rice from the Historic Charleston City Market on Market Street

Historic Rice Fields of South Carolina in the 18th to 19th Centuries

In South Carolina, rice became a profitable plantation crop in the 18th century as a result of the knowledge, tools, and techniques of enslaved West African farmers. Dark orange areas on the map indicate historic rice-growing areas.

"Whites actively sought African knowledge of rice growing, and slaves used that knowledge in the bargaining system of task labor to negotiate less plantation work so they might spend more time tending their gardens," writes William C. Whit in his chapter, "Soul Food as Cultural Creation," in *African American Foodways: Explorations of History and Culture*. The result: Enslaved laborers were categorized and assigned specific work dependent on their ability. If they met

their daily labor quota, they could carve out more free time. Though this system is often characterized as more "humane" than the pushing, or pulling, system that was common in cotton production, it remained a system of enslavement where even light offenses were punished by violence such as whipping.

The integral role of women to rice systems in West Africa was also replicated in the rice plantation system. Enslaved women were heavily involved in sowing seeds, weeding, and hoeing on rice plantations. Rice was milled by mortar and pestle through the colonial era, mirroring African processes and methods. Milling in this manner required skill to minimize breakage and immense manual labor to prepare the millions of pounds of rice that were sold. The winnowing, or fanner, baskets used in the rice preparation process derived from a design used by African women, one that differed from Native American designs found in the Southeast.

Black knowledge systems also permeated the preferences for rice preparation in the culinary arena. Rice remains an important part of diets in regions of West Africa today, where dishes such as jollof serve as the culinary cousins and forebearers of red rice, a common food in Charleston and the Lowcountry. Today, hoppin' John, the one-pot dish of rice and field peas, is consumed widely in the South and among Black peoples for New Year's. This dish, whose "contours are distinctly African, with the two main African ingredients and origins linked to slave dwellings and plantation kitchens of the South," as Judith Carney and Richard Nicholas Rosomoff write in *In the Shadow of Slavery*, has formed the basis of an enduring American culinary tradition.

Carolina Gold Rice

From the 1700s until a series of hurricanes decimated much of the crop, slavery ended, and its popularity among producers was overtaken by other varietals, Carolina Gold dominated American rice production. It's estimated that in South Carolina alone between 3.5 and 5 million bushels of it were grown at the onset of the Civil War.

Carolina Gold was the first long-grain rice that would become important to world commerce. The crop, fueled by enslaved labor and knowledge systems, was the cornerstone for the incredible wealth of Charleston and other rice-producing plantation economies. Famed for its fluffy grains and sweet, almost nutty flavor, Carolina Gold largely disappeared until recent projects in the early 2000s brought it back to the fore. Today, a group of Carolina growers and the Carolina Gold Rice Foundation are dedicated to preserving the famed rice crop, and Carolina Gold is seeing a resurgence. Cooking with it means continuing a part of Black history in the United States.

Rice in many West African societies is central to religious and daily rituals as well as to cultural identity.

OPPOSITE: "Loading a Rice Schooner" by Alice Ravenel Huger Smith depicts enslaved peoples carrying baskets of rice to a ship.

Black-Eyed Peas & Greens

Black-eyed peas, a common varietal of cowpeas, were brought to North America from Africa via the slave trade. At the onset of the trade between Africa and the Americas that would uproot millions of lives, they were a common part of African diets. Once they made their way to North America, black-eyed peas followed a similar progression as other foods connected to Black migration and African foodways. In the South they were a common crop in the subsistence gardens of enslaved peoples. Eventually, the use of black-eyed peas filtered outward, and they were consumed by Black and white peoples across the socioeconomic spectrum. By the 1800s black-eyed peas were a commercial crop in the United States, grown and plowed under to replenish the soil—and even used as livestock feed. Today, they are still widely consumed in the United States and thought to bring luck when eaten with greens on New Year's. Black-eyed peas are also now often used to make hoppin' John, replacing the field peas traditionally used in the dish in the Lowcountry, as black-eyed peas are more readily available throughout the United States.

Greens

Greens are another staple ingredient of Black culinary traditions. "Perhaps no other cooking traditions feature them so prominently," note Carney and Rosomoff in *In the Shadow of Slavery*. "In West Africa alone there are more than 150 indigenous species of edible greens." Historically, greens were used in West Africa for flavor, to add bitterness to a dish, and as a thickening agent. They were served cooked, made into soups, and more.

Enslaved peoples often grew greens in subsistence gardens and used a wide variety of types, including kale, collards, pokeweed, dandelion, mustard, purslane, and chard. Greens were a cherished and important aspect of the diet of Black peoples, serving as nutritional powerhouses that helped fill the gap between meager rations and dietary needs. The preferences and labor of Black peoples in the South undoubtedly contributed to greens' status as one of the pillars of southern cuisine. The Great Migration brought increased demand for greens to cities outside the South, and greens became a recognized soul food staple in the 1960s.

Today, greens are increasingly adapted to align with modern trends in American cuisine. Traditionally they were cooked with pork for seasoning, but preparations have shifted in response to growing health consciousness and veganism in Black communities and beyond. Many newer recipes utilize smoked turkey rather than pork or forgo animal products altogether. The embrace of greens by health-conscious communities is recognition of their nutritional density, and they are often touted as a superfood.

Enslaved cooks saved the nutrient-dense cooking broth of greens, known as pot likker, to give to enslaved children for extra nourishment. Eventually, pot likker became widely consumed in the South, often alongside cornbread. It was prescribed by southern doctors as medicine. In 1935, a senator even resorted to reciting his recipe for pot likker in attempts to filibuster a bill. "Greens have been there in every phase of the African American experience and haven't been rejected with the increased demand for healthy foods. The future certainly looks bright for dark, leafy greens," writes Adrian Miller in *Soul Food: The Surprising Story of an American Cuisine, One Plate at a Time.*

A farm grows rows of delicious and healthy kale.

Fried Chicken

Though soul food is often used as a reductive and negative symbol for Black foodways, fried chicken offers an example of how a dish traditionally associated with the canon can have deep historical meaning and also become part of modern American food culture. In the United States, the history of fried chicken is deeply entwined with Black labor and Black history. Fried chicken is considered a quintessentially southern food.

Though the exact genesis of southern fried chicken is hard to trace, Black labor, particularly in the South, had a hand in cooking and popularizing the dish. According to Adrian Miller in *Soul Food,* it's undeniable that "a particular type of fried chicken developed in the American South, that many times enslaved African Americans were doing the cooking, and that everyone was doing the eating."

Early cookbooks by wealthy white women whose kitchens were surely staffed by Black enslaved cooks, like *The Virginia Housewife* and *The Carolina Housewife,* include recipes for fried chicken and smothered fried chicken, though the origin of those recipes is not credited or discussed. Fried chicken ultimately became a common part of a "Virginia breakfast," an early 1800s spread featuring a hot bread and a fried or baked meat. Early cookbooks by Black authors, such as Rufus Estes's *Good Things to Eat* and *What Mrs. Fisher Knows About Old Southern Cooking,* also include fried chicken recipes.

Chicken has a long history and many complex meanings for Black communities, not all positive. Some enslaved peoples used chicken as a tool for self-empowerment, raising the birds and selling them and their eggs when permitted. Work as a chicken vendor was strictly regulated, but for those who could gain access to local markets, the sale of chicken and other goods provided vital economic resources. Chickens, and their eggs, also helped fill nutritional

Female waiter carriers serve hot meals to passengers at the Gordonsville train depot in Virginia.

gaps for Black peoples, who were given meager and often monotonous rations.

Chicken remained an important, though contested, symbol for Black communities long after emancipation. Fried chicken was commonly eaten at Black church functions and Sunday dinners, taking on the name "gospel bird" or "Sunday cluck." Fried chicken was also an important tool for Black entrepreneurship. In railroad towns like Gordonsville, Virginia, once called the Fried Chicken Capital of the World, Black women known as waiter carriers sold food, often fried chicken, to rail passengers on trains passing through. These enterprises provided for their families, enabled them to purchase homes and support other entrepreneurial ventures, and helped feed hungry children in the neighborhood. "Food serves more than its intended function to nourish and to satiate," writes Psyche A. Williams-Forson in *Building Houses Out of Chicken Legs*. "The trading and selling of these foods for commerce also provided relative autonomy, social power, and economic freedom."

Fried chicken was also an important part of meals during the Great Migration. Shoebox lunches, so named because the food was packed into empty shoeboxes, were a fixture of Black peoples' journey as they left the American South, when Black migrants did not have the luxury of using a dining car—even a segregated one. Maya Angelou's *I Know Why the Caged Bird Sings* describes fellow Black passengers feeding her fried chicken from their lunch boxes on a train journey in the segregated South as a child.

On the other hand, chicken has long been used to demonize and stereotype Black peoples. Narratives from the antebellum era often characterized Black peoples as chicken stealers whose theft was posited as part of their nature. These narratives placed blame on enslaved peoples without examining the institution of enslavement and the effects of systemic deprivation on decision-making. Some scholars also emphasize that while chicken theft was likely not so widespread, enslaved peoples may have engaged in theft as a means of regaining agency over an aspect of their lives and for vital sustenance.

Historical imagery abounds with these stereotypes well into the 18th century—on postcards, in minstrel shows, on sheet music illustrations, and beyond. Black women were represented as mammies and appeared as caricatures in chicken-fryer ads. The racist 1915 film *The Birth of a Nation* played a role in spreading the fried-chicken stereotype. In its entirety, the film attempts to portray Black people as aggressive and less than, and in one scene, a Black elected official gnaws on a piece of chicken while shoeless and drinking alcohol. Black men, often depicted as lazy, ignorant chicken stealers, were represented by a caricature known as a coon. That racist imagery proved popular in the early 1900s, with businesses like the Coon Chicken Inn restaurants demonstrating how widespread the caricature was. Coon Chicken Inn was founded in Salt Lake City, Utah, in the 1920s and expanded to multiple locations in Washington state, as well as in Portland, Oregon. To enter the restaurants, customers walked through a door situated within the red lips of the large caricature of a Black railway porter. Menus, napkins, promotional materials, and other items all displayed the same caricature. The popular restaurants capitalized on the stereotyped facade by selling, what else, fried chicken, until closing in 1957.

By no means do Black folks have the sole claim on southern fried chicken. However, Black peoples helped make fried chicken a staple southern dish, marking the development and popularization of it through their labor as cooks and vendors, and even in their migration patterns. Despite the stigma, fried chicken has now become a part of American culinary culture. And fried chicken is Black food as much as it is American food.

> By no means do Black folks have the sole claim on southern fried chicken. However, Black peoples helped make fried chicken a staple southern dish.

OPPOSITE: A hearty meal with African American culinary roots: fried chicken, coleslaw, corn, and beans

Barbecue

Barbecue is an iconic American food. Though numerous cultures smoke and slow-cook meat, barbecue remains a culinary tradition commonly associated with American cuisine. If you ask people from other countries to list what they consider to be American foods, barbecue often ranks up there, along with ubiquitous fast-food options, burgers, and apple pie. Much of that is thanks to modern food media, in which barbecue has become a focus of numerous TV shows, books, articles, and more. Much of that media has focused on white men, lending a white face to a food tradition with deep roots in Black and Indigenous communities. This lack of representation is ultimately what led Colorado native Adrian Miller to author his book *Black Smoke: African Americans and the United States of Barbecue* and explore the roots of the cuisine.

Black Barbecue Traditions

The exact genesis of American barbecue is murky. However, throughout its history, Black Americans have played a central role in its development. Writer and culinary historian Adrian Miller frames Black peoples as shepherds of American barbecue culture rather than its originators. In *Black Smoke,* Miller notes that African populations did smoke meat in the precolonial era, but there's limited evidence of cooking traditions similar to what would eventually emerge as barbecue in the United States. "The stronger arguments for West African influence on barbecue are the cooks' deftness with seasoning and saucing and cumulative years of honed expertise that were added to what they learned from their Native American teachers," he writes. "Equipped with that knowledge, barbecue flourished thanks to the handiwork of Black barbecuers."

In short, American barbecue draws on Indigenous methods of cooking that coalesced with Black and European traditions. Indig-

A vintage photograph of men and women roasting meat over a shallow barbecue pit

enous cooks used shallow pits and spit-roasting methods for meats. Those methods, the basis for barbecue, were then adapted and changed by colonization. Black peoples were the stewards of this process of adaptation, acting as the primary barbecue practitioners for a significant portion of American history.

Barbecue spread as slavery did, from the early Virginia colony outward. Barbecue cooks had a special status during enslavement, their high value was acknowledged, and they were "loaned" to other plantation owners for special occasions. During the colonial era, barbecue emerged as a common means to celebrate feasts or special occasions with large groups of people. It also served as an important avenue of Black entrepreneurship following emancipation.

Many Black barbecuers, who we'd call pitmasters today, earned a living crafting barbecue for events and gatherings or selling it from their businesses. Pitmasters and barbecue cooks were hired to cook for large political rallies and social events, at times serving tens of thousands of people. Some operated barbecue stands as a side hustle. In reality, Black barbecuers were considered the source of the most "authentic" barbecue for much of American history.

Take, for example, Marie Jean, who was born enslaved in the late 1700s in Arkansas and went on to become a pitmaster known for catering large gatherings. She presided over events such as the 1840 Fourth of July barbecue in Pine Bluff, Arkansas (well before the Civil War), and eventually bought her freedom for $800—more than $28,000 in today's currency. After her emancipation, Jean operated a boardinghouse known for its cuisine, and her life and cooking were eulogized in the *Weekly Arkansas Gazette* after her death.

As Black peoples migrated out of the South following the end of enslavement, they brought barbecue with them. As a result, barbecue became one of the focal points of class-related and racial struggles during the Great Migration. As middle class and wealthier Black peoples, and the media, grappled with the influx of newcomers, barbecue was often used as a symbol for everything deemed "wrong" with working-class Black migrants making their way out of the southern United States. But over time, barbecue overcame these barriers and grew to national acclaim, becoming a fixture at family gatherings, churches, and events. As barbecue spread, regional barbecue styles popped up. These styles are often known by location names, like Memphis, Kansas City, and Carolina, though even within regions, practices vary.

Black barbecue has some distinctive elements, according to Adrian Miller. He points to charcoal flavor; not always adhering to the low-and-slow cooking method; typically being served with white bread; and the use of or focus on sauce. Many point to saucing methods as the most prominent of Black contributions to U.S. barbecue traditions. Descriptions of barbecue sauces from the 19th century note it was often spicy, with recipes that utilized red chili pepper. Over time, tomato was added to sauces, and the multifaceted sauce variations we know today grew as barbecue itself expanded.

Beginning in the 1990s, media narratives began to shift toward what Miller calls the "four types of White Guys Who Barbeque," emphasizing hipster pitmasters, rural artisans, those with fine-dining experience, or a combination of the above. Suddenly barbecue was considered a craft worthy of investment

> *In short, American barbecue draws on Indigenous methods of cooking that coalesced with Black and European traditions.*

OPPOSITE: Barbecue has become synonymous with American cuisine—and a pulled-pork barbecue sandwich and a cold beer is an unbeatable combination.

and media coverage. Mirroring this shift, more white pitmasters and barbecuers entered the space. Many early white barbecuers had Black staff and assistants. It's unclear how much expertise was transferred or absorbed from those Black assistants as the demographics shifted, but it's important to note the possibility. Some also propose that as barbecue shifted from primarily whole-animal cooking over outdoor setups to smaller cuts cooked indoors, it helped new faces gain entry into the space and supplant historically Black labor. In barbecue, as in so many other aspects of American foodways, Black pitmasters often have not been credited for their contributions.

No matter what caused the shift to the barbecue environment of today, where Black pitmasters seem few and far between, Black expertise helped build the foundation of what American barbecue is today. Work to recognize both the current Black barbecue community and the Black barbecue legacy is ongoing. In 2019, Miller joined the board of the American Royal Barbecue Hall of Fame and made the very significant point that of 27 inductees in 11 years, only one was Black. Since Miller gained his seat on the board, more Black barbecuers have been inducted, including James Beard Award winner Rodney Scott, who was inducted in 2021.

Jones' Bar-B-Q Diner

One of the oldest Black-owned businesses in the United States is a James Beard Award–winning barbecue restaurant in Marianna, Arkansas. Walter Jones began selling barbecued pork in 1910, before the start of the Great Migration and about 50 years after emancipation. The business began small—its barbecue was sold from a washtub. In 1964, it moved to a small shotgun-style building, where it still operates today. Walter Jones's grandson James Jones runs the family business now, known as Jones' Bar-B-Q Diner.

The James Beard Award–winning Jones' Bar-B-Q Diner in Marianna, Arkansas, one of the oldest Black-owned businesses in the country

Celebrated Black Pitmasters & Barbecue Styles

Selected regional styles:
① Chicago Southside ② Deep South ③ East Texas ④ Eastern North Carolina ⑤ Kansas City ⑥ Memphis ⑦ Western South Carolina ⑧ Midwestern ⑨ Eastern South Carolina ⑩ Southern Kentucky ⑪ Southwestern Kentucky ⑫ St. Louis ⑬ Virginia ⑭ Western North Carolina

The no-frills restaurant sits on a residential street in a small town with a population of fewer than 4,000 people, 25 miles from the Mississippi River. This region of Arkansas was once part of the state's cotton belt (and the black belt). Its rich, dark soils supported cotton production, and enslaved Black peoples were forced to work there harvesting the cash crop.

Today, Jones' Bar-B-Q Diner reminds us of the rich history of American barbecue, a culinary tradition deeply connected to southern Black expertise. The diner, renowned for the delicious simplicity of its offerings, draws customers

> ### Focus On: Painful Barbecue Legacy
>
> Images of savagery related to barbecues and propaganda portraying grotesque Native American barbecue habits were used by colonists to help justify enslaving Indigenous peoples. Eventually, Black enslaved peoples replaced Indigenous laborers in the colonies, and barbecue was used against them as a tool of control. Roasting or burning Black peoples alive was a punishment inflicted on some after rebellion or misbehavior. If a lynching involved fire, it was called a "Negro barbecue," and for some of these events white spectators dressed in their best clothing, accompanied by their children, to gather and watch. They would take photos and sometimes cut off pieces of burnt corpses to take as mementos, or the remains would be displayed publicly. A mixture of vinegar, red pepper, and salt—reminiscent of barbecue sauce—was also used to torture enslaved peoples. It was applied to cuts and lashes after the individuals had been whipped or beaten, causing a searing, stinging pain on top of the immense abuse already inflicted. As with other foods such as fried chicken, barbecue was often used to stereotype and degrade Black peoples and reinforce Black peoples' place at the bottom of the social hierarchy.

from far and wide, including former president Bill Clinton. Indoor seating is limited, and most orders are placed for carryout from a window. Chopped pork barbecue cooked over oak and hickory is available two ways: by the pound or in a sandwich wrapped in tinfoil. House-made slaw is offered, and you can purchase vinegar-based sauce by the pint. There is only a Facebook page and no online ordering. James Jones has kept his methods and recipes, passed down from his great-grandfather, a secret. But one known method hearkens back to the early barbecue traditions of enslaved peoples: Jones sauces the pork as it's cooking with a vinegar-based sauce and douses the sandwich with the same sauce to finish. This technique recalls early barbecue methods in the North American colonies that utilized a vinegar-based sauce for both cooking and serving. Of course, Black cooks were typically responsible for the barbecue preparation.

In 2012, the James Beard Foundation awarded Jones' Bar-B-Q Diner an America's Classics Award, given to restaurants "distinguished by their timeless appeal" and that "serve quality food that reflects the character of their communities." Jones' Bar-B-Q Diner was the first restaurant in Arkansas to be awarded a James Beard Award. It has also been recognized by *Food & Wine,* the Food Network, and other major media organizations.

Jones' Bar-B-Q Diner was badly damaged by a fire in early 2021 but reopened after an outpouring of community support raised nearly $100,000. It is open from 7 a.m. until it sells out, which could happen within a few hours on summer days.

OPPOSITE: **A chef adds ingredients to a slow cooker at Jones' Bar-B-Que Diner.**

Fish & Seafood

Black communities have a long history of consuming fish and seafood, as well as working in related industries. Just as they brought agricultural knowledge with them to the colonies, West Africans also carried knowledge of winds and currents, where certain fish were likely to be found, preparation preferences, and more. Enslaved peoples in North America, particularly those in coastal regions or with access to waterways for fishing, often incorporated seafood into their diets. Some enslavers encouraged or allowed fishing by enslaved peoples as a way to help keep provisioning costs down. Though fish and seafood were generally part of the diets of all peoples living near a body of water, during enslavement fried fish became a traditional Saturday meal for those permitted to fish after their work was done. Following emancipation, the tradition of fish fries continued in the Black community, as part of summer gatherings and church fundraisers, and as the basis of restaurants and food businesses started by Black migrants during the Great Migration. Many regional or subregional cuisines that draw heavily on Black inputs, such as Cajun, southern, and Lowcountry cuisines, also prominently feature seafood in dishes such as fried catfish, shrimp and grits, and gumbo.

In the Chesapeake Bay region, along the coastline from New York to Virginia, Black watermen were an integral part of the fishing industry and helped fuel the seafood-centric diet that continues to impact the region today. Black peoples have been associated with the seafood industry in the area since they were first brought to the Chesapeake Bay in the 1600s as enslaved laborers. Black peoples have oystered,

Young oystermen unload bags of shellfish from a fishing boat in Olga, Louisiana.

crabbed, hauled freight, shucked oysters, picked crabs, and built, operated, and crewed fishing boats and more for generations. Though their numbers have dwindled somewhat since, fourth-generation Black watermen still operate in the Chesapeake Bay, maintaining a long history of involvement with the local seafood industry.

In the 18th century, enslaved and free Black workers made up the majority of the labor force in the fishing industry, helping catch, process, and transport seafood. As noted, 100 or so years later in Charleston, South Carolina, Charles Leslie, a free Black man, became a notable fishmonger,

operating a large fishing operation reliant on a predominantly Black workforce. Leslie's organization eventually supplied foodstuffs throughout South Carolina and helped define seafood sustainability in local markets.

In New Orleans, Black oystermen dominated the industry in the 18th and 19th centuries. Enslaved workers would sell oysters and do street vending in the city, though their profits would go to their enslavers. After emancipation, Black peoples continued to play an outsize role in the local industry, with some even moving to New Orleans because the seafood industry there offered opportunities for employment. Black labor continued to dominate oyster processing in much of the United States through the 20th century.

Though oysters are not commonly associated with Black culinary traditions, a Black man is largely responsible for transforming the mollusk's reputation from that of a cheap food served in brothels and bars to one that is associated with high price points. Thomas Downing, the son of Virginia slaves, created an environment during the oyster boom of the 1800s that "helped elevate oyster consumption" and introduce it in spaces designed for families, women, politicians, and power players. Sadly, some of the same spaces that now serve oysters may not feel entirely welcoming to Black patrons, who have a long history of being targeted by uneven enforcement of restaurant dress codes.

The Gullah Geechee community has also played a significant role in fishing practices and seafood consumption in the United States. As part of the Georgia Black Fishermen oral history project, Dionne Hoskins interviewed Cornelia Walker Bailey, a prominent historian on Sapelo Island, Georgia, which is home to a historic Gullah Geechee community that includes the Hog Hammock community, believed to be one of the last intact island Gullah Geechee communities in the U.S. In the interview, Bailey recalled her mother fishing during the day while her father was at work, then her father returning home to fish at night. What they collectively caught—yellowtail, red drum, and mullet—was sold or shared within the community. Many of the fishing practices of the barrier island came from West African traditions, Bailey said, but as education and job options arose, there became a struggle between economic opportunity and preserving Gullah Geechee cultural traditions—a balance that is still at play today.

In New Orleans, Black oystermen dominated the industry in the 18th and 19th centuries.

OPPOSITE: David Bates's "Ed Walker Cleaning Fish" from 1982 portrays a man preparing the fresh catch of the day.

Sweet Potatoes & Yams

First, let's clear up some of the yam versus sweet potato confusion. Yams have been utilized in West Africa since before the Transatlantic Slave Trade. Those large and hairy tubers feature in origin myths for Igbo peoples and are the focus of harvest festivals, and some words that sound like "yam" in West African languages mean "to eat" or are close to the words for "food." Yams were common provisions for slaving ships and used to feed both enslaved peoples and traders on journeys across the Atlantic. By some estimates, yams were the only foodstuffs aboard ships, and upwards of 100,000 yams were used to feed 500 enslaved Africans at a time along the Middle Passage. That breaks down to just 200 yams per person on a months-long voyage. Today, the yam is still commonly eaten in West Africa, the Caribbean, and throughout Latin America—but it's been surpassed by the sweet potato in the United States.

Sweet potatoes, in contrast, are a much newer crop to the African continent. Sweet potatoes, which are not actually potatoes and come from a separate plant, have been cultivated in the Americas for thousands of years. They were introduced to Africa by European traders in the 1600s. However, they did not immediately become popular. African yams and other tubers were readily available, utilized widely, and retained their significance in community and cultural practices instead.

It was in the Americas that sweet potatoes were more widely adopted by diaspora communities.

OPPOSITE: **A vendor sells fresh produce on the streets of Harlem in 1927.**

> "Centuries after black and white southerners figured it out, the broader American public is now catching on to the fact that the sweet potato is a 'superfood.'"
>
> —ADRIAN MILLER, SOUL FOOD: THE SURPRISING STORY OF AN AMERICAN CUISINE, ONE PLATE AT A TIME

The root vegetable has origins in Central and South America dating back to 2500 B.C. Sweet potatoes were an incredibly convenient food and became a staple part of the diets of enslaved peoples. They were easy to store and highly nutritious, often grown and used to round out rations. Their sweetness was also a treat. Enslaved peoples cooked them in the ashes of a fire or ate them mashed with spices. Most important, they grew well in temperate climates, unlike African yams. Over time, sweet potatoes became an integral part of southern foodways, finding their way to the planters' table, as did many other staple foods of enslaved peoples. Sweet potato farming spread north in the late 1800s and throughout the nation via the Great Migration. The vegetables became popular in cities as an affordable street food, one familiar to Black migrants. They also became an important part of the soul food canon in dishes such as sweet potato pie and candied sweet potatoes (commonly called candied yams). According to chef and culinary educator Scott Alves Barton, "As the sweet potato takes up the role of the yam—foodstuff for sacred twins and ancestors—it epitomizes the adaptive creativity of the diaspora."

Today, "sweet potato" and "yam" are often used interchangeably. There's debate over how sweet potatoes came to be called "yams" in the United States. Some point to a marketing effort in the 1930s meant to distinguish orange-fleshed sweet potatoes from other varietals. However, there's also limited evidence that some Black communities called them "yams" as early as the 18th century, which predates the marketing effort.

Sweet potatoes have become a modern American dining staple—even if the confusion between yam and sweet potato persists. For many Black families in the United States, sweet potato pie in particular is considered an essential part of holiday meals, church functions, family reunions, and other communal events. In a sense, sweet potatoes have retained some of the cultural significance held by true yams in West Africa. They appear on menus in the form of fries, tots, and hashes. They've also taken on new currency as an increasing emphasis on plant-based eating and nutrition has led many to eat sweet potatoes. "Centuries after black and white southerners figured it out, the broader American public is now catching on to the fact that the sweet potato is a 'superfood,'" writes Adrian Miller in Soul Food.

OPPOSITE: Nutrient-rich sweet potato hash with onions and bell peppers

Baked Goods

At first glance it would be easy to assume that cakes, pies, breads, muffins, and rolls are creations drawn solely from European foundations and techniques. Many popular baked goods don't draw on ingredients that immediately tie back to the African continent. Yet cuisine is much more nuanced than just ingredients. It's a result of trade, infrastructure, and economic factors that coalesce to shape how

people are able to interact with food in a certain market. Cuisine is also a result of culture, history, personal preference, and popular consciousness, which all impact how makers, cooks, bakers, sellers, growers, and doers in the food space bring a cuisine together.

Black peoples often supplied the labor and expertise that underpinned early southern cuisine, including baking. "Black women, in particular, originated many of the innovative recipes that the white women they cooked for would publish and profit from," writes Chala June in the Bon Appétit article "Cheryl Day Just Wrote the Definitive Book on Southern Baking." "This whitewashing erased generations of Black women's contributions to Southern culinary culture, a long legacy that chefs and food historians are working to fully uncover to this day." Through their decision-making and judgment of just how much of an ingredient to use, how long to leave something to bake, how to regulate temperature (whether over a fire or in an early oven), and what combinations of spices to add for just the right touch, Black bakers in the South imparted their presence on the dishes they labored over.

In cities like Charleston, Black women have a long history of making their name as cooks and bakers. Pastry cooks were

highly valued enslaved laborers and could make or break the reputation of a well-to-do family. As free men and women, Black bakers used their skills for income, to feed their families, and to build businesses. In a region where baking has been called a "way of life," pies compete with a multitude of variations of biscuits, cakes, cobblers, and sweets that Black cooks and bakers helped develop.

Zephyr Wright, the longtime cook for President Lyndon B. Johnson and Lady Bird Johnson, pulls freshly baked bread out of the oven.

Early cookbooks point us to their contributions. The art of southern baking, as shared in *The Virginia Housewife* and *The Carolina Housewife*, required cooks to master a diverse array of baking skills and techniques. Originally published in 1824 and 1847, respectively, the two books can be viewed as likely repositories of the baking expertise of enslaved cooks in the early American South. Recipes for biscuits, yeasted breads, buns, muffins, rolls, cakes, and other baked goods are abundant in the books, and would have been part of the expected repertoire and labor of Black cooks. The earliest cookbooks published by Black cooks, from the 1800s and early 1900s, also demonstrate this expertise, with extensive sections on cakes, breads, pies, puddings, and biscuits.

On some plantations, enslaved peoples were given permission to make special foods around the Christmas holiday. One such food was the tea cake. Enslaved peoples' versions of the recipe are believed to have been interpretations of the European tea cakes served by plantation owners. Unable to read or write, enslaved peoples passed these recipes on by word of mouth. "Over time, when more Black people started reading and writing, they didn't necessarily write about things like the tea cake, because they were so focused on moving forward and getting a job," writes Etha Robinson in "Tea Cakes and Black History: Reclaiming a Legacy," a post for National Geographic's Education Blog. As is happening with so many forgotten or underrecognized Black contributions to foodways and recipes, today's historians and culinarians are now rediscovering the tea cake and its significance. "It is the commemoration of a removal of a shackle that prevented people from becoming their true selves," writes Robinson. "The tea cake is symbolic of that removal and the future we hope to create."

In a nation where Black peoples remained intertwined with the food space for generations and Black women in particular were renowned for their baking prowess, Black peoples must surely be able to claim some credit for the development of the nation's many sweet treats and dishes. Black peoples helped define American baking through their deftness making pie crusts and their confidence with cakes for white employers and enslavers. They helped define southern baking and spread a taste for quintessentially southern baked goods, such as biscuits, throughout the entire nation. And for many Black bakers, their sales and marketing skills fueled social movements, turning simple ingredients into pies and cakes that provided funds for boycotts and civil rights marches.

> In a nation where Black peoples remained intertwined with the food space for generations and Black women in particular were renowned for their baking prowess, Black peoples must surely be able to claim some credit for the development of the nation's many sweet treats and dishes.

OPPOSITE: **Americans began to view Black bakers, particularly women, as uniquely adept with baked breads, pies, and cakes.**

Cocktails, Distilling & Brewing

West Africans traditionally brewed drinks from available plants, such as palm trees and native grains. During the antebellum period in the colonies, alcohol was often part of rations given to the enslaved or granted as a gift during harvest festivals, intended to pacify them. While working, enslaved laborers and field-workers would be brought beers or other distilled beverages, common drinks in the colonial world. There is also a long history of mixology and fermentation by Black peoples in service of white employers and as entrepreneurs marketing their skills broadly.

In many American cities, Black bartenders and beverage professionals became part of a respected service class and earned legendary reputations for themselves. Formerly enslaved, Cato Alexander ran a New York inn famed for its punches in the early 1800s. In the late 1800s, and early 1900s, Hancock's bar in D.C. was renowned for the craft of its Black bar staff. Dick Francis earned enough through his work at Hancock's and as bar manager for the U.S. Senate to send his son to medical school and amass a small fortune.

The life and work of the Black bar professional Tom Bullock offers another example. Bullock was a bartender at the St. Louis Country Club and published *The Ideal Bartender* in 1917, the first book by a Black bar professional. Bullock's acclaim was also embroiled in a presidential scandal. In the early 1900s, former President Theodore Roosevelt came under fire for alleged heavy drinking. In testimony Roosevelt claimed to have consumed only a portion of a mint julep prepared by famed bartender Tom Bullock. Though Roosevelt eventually won the lawsuit, a 1913 *Saint Louis Dispatch* editorial remarked incredulously, "Who was ever known to drink just a part of one of Tom's?"

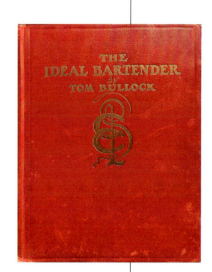

ABOVE: **Tom Bullock's** *The Ideal Bartender* is the first book published by a Black bartender.
OPPOSITE: **A group of friends share a drink at a bar in Clarksdale, Mississippi, in 1939.**

Voices in Black Food

This book is just a starting point to exploring Black foodways in the United States, an entrée into a vast array of knowledge and expertise. And as much as it's vital to look backward to understand the foundation of American cuisine, it's also important to look to the present and future. Here you'll find a much-too-short sampling of chefs, writers, historians, and other culinary luminaries who are informing our understanding of Black food today. The work of these folks, and countless others, is laying the foundation for the continued development of American cuisine far into the future.

While I attempted to ensure gender equity among the voices represented in this book, sensitive to the fact that Black women have done immense, often unrecognized labor in the American food landscape, I ultimately solicited quotes and insights from more women than men. However, male chefs, writers, and interviewees were far more responsive to my inquiries. My deep suspicion is that professional women in food, like many women today in the United States, according to numerous studies, continue to take on more underpaid or unpaid labor, and as a result may be too busy or unable to contribute time, recipes, or thoughts to this book or other projects like it.

OPPOSITE: Chef Benjamin "BJ" Dennis (standing) serves a meal at Joseph Fields Farm in Johns Island, South Carolina.

Jessica B. Harris
Culinary Historian

Jessica B. Harris is one of the United States' most celebrated culinary historians, as well as an author, a journalist, and a frequent food media commentator. Harris was featured as an expert on the groundbreaking Netflix series *High on the Hog*, which was adapted from her eponymous book on the history of African American cuisine. She was the lead curator for the exhibit African/American: Making the Nation's Table at the Museum of Food and Drink in New York and has consulted for the Smithsonian National Museum of African American History and Culture. She's won multiple James Beard Foundation Awards, including a Lifetime Achievement Award in 2020, and was named one of *Time* magazine's most influential people in 2021.

Much of Harris's work illustrates the richness, diversity, and complexity of Black foodways and Black contributions to cuisine in the United States and beyond. In *High on the Hog: A Culinary Journey From Africa to America*, she takes readers on a multigenerational exploration spanning multiple continents, colonial North America, the American West, urban and rural food cultures, Black entrepreneurship, and more to illustrate how interwoven Black history, labor, and contributions are with American cuisine and culture. In it, she describes how Black peoples "have cooked our way into the hearts, minds, and stomachs of a country."

In other works, such as *Beyond Gumbo: Creole Fusion Food From the Atlantic Rim*, Harris pushes us to consider just how broadly culinary contributions from the African diaspora have spread. She proposes a framework of ingredients, techniques, and even social roles tied to the diaspora that are now interwoven into creolized cuisines throughout North and South America and the Caribbean. Through her work, Harris has helped redefine soul food, expand the history of American cuisine, and connect ties from the Black diaspora to cuisines and cultures around the world.

Much of Harris's work illustrates the richness, diversity, and complexity of Black foodways and Black contributions to cuisine in the United States and beyond.

Adrian Miller

Soul Food Scholar

Adrian Miller, known as the Soul Food Scholar, is a former attorney, certified barbecue judge, and food writer. Miller describes his work excavating and exploring Black foodways as "dropping knowledge like hot biscuits." Through his numerous award-winning books he highlights the breadth and depth of Black contributions to the cuisine of the United States through generations of labor, innovation, and leadership in the culinary space.

"Enslaved Africans and later African Americans have had a transformational influence on American food, in terms of ingredients that have been added and really how cuisine was performed," Miller says. "Our stamp on the cuisine is profoundly transformational." Miller's work does much to share stories of Black influence and talent beyond soul food and the cooking traditions of the southern United States. "With the exception of French chefs, African Americans did much to establish fine dining in early America," he notes. "Some of the most well received restaurants, culinary establishments, and caterers were African Americans."

The White House was another place where Black culinary talent has long made its mark. In *The President's Kitchen Cabinet: The Story of the African Americans Who Have Fed Our First Families, From the Washingtons to the Obamas,* Miller illustrates how Black culinarians and laborers have long acted as tastemakers for America's leaders. Through their roles as White House chefs, stewards, cooks, butlers, and servers, Black peoples were often the first to leverage new culinary technologies and helped shape dining at the highest levels of political and social spheres of the United States.

For example, *The President's Kitchen Cabinet* traces the story of formerly enslaved cook Daisy Bonner, who introduced President Franklin Roosevelt to many southern delicacies, including pigs' feet. Roosevelt enjoyed pigs' feet so much, he eventually served them to Winston Churchill. By detailing the lives and work of often forgotten Black figures, Miller demonstrates how Black peoples have long influenced fine dining.

Miller emphasizes, "The shame of all of this is that in our present context, African Americans are not associated with fine dining." But he says, "Black history is American history," especially when it comes to food.

"Black food means anything made by African heritage people in the broadest sense."

Hibiscus Aid

Recipe from *Native Recipes*, provided with permission from the University of the Virgin Islands

Cook time: 20 minutes | *Makes about 3 quarts*

30 dried red hibiscus blooms

½ ounce ginger (about 1½-inch piece), peeled

½ gallon plus 1 quart water

Juice from 6 limes

Sugar, for sweetening

Wash hibiscus and ginger. Cut ginger into very small pieces or grate it. Boil ginger in 1 quart water for about 2 minutes. Add hibiscus, remove from heat and cover.

When cool, strain liquid into a large pitcher. Add ½ gallon of water and lime juice. Sweeten to taste.

Chill and serve cold. If you wish, add a dash of rum or your favorite liquor.

Gregory & Subrina Collier

Founders of BayHaven Restaurant Group

Much of the increasing recognition and resources available to Black culinarians today is directly the result of Black writers, chefs, food service workers, historians, bloggers, and restaurateurs. Chef Gregory Collier and his wife and business partner, Subrina Collier, are two such figures. In 2016, the duo helped found Soul Food Sessions, a dining series aimed at promoting and supporting Black hospitality workers. Gregory, a James Beard Award semifinalist, and Subrina, a James Beard Foundation Women's Entrepreneurial Leadership Fellow, both served on President Joe Biden's Small Business and Entrepreneurs Advisory Council. Through their restaurant group, BayHaven, the Colliers have also launched numerous projects that not only win awards but also seek to uplift Black food culture and empower Black food professionals.

Gregory emphasizes that BayHaven's ethos focuses on "empowerment through the hospitality industry." Leah & Louise, a highly awarded restaurant founded by the Colliers in Charlotte, North Carolina, serves southern food through the lens of the Mississippi River Valley, layering history into the concept and menu. There, a service charge takes the place of tipping, which goes to support higher wages, health insurance, paid time off, retirement contributions, and a holiday bonus for staff. In 2021, the Colliers launched the BayHaven Food and Wine Festival in Charlotte. More than 2,000 attendees and 62 chefs, mixologists, and winemakers took part in the three-day festival designed to showcase Black excellence in food and beverage. In addition to highlighting a broad array of Black culinary and beverage talent from around the country, the festival also sought to provide spaces to predominantly Black attendees that they may not get elsewhere. As Subrina says, "I want us to have our own festival, celebration, moments of luxury, tasting tents, 'cause we don't always get that."

> "Black food is everything touched by people of the African diaspora, especially in the Americas via the slave trade. Our influence on the world's cuisine is incalculable."
> —CHEF GREGORY COLLIER

BBQ Chicken & Field Peas, p. 232

BBQ Chicken & Field Peas

Recipe by Greg and Subrina Collier

Cook time: 1 hour 20 minutes, plus overnight prep | Makes 6 to 8 servings

This all goes down in a cast-iron pan—one-pot style. This is our version of the classic French duck and white bean cassoulet. At home we like to fire up the grill and "bake" this dish on it to give the peas a smoked flavor, but here we use a good smoked bacon.

For the Memphis dry rub
1 cup brown sugar

½ cup smoked paprika

3 tablespoons lightly toasted peppercorns (cracked with back of pan or in spice grinder)

3 tablespoons kosher salt

¼ cup granulated garlic

1 tablespoon ground cumin

¼ cup granulated onion

1 tablespoon cayenne pepper

1 tablespoon dry mustard

For the chicken and field peas
Whole chicken, cut into 8 pieces

½ pound slab not-too-smoky bacon, cut into ½-inch chunks

2 tablespoons butter

2 tablespoons oil

1 cup medium-diced carrots

1 cup medium-diced peppers

1 cup medium-diced onions

1 cup medium-diced celery

4 cups chopped tomatoes

1 cup dried purple hull peas, soaked overnight

1 cup dried sea island red peas, soaked overnight

1 cup dried Austrian green peas, soaked overnight

1 cup dried cream peas, soaked overnight

1 cup apple cider vinegar

Small bunch fresh parsley, leaves chopped, stems saved

10 sprigs fresh thyme

2 bay leaves

1 teaspoon whole cloves

2 cups chicken stock

2 cups brown sugar

1 tablespoon tomato paste

1 tablespoon chopped garlic

1 tablespoon chopped ginger

1 tablespoon coriander

2 tablespoons smoked paprika

1 tablespoon crushed red pepper

¼ teaspoon cayenne pepper

Salt

Freshly ground black pepper

For the Memphis dry rub: Combine all Memphis dry rub ingredients in a small bowl. Coat chicken all over heavily in dry rub. Place in a large bowl and refrigerate overnight. Reserve leftover rub in an airtight container.

For the chicken and field peas: Preheat oven to 325°F.

Add bacon chunks to a large cast-iron pan and cover in water. Heat over medium heat, until the water begins to boil. Turn heat down to a gentle simmer; cook for about 30 minutes, until the bacon is crisp. Remove bacon, placing on a paper towel–lined plate.

Return the pan back to medium heat and add butter and oil. Once melted and frothy, add chicken, skin side down. Cook until skin is nicely browned, about 5 minutes, and turn over. Cook for an additional 2 minutes. Remove chicken from pan.

In the same pan add diced veggies and sauté for 1 minute. Add chopped tomatoes and peas to the pan and sauté until dry, about 7 to 10 minutes.

Add vinegar to deglaze the pan, scraping up brown bits from the bottom with a wooden spoon.

Make a bouquet garni by rolling the parsley stems, thyme, bay leaves, and whole cloves in a piece of cheesecloth and tying it into a bundle with butcher's twine.

Add bouquet garni, remaining ingredients, including salt and pepper to taste (be careful; the salt from the bacon will come out as the dish bakes), and browned chicken to the pan, arranging chicken in a single layer nestled in the peas—try not to cover the skin. Bring to a boil, then reduce heat to a gentle simmer.

Place cast-iron pan in preheated oven and cook until chicken thigh reads 183°F on a thermometer, about 20 to 30 minutes.

Remove bouquet garni before serving. Serve with toasted bread and pickled veggies.

Dirty Rice

Recipe by chef and business owner Ederique Goudia

Cook time: 35 minutes | *Makes 6 servings*

2 tablespoons vegetable oil, divided

1 pound chicken livers

1½ pounds ground beef

2 cups onion, chopped fine

1 green bell pepper, seeded and chopped fine (1 cup)

1 cup finely chopped celery (about 2 medium stalks)

2 cloves garlic, minced

4 tablespoons finely chopped parsley

1½ tablespoons Worcestershire sauce

1½ tablespoons kosher salt

½ to ¾ tablespoon freshly ground black pepper

4 cups cooked white rice

Heat 1 tablespoon oil in a large skillet over medium heat. Sauté chicken livers until cooked through, about 3 to 5 minutes per side, until browned on the outside but still pink on the inside. Using a fork or serving spoon, grind or mash chicken livers into fine grounds. Remove livers from skillet and set aside.

In the same skillet, add ground beef and brown until meat is cooked through, about 7 to 10 minutes. Remove meat from skillet, draining any excess fat, and set aside.

Add remaining 1 tablespoon oil to the skillet and sauté onions, bell pepper, celery, garlic, and parsley until vegetables are soft and translucent, about 8 minutes. Lower the heat to medium-low and add chicken livers and ground beef back to the skillet. Add Worcestershire sauce, salt, and black pepper; stir, cover skillet, and cook for an additional 10 minutes. Remove from heat and fold in cooked rice.

Frederick Douglass Opie
Professor & Author

Frederick Douglass Opie is a podcaster, author, and professor of history and foodways at Babson College. Opie's work emphasizes the historical context that connects food to our lives and cultures. Many of his projects focus on food in connection to protest and social movements. In his book *Hog and Hominy: Soul Food From Africa to America*, Opie traces the evolution and adaptation of African foodways in America and tackles issues of migration, identity, and power as he constructs a history of the development of soul food in the United States. In *Southern Food and Civil Rights: Feeding the Revolution*, he traces how southern cuisine was interconnected with the civil rights movement and how food tied into negotiations and debates about Black culture in the United States. His work challenges us to consider the significant interplay of food, power, and culture.

When discussing Black foodways in the United States, Opie notes, talking about Black peoples without also getting into the "good, the bad, and the ugly" tells an incomplete story that obscures vital context and nuance. Opie also emphasizes that the contributions of Black peoples to American cuisine are part of an interwoven tapestry. "If Black folks didn't come to this country, there wouldn't be a cuisine," he says. "The same could be said of Native American and also of European contributions."

Opie also notes that the interwoven nature of American cuisine and Black foodways is incredibly complex. He points to Gullah Geechee cuisine as an example, a cuisine distinct from that of the rest of South Carolina. According to Opie, while some parts of the two cuisines are the same, the differences come out of the historical circumstances of the Gullah Geechee peoples: "The Gullah country was a region in which the plantations were operated by absentee landlords. African culture was established and renewed as people from Africa continually disembarked on boats there. The concentration of people of African descent was much stronger there than other regions of the South. So, you're talking about a Black majority, and a majority whose culture remained intact."

When considering today's cuisine, Opie directs us to add nuance to our examinations of food cultures and culinary practices. His work demonstrates that through history we can gain vital contextual insights and begin to trace how numerous cuisines—national, regional, hyperlocal, and in between—may draw on shared elements of Black history and culture in unique ways.

"'Black food' is an understatement. It is so complex. Every region has its complexities."

Jennifer Hill Booker

Chef

Chef Jennifer Hill Booker's work encompasses a range of culinary techniques, continuing the history of Black culinarians in the United States who blend Black and other culinary influences in their careers. Booker trained at Le Cordon Bleu in Paris, is a James Beard Foundation Impact Fellow, and has published multiple books. Booker combines French and European cooking styles, influences from the Mississippi Delta, and other cooking traditions rooted in Black experiences into a style she calls "southern with a French accent." Booker's two cookbooks explore the overlap between French and southern cuisines, two culinary traditions historically rooted in Black labor and expertise in their practice in the United States.

Booker draws on Black culinary traditions and historic expertise that are relatively unrecognized in the broader discussion of food in the United States, like the long history of Black labor in fine dining and Black practitioners of French cooking. Booker says people are often surprised by her work. "I make it a point to remind them that the colonization of America depended on slaves who cooked the food their owners ate, be they French, German, or British. We married the dishes of our owners with the techniques, ingredients, and influences of our West African origin."

Booker previously lived in Bavaria and Heidelberg, Germany, where she was a personal chef for both military and German families. That expertise and experience informs the Bauhaus Biergarten, a restaurant project she co-owns and opened in Springdale, Arkansas, that challenges common conceptions of what Black chefs are qualified to do. The German-style beer garden offers outdoor seating, community tables, traditional European beer, bratwurst, and pretzels. Booker says, "I have to teach people that as a trained professional there's a huge range of culinary things I can do. If you think about Black chefs, our heritage draws on so many different cultures and histories. We can draw on all of those, which is evident in our cuisine."

"I'm from the South, so when you say 'Black food,' I automatically think southern food—fried catfish, beans, greens. But we also lived in Detroit, so I also think block parties, barbecue, red pop."

Succotash With Tarragon & Crème Fraîche

Recipe from *Dinner Déjà Vu: Southern Tonight, French Tomorrow,* by Jennifer Hill Booker

Cook time: 35 minutes | Makes 6 to 8 servings

This dish reminds me of summers in the Mississippi Delta and time spent wandering the produce market stalls of Paris. It's the perfect combination of fresh produce, tender beans, fragrant tarragon, and cool crème fraîche.

2 cups butter beans (fresh or frozen)

1 tablespoon unsalted butter

½ cup thick-cut hickory smoked bacon, about 6 strips; cut into ¼-inch lardons

1 small sweet onion, chopped fine, about ½ cup

3 celery ribs, chopped into ¼-inch dice

1 medium red bell pepper, seeded and cut into ¼-inch dice, about ¾ cup

2 cups fresh or frozen corn kernels

2 large garlic cloves, minced

4 scallions, white and green parts, chopped fine

1 cup heavy cream

2 tablespoons fresh tarragon, coarsely chopped

Salt

Freshly ground black pepper

¼ cup crème fraîche, for garnish

1 teaspoon fresh tarragon leaves, for garnish

Bring 1 quart of salted water (about 2 teaspoons of salt) to a rolling boil.

Add butter beans and cook for 3 to 5 minutes for fresh beans and 5 to 10 minutes for frozen.

Remove from heat, drain, and reserve until needed.

Melt the butter in a large sauté pan over medium heat.

Add the lardons and cook until crisp, about 7 minutes. Stir in the onion, celery, and bell pepper, stirring to coat with the butter and bacon fat. Cook until tender, about 5 minutes.

Add the corn, garlic, and scallions and cook an additional 5 minutes, stirring occasionally.

Add the cooked butter beans to the mixture and stir to combine.

Stir in the heavy cream and tarragon. Reduce heat to low, and cook uncovered for 5 more minutes, or until succotash is heated through.

Season liberally with salt and black pepper and serve garnished with crème fraîche and tarragon.

Chris Williams

Chef & Restaurateur

Chef and restaurateur Chris Williams, along with his brother Ben, founded Lucille's restaurant in Houston in 2012 as a tribute to his great-grandmother, culinary entrepreneur Lucille Bishop Smith. The restaurant replicates and draws on some of Smith's recipes and also serves a variety of innovative southern dishes. In addition to Lucille's, Williams founded a nonprofit (also named for his great-grandmother) in 2020 during the COVID-19 pandemic. The nonprofit has served more than 200,000 meals to those in need, first responders, poll workers, and others. While Williams's community work has not abated, his restaurant group is also growing. Their newest Houston outlet was included in the Michelin Guide's expansion into Texas in 2024.

Williams is no stranger to the long and diverse history of Black culinary expertise and entrepreneurship in the United States. When it comes to American food, he says that Black peoples were "the ones tasked with cultivating the art form, with mastering the harvest from the land, and figuring out the best ways to preserve, utilize, and make it delicious." Williams is keenly aware of that legacy—his great-grandmother Lucille founded a commercial food-training program and created the first hot-roll mix (distributed in the United States in the 1940s). Smith was a highly trained culinary professional who spent considerable effort teaching and creating opportunities for others and succeeding, despite deeply rooted segregation and Jim Crow laws, until her death in 1985.

Today, Williams considers his work as an extension of his great-grandmother's legacy. That means going beyond the limited lens with which we commonly view Black food. A narrow focus on barbecue or soul food doesn't fit with Williams's professional experiences or his family's history. He notes that in his great-grandmother's cookbook, *Lucille's Treasure Chest of Fine Foods,* which is now a rare collector's item, she included a whole section on meat substitutes and even a recipe for guacamole. Though both would be considered far outside the stereotypical canon of Black culinary expertise, Smith worked with and had a deep knowledge of many cuisines and ingredients.

"We've always done more than soul food," Williams said. While white chefs have historically been allowed to demonstrate expertise in cuisines far and wide, that same space has not often been granted to Black chefs and other chefs from marginalized backgrounds. Williams continues to work to change that.

"Black food is loaded. Soul food, barbecue, West Indian, breakfast. That's how America sees it."

Upright Roasted Duck

Recipe by Chris Williams

Cook time: 1 hour 40 minutes | Makes 6 to 8 servings

For the duck
1 duck (5 to 6 pounds)

3 tablespoons kosher salt, divided

4 medium shallots, halved lengthwise

1 pound baby potatoes, whole

4 stalks celery, cut crosswise into 3 pieces

12 ounces carrots, peeled, cut crosswise into 3 pieces, thick pieces halved lengthwise

2 small apples, cored, cut into 8 wedges

2 cloves garlic, finely minced

2 teaspoons finely minced fresh thyme

3 teaspoons finely minced fresh parsley

3 tablespoons olive oil

2 teaspoons white pepper

1 (24-ounce) can of beer, preferably pilsner or lager (Stella, Heineken, PBR)

¼ cup chicken or vegetable stock

For the glaze
½ cup fig jam

3 tablespoons orange juice

2 tablespoons balsamic vinegar

1 tablespoon Worcestershire sauce

1 tablespoon butter

2 teaspoons white pepper

2 teaspoons red chili flakes

2 cloves garlic, minced

Preheat oven to 450°F. Place a rack at the lowest position of the oven to give the duck enough room to stand as it roasts.

Remove excess fat from the body cavity and neck of the duck. Slipping your hand under the duck breast skin, gently pull the duck breast skin from the duck breast meat, leaving the skin on the bird intact. Take care to not rip holes in the duck skin.

Bring 2 cups water to a boil. Pour boiling water over the duck to tighten the skin. Pat the skin and the inside of the cavity dry. Season all over with 2 tablespoons kosher salt. Set the duck aside and let cool while preparing remaining ingredients.

In a small saucepot, whisk together all glaze ingredients. Warm over low heat and let flavors mingle for about 10 minutes. Add water 1 tablespoon at a time to loosen if glaze becomes too thick. Set aside.

In a large bowl, toss together the shallots, potatoes, celery, carrots, apples, garlic, thyme, parsley, and olive oil. Season with remaining 1 tablespoon kosher salt and 2 teaspoons white pepper. Set aside.

Open and reserve ½ cup of the beer. Lightly oil the outside of the beer can. Place the beer can, with remaining beer, in a deep roasting pan. Slip the duck cavity over the beer can so that the duck is upright. Cover wing tips with foil and gently move to the oven.

Roast the duck for 15 minutes to gain some color. Reduce oven temperature to 350°F.

Pull the rack out of the oven carefully. Add the vegetables around the duck and pour in the reserved beer and stock.

Roast the duck for another 45 minutes. Carefully remove the duck from the oven. Brush all over with glaze and return to the oven to cook for an additional 15 to 20 minutes, until a thermometer reads 165°F.

Remove duck from the oven and brush with additional glaze. Let rest for 10 minutes before carving.

Thérèse Nelson

Writer & Chef

Through her work as a writer, chef, and founder of Black Culinary History (a space dedicated to the preservation of the Black community's culinary heritage), Thérèse Nelson works to carve out agency and space to explore Black foodways among larger historical narratives. Nelson is particularly aware of the legacy of many diverse groups and emphasizes the importance of those contributions to American cuisine. "We forget that this was a place before we got here," she says and cautions against forgetting the contributions of Indigenous peoples in an effort to make space for Black narratives.

Nelson founded Black Culinary History in 2008 as part of her own journey to investigate Black culinary heritage. On social media and the Black Culinary History website, as well as through special projects like the *Black Desserts* podcast that she hosts, Nelson showcases a vast array of historical narratives, profiles, and resources to help people learn more about Black foodways in the United States. Her work, including curating resources and advice for new Black writers, is a prime example of the way new media is changing how and what narratives are told.

Nelson is acutely aware of how social media, podcasts, independent websites, and blogs—and even Netflix—have democratized what stories gain wider traction and have narrowed the space between legacy publications and new upstarts. Black Culinary History is itself a product of new media platforms, independent and driven by the resources and interests of a passionate founder.

According to Nelson, "Folks who are so fly, so brilliant, and so clear about who and what they are have been able to circumvent systemic bias and systemic racism in a way that has gotten the core mission of their work out there." She emphasizes that new media spaces have the potential to redefine what success looks like: "Media is a powerful tool that essentially gives us mobility, especially Black folks in this world."

"As a chef, Black food means how my cultural roots show up in the food I cook and the food I eat. That gives me enough latitude to be curious about the rest of the diaspora, to look outside of my own personal roots, which are a particularly American story, but also one that's partly unwritten because of how much I do know."

Peter Prime

Chef & Restaurateur

Chef and restaurateur Peter Prime co-founded Cane, a popular Trinidadian restaurant in Washington, D.C., with his sister Jeanine in 2019. Cane explores the multiculturalism embedded in Trinidadian cuisine, which encompasses influences from Indigenous peoples, Africa, East Asia, Europe, and India. A small but mighty presence in the D.C. dining scene, Cane has a maximum capacity of only 33 guests. In 2020, Cane was awarded a New Restaurant of the Year award from the Restaurant Association of Metropolitan Washington, and Prime was named Eater D.C.'s Chef of the Year. He has since departed Cane and taken on a role as partner and chef at Bammy's Modern Caribbean, also in D.C.

Prime knows firsthand how the American food landscape has shifted to more fully embrace foods of the Black diaspora. Originally from Trinidad and Tobago, he came to the United States in 2000 for college. While studying accounting and finance, Prime worked in a professional kitchen and found the environment invigorating. He switched his focus to hospitality management and began a career in food. "The way Americans perceive food, in general, has changed significantly in the last 20 years," he says. He points to an expanding awareness of social justice, a broadening definition of fine dining, and more openness to other cultures as factors that have expanded the realm of opportunity for Black and other marginalized food folks.

Prime was turned down multiple times while trying to find a space and investors for Cane. "People would say, 'D.C. is not ready for that type of food.'" Just a few years after opening Cane, more opportunities for Caribbean projects and others connected to the Black diaspora exist than ever, as people's awareness of culinary diversity has expanded rapidly. New outlets such as Yelp, blogs, and other online communities helped drive that awareness, making the food space more democratic and shifting power away from traditional food critics and legacy publications. "Whether you got reviewed or not, good food became harder and harder to deny. The word got out there. If you got one bad Yelper, they would be swallowed by the good reviews if the food is good."

> "I think of Black food as food of the African diaspora … Growing up in the Caribbean, we would rarely use the term 'Black food,' as we know how heavily our cuisine has been influenced by the African diaspora, and we'd simply refer to it as Trinidadian or Caribbean."

Jerome Grant

Chef

Chef Jerome Grant is connecting cultures and telling profoundly personal stories through food. He believes that food can act as a flag—a cultural, familial, and communal symbol that ties us together as human beings. His grandmother, a Jamaican immigrant who worked in the hospitality industry shortly after arriving in the United States, helped teach him how to cook and was integral in shaping his view of food as a connecting force.

Many of Grant's culinary projects have delved into the connections between food and history. He worked as a sous chef, then executive chef, at Mitsitam Native Foods Cafe at the National Museum of the American Indian. Later, he served as the inaugural chef of the Sweet Home Café inside the Smithsonian's National Museum of African American History and Culture, dubbed the "Blacksonian" by some. Sweet Home Café was nominated for a James Beard Award for Best New Restaurant in 2017 and operates as an edible, curated exhibit, introducing guests to various aspects of Black cuisine through themed menus rooted in history and organized by geographical region.

Grant describes being the inaugural chef of the National Museum of African American History and Culture as a daunting and challenging learning experience. The museum café team worked for months to ensure that they could do justice to Black food history. They carefully considered stories from various entry points and migration. By working with historians and experts, Sweet Home Café curated a menu based on hundreds of years of Black history. Grant says that the hardest part was capturing nuance, the regional differences and ways that recipes vary over time and place. A good example of this is the café's son of a gun stew, often made by free Black cooks on trail drives and ranches in the American West. "How do we introduce that to Northerners who have never heard of it? How do we go from dialogue among professionals to telling the story to the great-great-grandmothers from Houston that have saved up their whole lives for an event like this?"

Grant emphasizes the significance of the labor of his family members and the long history of Black food folks as enslaved laborers and free people in shaping American cuisine. As he notes, Black peoples, especially women, have always been in hospitality, feeding children, cooking for others, and performing domestic labor, then going home to take care of their own families. And yet, Black foodways and Black food folks have historically not been granted the same respect by formal institutions.

Ultimately, Grant realized that projects like Sweet Home Café will never please everyone. Personal relationships to food are incredibly complex. However, Grant says that exploring history through cuisine remains vital, particularly for marginalized groups often left out of mainstream narratives. An immense amount of history and traditions can be unearthed and preserved through such projects. Grant continues that exploration through his current venture, Mahal BBQ, which draws on both his African American and Filipino heritage.

"Black food is food from the women and the hands that helped nurture America, that made America what it is and helped shape it."

Jerk Pork Lumpia

Recipe by Jerome Grant

Cook time: 35 minutes | *Makes 25 to 30 lumpia*

New Year's Eve is one of my family's favorite holidays because it is filled with various traditions that reflect our multicultural roots. The most anticipated tradition my kids look forward to is lumpia rolling with their grandparents. From speed rolling to competing over who rolls the most perfect lumpia—we all know it only ends one way: everyone enjoying a delicious, golden, and crispy snack! Lumpia is a fried spring roll that was introduced to the Philippines by Chinese immigrants in the 17th century. Their fillings range from savory to sweet, and they are eaten during New Year celebrations to symbolize wealth and prosperity. This lumpia recipe infuses my Jamaican upbringing into a classic Filipino dish to create a flavorful punch with every crunch!

You can substitute and experiment with different vegetables and fillings to create your own version. For an extra push of good luck, add some noodles into the filling to symbolize longevity.

- 2¼ cups canola oil, divided
- 1 small onion, finely chopped, about ⅔ cup
- ½ cup finely chopped carrots, about 1 medium carrot
- 1 pound ground pork
- 3 tablespoons jerk seasoning
- ½ cup finely chopped cabbage
- Salt
- Freshly ground black pepper
- 3 whole scallions, thinly sliced
- ¼ cup finely chopped cilantro
- 2 eggs
- 1 package lumpia wrappers, about 25 to 30 wrappers

Heat ¼ cup of canola oil in a sauté pan over medium heat, add onion and carrots, and cook for 2 or 3 minutes.

Add pork, jerk seasoning, cabbage, and salt and pepper to taste, and continue cooking until pork is fully browned, about 5 to 7 minutes.

Remove mixture from pan and let cool to room temperature. Once at room temperature, fold in scallions and cilantro.

Whisk eggs in a small bowl to create your egg wash. Set aside. Remove lumpia wrappers from package and cover with a damp paper towel or napkin to prevent the wrappers from drying out while not in use.

Place one lumpia wrapper on a work surface with one corner facing you. Place 1 heaping tablespoon of filling in center of wrapper and shape filling into a thin horizontal 5-inch-long log.

Lightly brush the edges of the wrapper with the egg wash. Roll bottom corner of wrapper up and over the filling, then tuck under filling. Fold left and right corners in tightly over filling to enclose it. Continue to roll filled wrapper away from you. Both sides should be as close to sealed as possible; use additional egg wash to seal, as necessary. Repeat until lumpia wrappers are completely filled and rolled.

Pour remaining 2 cups of canola oil into a large nonstick, high-sided pan. (The oil should cover the lumpia at least halfway when frying. Adjust the amount of oil if needed.)

Heat pan over medium-high heat. The oil is hot enough if the oil bubbles immediately when you place the tip of a lumpia into the oil.

Fry the lumpia in batches in the pan until they are deep golden brown and crispy on all sides, approximately 2 to 3 minutes per side. Remove to a wire rack lined with paper towels. Serve immediately.

Benjamin "BJ" Dennis

Chef & Cultural Preservationist

Chef Benjamin "BJ" Dennis IV is a Gullah Geechee chef, caterer, and steward dedicated to studying and preserving his community's cuisine and culinary history. The Gullah Geechee are descendants of enslaved peoples of the coastal plains and sea islands of the Lowcountry. In those areas white planters would leave during the summer months, fleeing high malaria rates. This environment allowed enslaved communities there to develop in relative isolation and maintain more of their African roots and traditions. A creolized culture developed with elements of various West and Central African traditions. This heritage is reflected in the Gullah Geechee language and cuisine. Dennis has been called the "de facto ambassador of its legacy" as he works to preserve traditional foodways and teach them to the next generation.

By soliciting recipes and seeds from neighbors and community members, poring through old cookbooks and records, and extensively traveling and studying, Dennis keeps vital traditions of Gullah Geechee foodways and an essential part of Lowcountry food culture alive. He hosts teaching programs, workshops, dinner events, parties, and more to share his love for and knowledge of Gullah Geechee cuisine with his community and beyond.

Dennis characterizes Gullah Geechee cuisine as "one of the OGs of the 'New World,' of America, a

"When we think of Black food in this country, it's the food of those who were brought here enslaved, food of the southern region of the country. It's very broad and will take you so many different places."

> **Focus On:** Pilau
>
> Pilau, a rice cooked in a seasoned stock and usually served with additional ingredients such as chicken, is a tradition shared among many cultures. Plov, the national dish of Uzbekistan, is a form of pilau. So are Caribbean rice and peas, West African jollof rice, Spanish paella, and the Palestinian rice dish maqluba. Red beans and rice, jambalaya, and hoppin' John are all southern pilau variations strongly connected to Black history. In the Lowcountry and for Gullah Geechee peoples, pilau is typically called perloo or purloo.

cuisine that tells a story of a difficult relationship. On one hand it was the food that mainly Gullah women were serving that became, in a broader sense, Lowcountry cuisine. Gullah is the mother of Lowcountry cuisine, and Lowcountry cuisine is one of the most popular foodways in America.

"Black contributions are not really visible or recognized," Dennis says. "But that's the history of Black Americans in general. The country as a whole doesn't understand the magnitude of our imprint on the foodways and agriculture." Dennis points to rice as an example of this magnitude. Rice is an essential part of Gullah and Lowcountry foodways largely because of the labor and knowledge of Gullah Geechee peoples who helped develop the region's rice culture. "Rice tells a story of math, science, technology, and astronomy, and many don't think that West Africans had those things," Dennis explains. "When you tell the story of rice, it proves the ingenuity of those who were enslaved, who came with this knowledge."

Gullah food and culture are deeply rooted in American foodways. "It's a cuisine that is part of the American fabric," he says, "but part of the fabric that people want to hide, want to shun. When you come to South Carolina, you see okra soup being eaten by someone who's not Gullah Geechee because it's part of their DNA, because it's the food of the Gullah Geechee that really resonated with all different backgrounds and races. It's American food."

Chef and cultural preservationist BJ Dennis checks on the rice he's cooking with traditional Gullah Geechee methods outside at Joseph Fields Farm.

Chicken Purloo

Recipe by Benjamin "BJ" Dennis

Cook time: 2 hours | Makes 6 to 8 servings

Purloo is a dish that is ingrained in the Gullah Geechee culture. It's the legacy of those who came from the rice-growing regions of West and Central Africa. Chicken purloo is one that is popular in homes and local eateries throughout the Gullah Geechee corridor.

- 1 large onion, diced
- 2 tablespoons minced garlic
- 3 tablespoons bacon grease or oil of choice
- 1 whole raw chicken, cut up
- 4 cups chicken broth or water
- 1 bay leaf
- 2 sprigs fresh thyme
- Salt
- Freshly ground black pepper
- 2 cups white rice
- 2 smoked sausage links (pork, chicken, or turkey), sliced ½ inch thick

In a large cast-iron or heavy-bottomed pan, sauté onion and garlic in bacon grease over medium-high heat until onion is translucent, 3 to 5 minutes.

Add chicken, broth, bay leaf, and thyme to the pan. Season with salt and pepper and bring everything to a boil. Reduce heat and simmer until chicken is cooked through, about 1 to 1½ hours.

Remove chicken and debone. Measure out 4 cups of broth (add more broth or water if needed for 4 complete cups), add salt and pepper to taste, and return to a boil. Add rice and sausage to pot. Cover and simmer until grains are tender, 25 to 30 minutes. Remove thyme and bay leaf and fluff rice with a fork. Add chicken back to the pot and fold to combine before serving.

Jambalaya

Recipe by Renae Wilson

Cook time: 50 minutes | Makes 8 to 10 servings

- 1 pound large raw shrimp, peeled and deveined
- Zest and juice of 1 lemon
- 2 tablespoons Cajun seasoning, divided
- 2½ cups dry long-grain white rice
- 1 tablespoon olive oil
- 16 ounces andouille sausage, sliced into 1-inch rounds
- 1 small green bell pepper, seeded and chopped
- 1 small red bell pepper, seeded and chopped
- 1 stalk celery, chopped
- 1 carrot, peeled and chopped
- 1 bunch scallion whites, chopped
- 2 tablespoons finely chopped parsley stems, plus chopped leaves for garnish
- 3 cloves garlic, minced
- 1½ teaspoons white pepper
- 1 teaspoon smoked paprika
- 1 teaspoon salt
- 1 or 2 jalapeños, serranos, or Fresno chilies, seeded and chopped (optional)
- 3 cups vegetable, chicken, or fish stock
- 1 (8-ounce) can tomato sauce
- 3 sprigs fresh thyme
- 8 ounces crabmeat

In a medium bowl, toss shrimp, lemon zest, and 2 teaspoons Cajun seasoning to coat shrimp; cover and let marinate at room temperature while preparing the jambalaya.

Rinse rice until water runs clear and set aside.

Heat the oil in a large Dutch oven over medium-high heat. Add andouille and cook, stirring occasionally, until browned in spots, 5 to 6 minutes. Using a slotted spoon, transfer andouille to a bowl and set aside.

Add rice to Dutch oven and stir until toasted, about 4 minutes. Add bell peppers, celery, carrot, and scallion whites. Cook, stirring often, until vegetables begin to soften, about 2 minutes. Add parsley stems, garlic, white pepper, smoked paprika, remaining Cajun seasoning, salt, and chilies (if using). Cook, stirring often, until fragrant, about 2 minutes. Drizzle stock and tomato sauce over rice and vegetables (do not stir). Add sausage and thyme sprigs, and bring everything to a boil. Cover pot.

Reduce heat to low and let simmer vigorously for 18 minutes. Remove lid. Scatter shrimp and crabmeat on top in an even (if possible, single) layer. Cover and let seafood steam until shrimp is just cooked through, 5 to 6 minutes more. Turn off heat and let stand, covered, for 10 minutes.

Remove lid and discard thyme sprigs. Fold the seafood into the rice, sausage, and vegetables. Adjust salt to taste. Garnish with parsley leaves and lemon juice.

Kevin Curry

Creator of Fit Men Cook

Kevin Curry founded digital platform Fit Men Cook in 2012 as a way to build community around healthy eating and cooking while he focused on his personal health journey. In the more than 10 years since, Fit Men Cook has amassed millions of followers across numerous platforms. Initially focused on recipes, Fit Men Cook has expanded to include travel storytelling and nuanced discussions of health topics like diabetes, mental health, and implicit bias in health care. Curry has also shared personal stories of family members' health journeys as they relate to food. He often provides content in both English and Spanish, a choice that, he emphasizes, allows him to reach as many folks in Black and brown communities as possible—people who generally have higher rates of heart disease, diabetes, and other illnesses connected to poverty and food apartheid.

Curry uses new media, and the opportunities for expanded reach it provides, to engage in vital conversations about food, culture, and health. He says that Black communities "take a lot of pride in our food, in our preparation, in how our grandmas and ancestors did it. I wanted to show that healthier eating is not boring, it's flavorful, and we can still have the same foods that Grandma used to make." He adds that though it has its drawbacks, social media is a powerful tool: "Now social media has turned moms, grandmas, uncles, everyone into a creator or photographer. You can see literally see inside someone's kitchen, learn how to cook directly from someone, get their perspective, and then even compare it to how you do it at home or to other communities."

Curry's work, which emphasizes health and empowerment, innovation in food, and food's connection to culture, weaves together long-standing threads in the Black community. He says, "We can draw on the historic ingenuity of Black cooks as we explore what it means to be Black, what it means to have soul food." Noting the interplay between culinary traditions and innovation, Curry says that there is so much room to explore for Black food folks, as "we are the soul, we are the spice, the sauce, the seasoning."

"When you say 'Black food,' I immediately think of southern food. When you look at the history of the country, Black food evolved into southern food."

New Year's traditional dishes: Hoppin' John (left), p. 265, and Collard Green Medley Salad (right), p. 264

Collard Green Medley Salad

Recipe by Kevin Curry

Cook time: 40 minutes | Makes 4 servings

- 1 pound collard greens, washed and chopped, divided
- 1 slice thick center-cut bacon, chopped (I prefer smoky to add more flavor)
- 1 tablespoon olive oil
- 1 leek (bulb only), sliced into rounds
- 1¼ cups no-salt-added chicken broth, divided
- ¼ cup apple cider vinegar
- 1 large bundle chard, stemmed and chopped
- 1 large bundle kale, stemmed and chopped
- Sea salt
- Freshly ground black pepper

Wash the collard greens in a large pot or sink to remove dirt. Remove the stems. Stack the leaves on top of one another, roll them up, then chop into pieces. Grab 3 stems and dice into pieces; set aside.

Set a large pot on medium-high heat, then add bacon, oil, leek, and chopped collard green stems. Cook until leek is tender and the edges have browned, about 3 to 5 minutes.

Add half the collard greens to the pot and reduce heat to medium. Add half the chicken broth to the pot and all the vinegar, and cook 2 to 3 minutes, or until the greens wilt enough to allow you to add remaining collards and broth to the pot. Stir.

Cover and simmer over medium-low heat until tender, about 15 to 20 minutes. Add chard and kale and cook for an additional 10 minutes. The longer you cook them, the better they'll taste.

Season with salt and pepper and enjoy! (Consider serving with air-fried fish nuggets.)

Hoppin' John

Recipe by Renae Wilson

Cook time: 1 hour 5 minutes, plus overnight prep | Makes 6 servings

Though hoppin' John is traditionally made with field peas, a dish of rice and black-eyed peas is also often now called hoppin' John, marking a blending of two culinary traditions connected to the Black American experience.

- 1 pound crowder beans (also called crowder peas) or black-eyed peas
- 1 tablespoon plus 1 teaspoon salt, divided
- 2 tablespoons butter
- 1 medium onion, chopped
- 1 medium carrot, peeled and chopped
- 1 celery stalk, chopped
- ½ green bell pepper, seeded and chopped
- ½ red bell pepper, seeded and chopped
- 2 tablespoons chopped fresh parsley
- 2 cloves garlic, chopped
- 1 tablespoon tomato paste
- 1 tablespoon smoked paprika
- 2 teaspoons mustard powder
- 1 teaspoon freshly ground black pepper
- 6 cups vegetable or chicken stock
- 3 sprigs fresh thyme
- 1 bay leaf
- Cooked rice (for serving)

In a large pot, add beans, 1 tablespoon salt, and enough water to cover beans by 6 inches. Let soak at room temperature overnight, then drain beans. Alternatively, bring beans, water, and salt to a boil, remove from heat, and cover. Let stand at room temperature for 1 hour. Drain and rinse beans.

In the same pot, melt butter over medium-high heat. Add onion, carrot, celery, bell peppers, parsley, and garlic. Cook, stirring often, until fragrant, about 2 minutes. Add tomato paste, smoked paprika, mustard powder, black pepper, and 1 teaspoon salt. Cook, stirring often, until beginning to brown, about 3 minutes.

Add beans, stock, thyme sprigs, and bay leaf. Bring beans to boil, then reduce heat to medium-low and simmer, stirring occasionally, until beans are tender, about 1 hour. Remove thyme sprigs and bay leaf before serving. Serve over rice.

Pork Loin Roast

Recipe by Renae Wilson

Cook time: 4 hours 30 minutes | Makes 6 servings

For spice rub

2 teaspoons light brown sugar

2 teaspoons garlic powder

2 teaspoons kosher salt

1½ teaspoons ground cumin

1 teaspoon freshly ground black pepper

1 teaspoon smoked paprika

½ teaspoon ground ginger

¼ teaspoon ground cinnamon

For pork roast

3½ pounds boneless pork roast, tied (as shown opposite)

3 tablespoons butter, softened, divided

3 tablespoons oil, divided

2 sprigs fresh rosemary

6 sprigs fresh thyme

2 bay leaves

¾ cup chicken or vegetable stock

¾ cup apple cider

¼ cup apple cider vinegar

4 cloves garlic, smashed

1 pound baby potatoes, whole

12 ounces carrots, peeled, cut crosswise into 3-inch pieces, top thick pieces halved lengthwise

3 medium leeks, white and light green parts only, washed and quartered lengthwise

4 celery stalks, cut crosswise into 3-inch pieces

Kosher salt

Freshly ground black pepper

2 teaspoons garlic powder

2 tablespoons all-purpose flour

In a small bowl, whisk together all ingredients for spice rub. Pat pork dry. Rub pork all over with 1 tablespoon butter, 1 tablespoon oil, and spice rub. Let stand at room temperature for 1 hour.

Using kitchen twine, tie rosemary, thyme, and bay leaves together. Alternatively, wrap in cheesecloth and tie up with kitchen twine. In a medium bowl, stir together the stock, apple cider, and apple cider vinegar. Set aside.

Preheat oven to 325°F.

Place pork roast in a 5- to 6-quart Dutch oven. Add herb bundle and smashed garlic to pot. Pour half of the stock-and-cider mixture into the pot. Cover the pot and place in the oven. Roast for 2½ hours. Remove the pot from the oven.

In a large bowl, toss together the potatoes, carrots, leeks, celery, and remaining 2 tablespoons of oil. Season with salt, pepper, and garlic powder. Arrange vegetables around pork roast. Cover the pot and return to the oven. Bake until an instant-read thermometer registers 175°F to 180°F when inserted into the center of roast, and vegetables are tender, about 1 hour more.

Remove pot from oven and let roast rest for 10 minutes. Transfer pork to a cutting board, and vegetables to a platter; tent with foil to keep warm. Discard the herb bundle, and scoop out about ¼ cup of liquid from the pot, whisk flour into the ¼ cup liquid, and set aside. Heat pot with the drippings and remaining liquid over medium heat. Add remaining 2 tablespoons butter to the pot and stir until melted. Whisk flour mixture into pot. Bring to a boil over medium-high heat and cook, whisking often, until thickened. If there is not enough gravy, add additional stock whisked together with 1 or 2 teaspoons of flour to make more.

Using two forks, shred the pork. Serve with vegetables and gravy.

Rock Harper

Chef & Restaurateur

Rahman "Rock" Harper is a chef and restaurateur and winner of the third season of *Hell's Kitchen*. Formerly the executive chef at Ben's Next Door and B. Smith's in Washington, D.C., he went on to establish his own venture, Queen Mother's Kitchen, a fast-casual restaurant that specializes in fried-chicken sandwiches, in Arlington, Virginia. For Harper, food is more than just calories. Food is a representation of history, an embodiment of culture, and a source of community.

Long popular in the United States, fried-chicken sandwiches gained viral popularity in 2019. Popeyes debuted its craze-inducing fried-chicken sandwich that year, Chick-fil-A tweeted that its version was the original, long lines marked buzzy debuts of popular variations, and billions of the crispy fried sandwiches were consumed. From Wendy's to KFC to Jack in the Box, major chains upgraded or debuted fried chicken sandwiches in rapid succession. Harper debuted Queen Mother's in that same time period, as a deliberate nod to how Black peoples were integral to the development and proliferation of fried chicken in the United States. Harper calls fried chicken "extremely powerful," in part because it has been an avenue for empowerment and a tool for community building among Black peoples.

Harper has been explicit about his desire to reclaim fried chicken, move past its stigma, and honor the examples of Black women, like his mother and grandmother, the waiter carriers of Virginia (see p. 195), and others. In discussing Queen Mother's, Harper emphasizes his desire "to embrace the thing that was most polarizing," a dish that some Black peoples have refused to eat in public because of such deep racial stereotypes. He acknowledges that stigma, but also points to fried chicken's long association with Black churches and Sunday service, with Black community groups, and with Black entrepreneurship. Through Queen Mother's, Harper seeks to remind consumers of those more positive aspects of fried chicken's history and reclaim the narrative.

"Civilization began in Africa. Black people built the United States. 'What is not Black food?' yields simpler answers."

Southern Potato Salad (left), p. 273, and Brined Fried Chicken (right), p. 272

Brined Fried Chicken

Recipe by Rock Harper

Make time: 2 hours, plus 12 to 24 hours brining time | *Makes 16 pieces*

For the brine

2 quarts water (8 cups)

¼ cup brown sugar

¼ cup kosher salt

1 teaspoon black peppercorns

1 garlic clove, smashed

1 small onion, peeled and quartered

For the chicken

2 (3- to 4-pound) antibiotic-free chickens, cut into 8 pieces each

6 cups flour

½ cup rice flour

2 tablespoons sea salt

2 tablespoons smoked paprika

1 tablespoon onion powder

1 teaspoon garlic powder

1 tablespoon freshly ground black pepper

Vegetable oil for deep frying

To make the brine, mix all brine ingredients in a bowl until combined.

Put the chicken in a large roasting dish and pour the brine over the chicken. Cover with plastic wrap and refrigerate for 12 to 24 hours.

Remove the chicken from the brine and let it dry slightly on a wire rack while preparing the batter.

In a large bowl, stir together the flours, salt, and spices. Dredge the chicken, 4 pieces at a time, in the flour. Gently shake the bowl to coat the chicken with flour, and then transfer the pieces to a wire rack, being careful not to scrape off the batter. Repeat with remaining pieces of chicken and let dry on the wire rack for 30 minutes.

Pour the oil into a deep fryer or 5-quart pot and heat it to a temperature of 350°F.

In batches, add chicken to the oil, frying the white and dark meat separately, until they reach an internal temperature of 165°F (approximately 15 minutes for white meat, 18 minutes for dark). Cook only about 4 to 6 pieces per batch. Overcrowding the oil will drop the temperature too much and yield a greasy product. Drain on paper towel–lined plates and serve with plenty of napkins!

Southern Potato Salad

Recipe by Renae Wilson

Cook time: 10 minutes, plus 2 hours cooling time | *Makes 6 to 8 servings*

- 3 pounds small potatoes, quartered
- 1 tablespoon plus 1 teaspoon salt
- 1 stalk celery, finely chopped
- ½ onion, finely chopped
- ⅓ cup bread-and-butter pickles, finely chopped, plus 1 tablespoon pickle juice
- ⅓ cup mayonnaise
- ¼ cup yellow mustard
- 2 tablespoons sour cream
- 1½ tablespoons sugar
- 2 cloves garlic, finely chopped
- 1 tablespoon Cajun seasoning
- 1 teaspoon celery seeds
- 1 teaspoon freshly ground black pepper

In a large pot, add potatoes, 1 tablespoon salt, and enough water to cover potatoes by 2 inches. Bring to a rolling boil, reduce heat slightly, and boil until potatoes are tender, 8 to 10 minutes. Drain potatoes and transfer to a medium bowl. Add celery, onion, and chopped pickles.

In a medium bowl, whisk together pickle juice, mayonnaise, mustard, sour cream, sugar, garlic, Cajun seasoning, celery seeds, the remaining 1 teaspoon of salt, and the pepper. Add dressing to the potatoes and fold to coat. Cover and refrigerate for 2 hours. Season to taste with additional salt and pepper before serving.

Corn Ribs with BBQ Sauce (left), p. 276, and Southern Baked Beans (right), p. 277

Corn Ribs

Recipe by Renae Wilson

Cook time: 25 minutes | Makes 4 servings

- 3 ears fresh corn on the cob, shucked
- 2 tablespoons olive oil
- 1 tablespoon butter, melted
- 1 tablespoon light brown sugar
- 2 teaspoons kosher salt
- 1½ teaspoons smoked paprika
- 1 teaspoon ground cumin
- ½ teaspoon cayenne
- BBQ sauce (see recipe below)

Preheat oven to 425°F. Line a baking sheet with parchment paper.

Slice corn in half lengthwise, then cut each half into 4 strips.

In a large bowl, whisk together oil, butter, brown sugar, salt, paprika, cumin, and cayenne. Toss corn ribs into the mixture until coated.

Place ribs in a single layer on prepared baking sheet. Bake for 15 minutes, until corn ribs begin to curl.

Remove from the oven and brush ribs with BBQ sauce. Return to the oven and bake until charred in spots, about 7 minutes more. Alternatively, grill the baked ribs for 4 minutes, until charred in spots.

Brush with more BBQ sauce before serving, if desired.

BBQ Sauce

Recipe by Renae Wilson

Make time: 5 minutes | Makes about 2 cups

- ⅔ cup apple cider vinegar
- ⅓ cup plus 1 tablespoon packed light brown sugar
- ¼ cup molasses
- 2 canned chipotles in adobo, finely chopped
- 2 tablespoons tomato paste
- 2 tablespoons yellow mustard
- 1 tablespoon Worcestershire sauce
- 1 teaspoon garlic powder
- ¾ teaspoon dried oregano
- ½ teaspoon onion powder
- ½ teaspoon smoked paprika
- ¼ teaspoon salt

In a medium bowl, whisk all ingredients together. Store in pint or half-pint mason jars. Refrigerate for up to 1 month.

Southern Baked Beans

Recipe by Renae Wilson

Cook time: 6 hours 30 minutes, plus overnight prep | Makes 8 to 10 servings

1 pound dried navy beans

8 ounces thick-cut bacon, chopped into ½-inch pieces

1 medium red onion, finely chopped

3 cloves garlic, finely chopped

¾ cup tomato puree

¾ cup tawny port

⅓ cup packed dark brown sugar

⅓ cup unsulfured molasses

3 tablespoons Worcestershire sauce

2 teaspoons kosher salt

¼ cup yellow mustard

1 teaspoon chili powder

1 teaspoon smoked paprika

In a 5-quart Dutch oven, add beans and enough water to cover by 6 inches. Let soak overnight. Drain beans.

Preheat oven to 325°F.

In the same Dutch oven, cook bacon over medium-high heat, stirring often, until beginning to crisp, about 7 minutes. Reduce heat to medium. Add onion to pot with bacon and drippings. Sweat for 3 minutes. Add garlic and cook until fragrant, about 1 minute. Stir in tomato puree and tawny port and cook until slightly reduced, about 2 minutes. Stir in brown sugar, molasses, Worcestershire sauce, salt, yellow mustard, chili powder, smoked paprika, and 1 cup water. Stir in beans. Reduce heat to low and simmer, uncovered, for 20 minutes.

Remove pot from heat. Add 2 cups water, cover the pot, and bake in the oven until the beans are tender, about 5 to 6 hours. Check beans for doneness every hour, adding additional water 1 cup at a time if too dry, up to 6 cups total.

Oyster & Salmon Croquettes

Recipe by Renae Wilson

Cook time: 10 minutes | *Makes 8 croquettes*

1 medium potato, peeled

½ teaspoon salt, plus more for salting potato

1 small onion, quartered

1 cup finely ground cornmeal, divided

1 (13.5-ounce) can salmon, bones removed

2 (3.7-ounce) cans oysters, drained

1 stalk celery, coarsely chopped

3 tablespoons chopped parsley leaves and stems

1 teaspoon dried dill or 2 teaspoons chopped fresh dill

¾ teaspoon mustard powder

½ teaspoon freshly ground black pepper

¼ teaspoon cayenne (optional)

2 cups vegetable oil for frying

Rémoulade (for dipping)

Grate potato with a box grater onto a paper towel–lined plate. Lightly salt potato and let stand for 30 minutes.

Place onion in a food processor and pulse until finely chopped and juicy. Add ⅓ cup of cornmeal, grated potato, salmon, oysters, celery, parsley, dill, mustard powder, pepper, cayenne (if using), and ½ teaspoon salt. Pulse until mixture is coarsely ground.

Form seafood mixture into 8 croquettes (about 3 tablespoons each). Place remaining ⅔ cup cornmeal on a plate. Working in batches, coat croquettes with cornmeal, turning and pressing to adhere. Transfer to a plate and let rest at room temperature for 20 minutes.

Heat oil in a medium saucepan over medium-high heat until oil registers 375°F on a deep-fry thermometer. Working in 2 batches, fry croquettes until golden, 3 to 5 minutes per batch. Transfer to a paper towel–lined plate to drain. Serve with rémoulade.

Joseph "JJ" Johnson
Chef & Restaurateur

Joseph "JJ" Johnson is a celebrated chef, entrepreneur, and James Beard Award winner. He's made a name for himself in recent years through numerous heralded projects that celebrate Black culture and also feature ingredients central to Black experiences in the United States and to communities worldwide. Johnson was named to both *Forbes*'s and *Zagat*'s "30 Under 30" lists in 2014 and currently helms Fieldtrip, a Harlem fast-casual restaurant focused on rice bowls that connects global cultures.

Johnson's family journey mirrors that of many Black peoples and food traditions that made their way out of the southern United States during the Great Migration. His grandmother came from North Carolina on a church bus and became a housekeeper and a bar maid in Harlem. His grandfather made his way from Mississippi. "The roots run deep in Harlem," he says. "I used to come to Harlem as a kid. I remember what it smelled like. I can remember the food. When you cook food and go to a prestige school like Culinary Institute of America, no one is telling you to cook in Harlem."

When Johnson decided to open his own restaurant, he ultimately wanted to do it in Harlem. He frames that choice as an opportunity to honor his family's ties and Harlem's history as a center of Black culture. He wanted to bring Black excellence to Harlem through Fieldtrip and create a place where everyone could feel welcome. Johnson continued that mission throughout the COVID-19 pandemic, providing tens of thousands of meals to essential workers and locals in Harlem.

Johnson says that American food is inseparable from Black history and that a focus exclusively on soul food, even within Black culture, blinds us to other forms of Black excellence in the food space. As he notes, Black chefs can make other styles of food—as they have historically done for presidents and at fancy hotels. Johnson credits, in part, increased travel for the recent expansions in understanding of Black foodways. "There's still a lot of education to be done," he says. "As people are traveling to West Africa, to Ghana, to Nigeria, to Senegal, to Nairobi, even Morocco, people are coming back and going, 'Oh my god, I want this food. Where can I find it?' I think that's what's helping really push the envelope on the exploration of what Black food looks like and is."

"Black food is American food. When you think about food in America, it is the American South, and the American South has then branched out into other parts of the country like Detroit, New York City, Oakland. We can follow the trail, and when Black people moved from the South, they brought those traditions with them."

Sweet Potato Cake With Cream Cheese Mousse & Candied Pecans

Recipe by Joseph "JJ" Johnson

Bake time: 18 minutes, plus 1 hour chilling time | Makes a 4-layer quarter sheet cake

For the sweet potato cake
1½ cups flour

1 teaspoon baking soda

1 teaspoon salt

1 teaspoon ground cinnamon

1 teaspoon ground ginger

½ teaspoon ground cloves

2 tablespoons orange zest

8 whole eggs

2 egg whites

2 teaspoons vanilla extract

1¼ cups sugar

1¼ cups finely shredded raw sweet potato (about 1 medium sweet potato)

For the cream cheese mousse
8 ounces cream cheese

1⅔ cups sugar

2 tablespoons lemon zest

7 gelatin sheets, bloomed in ice water*

1½ tablespoons honey

1½ cups heavy cream, whipped, plus 3 tablespoons heavy cream, divided

Candied pecans (store-bought or homemade)

*To bloom gelatin sheets, place in a bowl of ice water for 5 to 10 minutes until soft and pliable. Remove from bowl and gently squeeze out excess water before adding to recipe.

To make the sweet potato cake: Preheat oven to 325°F. Line two half-sheet trays with parchment paper.

In a large bowl, combine flour, baking soda, salt, spices, and orange zest. Whisk until well combined.

In a separate bowl, use an electric mixer on high speed to whip together eggs, egg whites, vanilla extract, and sugar until tripled in volume and thick, about 8 to 10 minutes.

Gently fold egg mixture into the dry ingredients. Then fold in the shredded sweet potato.

Divide batter into two half-sheet trays. Bake for 15 to 18 minutes. Remove from the oven and let cool.

To make the cream cheese mousse: Cream together cream cheese, sugar, and lemon zest in a mixer on high speed until light and fluffy, about 4 to 5 minutes.

In a saucepan, heat gelatin sheets, honey, and 3 tablespoons heavy cream over low heat until the gelatin dissolves, about 2 minutes. Let cool to room temperature, about 15 minutes, then fold gelatin mixture into the cream cheese mixture.

In a small mixing bowl, use an electric mixer to whip remaining 1½ cups heavy cream until light peaks form, about 3 minutes. Fold the whipped cream into the cream cheese mixture.

To assemble the cake: Cut each sheet cake in half. Place one layer on a cake plate, frost the top with one-quarter of the cream cheese mousse, then place another layer of cake on top. Repeat to make a 4-layer cake. Frost the entire cake with remaining mousse and refrigerate to set for 1 hour. Top with candied pecans.

Cheryl Day

Author & Baker

Cheryl Day is a *New York Times* best-selling cookbook author, baker, James Beard Award semifinalist, and co-founder of Southern Restaurants for Racial Justice, which works to support Black-owned restaurants in the South and beyond through grants and programming—and is an organization that I serve as an adviser for.

Day descends from a long line of bakers, and her culinary trajectory echoes the dynamics that have impacted many Black American families. She can trace her roots to her great-great-grandmother Hannah Queen Grubbs, who was born enslaved and known for her cooking and baking. "I'm a direct connection to all of it," Day says. "My grandmother was known for her biscuits, was known for making small cakes frosted in delightfully colored tints. I feel like history and legacy are so mind-blowing. I do feel a direct connection to my great-great-grandmother who was born enslaved, who was cooking all her life. To all of it, I feel that connection."

In addition to her multigenerational culinary legacy, Day's life was also impacted by the Great Migration. Her mother left small-town Alabama during the Great Migration and ultimately landed in California. Day grew up in Los Angeles and remembers how they kept community through food. "I grew up eating southern food. Collard greens, black-eyed peas, sweet potato pie, cornbread dressing—all of it." Day's aunt would prepare chitlins, a familiar southern dish that community members would revel in as they maintained historic food traditions in their new homes. In 2000, Day returned to the South. She now lives in Savannah, Georgia, where she co-owned Back in the Day Bakery with her husband, Griffith Day.

It's that long legacy of community through food, holding on to traditions throughout migration, and Black baking expertise that Day honors through her work. "Black folks should know that we created southern cuisine and baking, and it's something that we should be really proud of." It's a point she drives home in her 2021 book *Cheryl Day's Treasury of Southern Baking,* which features 13 chapters dedicated to various cakes, biscuits, and loaves, drawing from a variety of sources including family recipes and vintage community cookbooks. In the book's dedication, Day writes, "This book would not have been possible without the millions of enslaved laborers who worked in the fields, plantations, and kitchens of the United States."

As Day strives to ensure that Black cooks and bakers are not forgotten, her work calls for accountability in narratives on southern baking that obscure the real origins of recipes, whitewash history, and attempt to leave out Black stories for the comfort of others or to downplay the impact of slavery on local cuisine.

"Black food is community, family, history, legacy."

Blackberry Cobbler

Recipe by Cheryl Day

Bake time: 55 minutes | Makes 6 servings

For the topping
2 cups unbleached all-purpose flour

1 tablespoon baking powder, preferably aluminum free

½ teaspoon fine sea salt

3 tablespoons light brown sugar

6 tablespoons cold unsalted butter, cut into ½-inch cubes

¾ cup heavy cream, plus more for brushing on top

Turbinado raw sugar, for sprinkling on top

For the filling
½ cup granulated sugar

¼ teaspoon nutmeg

⅛ teaspoon ground cloves

1 to 2 tablespoons cornstarch

Zest of 1 lemon

6 cups fresh blackberries

Position a rack in the middle of the oven and preheat to 350°F. Butter a 9-inch deep-dish pie plate.

To make the topping: In a large bowl, whisk together flour, baking powder, salt, and brown sugar. Add in the butter cubes and, with a pastry blender or your fingertips, cut the cold butter cubes into the dough. You should have a mixture of sandy patches to pea-size chunks and some slightly larger bits as well.

Pour the cream over the flour mixture and toss together with a rubber spatula or your hands until you have a very soft dough. Gently knead the dough until it is fully combined.

Turn out the dough onto a lightly floured surface and gently pat the dough into a 9-inch roundish shape. Place the dough on a baking sheet and wrap in plastic wrap. Refrigerate while you make the filling.

To make the filling: In a large bowl mix together the sugar, nutmeg, clove, cornstarch (2 tablespoons will make for a less-runny filling), and lemon zest. Add the berries and coat with the sugar mixture. Pour the mixture into the prepared pie plate.

Remove the chilled dough from the refrigerator and cut a hole in the middle with a paring knife, in any shape you like, to create a steam vent. Gently place the dough on top of the filling. Brush it lightly with heavy cream and sprinkle with turbinado raw sugar.

Place pie plate on a parchment-lined baking sheet to catch any juices that fall while cobbler bakes. Bake until the top is a deep golden brown and the fruit is bubbling, about 45 to 55 minutes. Transfer to a wire rack to cool slightly, 10 to 15 minutes, before serving.

Serve the cobbler warm or at room temperature. The cobbler is best served the same day but can be covered with plastic wrap and refrigerated for up to 3 days.

Apple Cream Pie

Recipe by Renae Wilson

Bake time: 1 hour | *Makes 8 servings*

6 medium Granny Smith apples, peeled, cored, quartered, and thinly sliced

¾ cup plus 2 tablespoons dark brown sugar

3 tablespoons all-purpose flour, plus more for dusting surface

1 teaspoon cinnamon

½ teaspoon cardamom

¼ teaspoon salt

½ cup heavy cream

1 teaspoon vanilla

2 unbaked store-bought pie crusts

1 large egg, beaten

2 tablespoons turbinado raw sugar

Preheat oven to 425°F.

In a large bowl, gently toss apples, brown sugar, flour, cinnamon, cardamom, and salt.

In a small bowl, mix together cream and vanilla.

On a lightly floured surface, roll out pie crusts into two 13-inch rounds. Line a 9-inch deep-dish pie plate with 1 crust. Fill with apple mixture. Gently drizzle the vanilla-cream mixture over the apple mixture. Top with the second pie crust (decorate with lattice or leave whole and cut an X in center for venting). Seal edges of the pie crusts together, crimping decoratively using a fork or fingertips. Brush the top crust with egg and sprinkle with turbinado sugar.

Bake pie until the crust is golden brown and filling is bubbling, tenting with foil if browning too quickly, about 1 hour. Let cool 20 minutes before serving.

Justin Hazelton

Mixologist & Bar Professional

Justin Hazelton is a mixologist and bar professional who was named best mixologist in Charlotte, North Carolina, by *Charlotte Magazine* in 2021 and opened Lorem Ipsum in the city in 2023. The bar is modeled after listening bar concepts in Japan that focus on high-quality sound for the ultimate auditory experience, a space where sound is as important as the drinks. In these bars, thoughtfully curated music or DJ set lists are meant to enhance the atmosphere. Hazelton is one of many Black beverage professionals making waves in the United States today by centering Black stories through mixology.

Many of the contributions Black peoples have made to the beverage space have been devalued or ignored until recently. Hazelton points to the missing details of legendary Black bar figures like Tom Bullock as an example, noting that we don't even know Bullock's birthday, as historically so little of early Black life was deemed valuable or worth recording. Hazelton also notes that modern food and beverage spaces often co-opt aspects of Black culture without also providing a space for Black patrons and professionals to thrive. He says, "In so many of those spaces, the owners are not Black. They want our music but not us."

Hazelton seeks to remedy that gap through Lorem Ipsum, which he describes as a space for exploration and discovery, one that embraces and centers an expansive Black experience. The bar hosts album listening parties that feature works from artists such as Stevie Wonder, Beyoncé, and André 3000, as well as nights with live DJs spinning everything from house music to jazz. Drinks like the Florida Water offer a conversation point as well as a beverage. The cocktail is named after a cologne historically used by enslaved laborers in the South for scenting everything from linens to aftershave and which also made its way into some diasporic spiritual rituals and practices. Other drinks, like The Jerk, a nonalcoholic cocktail made with hibiscus (which originated in West Africa and has a long history in the diaspora), similarly spotlight ingredients or histories of Black communities. For Hazelton, Lorem Ipsum is an opportunity to interrogate new story lines in the beverage space, ones in which Black experiences take center stage.

> "Black stories don't always have to be about the past—we can talk about Black futurism and now. There are so many stories about what we can all possibly be, and we can tell those through cocktails as well."

F.U.B.U. Cocktail

Recipe by Justin Hazelton

Make time: 2 minutes | Makes 1 cocktail

The F.U.B.U. cocktail is the first cocktail I made for the restaurant Leah & Louise. The name F.U.B.U. comes from the Black-owned clothing line from the late 1990s, early 2000s that I loved to wear and wanted to pay homage to through this cocktail. This variation of a whiskey sour is made in a Black-owned restaurant in a haven of Black excellence and is also inspired by Nathan "Nearest" Green's mastery of the craft of distilling. I am so honored to be able to use my inspirations to inspire others.

1½ ounces Uncle Nearest 1884 whiskey

½ ounce Cardamaro

1 ounce raspberry simple syrup

½ ounce fresh lemon juice

1 ounce egg white (from 1 large egg)

Angostura bitters

Combine all ingredients except the bitters in a shaker; add ice, and shake vigorously. Strain contents into small tin, throw out leftover ice, and shake vigorously again with no ice (this is called a reverse dry shake).

Pour this foamy mixture into a coupe or martini glass. Garnish with 3 drops of Angostura bitters and enjoy!

EPILOGUE

Where Do We Go Now?

What Lies Ahead

Storytelling is a powerful medium to shape perception. The stories we embrace can confer authority, give credit, and help determine what is valued in our popular consciousness. Food is a vital aspect of cultural creation and connection, just as music, art, and language are. As such, the food stories we tell and their value will be contested, they will shift over time, and they will often reflect the power dynamics of our society.

Increasingly, Americans are beginning to recognize that Black food *is* American food and that American cuisine is, in part, Black cuisine. Black labor, knowledge systems, and practices are vital threads in America's culinary tapestry.

Exploring Black history and foodways can help us understand why sweet potatoes are also called yams, how dishes such as macaroni and cheese made their way into our shared culinary habits, and even why sugar is so prevalent in the American diet. These explorations also force us to confront some hard truths. Much of what we consume in the United States can be tied directly back to Black experiences of enslavement and to settler colonialism. So much of what we now think of as "modern" globalized culinary and economic systems has roots in those structures. Because of that painful truth, many have ignored or downplayed the Black impact on the American kitchen and economy and therefore denied much of the Black history of the United States.

Narratives that examine cuisine as a messy and complicated interplay of economic, social, and cultural dynamics are vital to understanding how we eat today and how we came to be as a nation and a community. That approach may make it hard to draw neat lines around our foodways and our history, but it also leads us to the richness of culinary practices we have in the United States today. It leads us to an understanding of American food as rooted in Blackness, but also in immigrant experiences, in Indigenous practices, and in immense ongoing culinary experimentation. That richness, which I consider one of the defining features of the American foodscape, is an immense privilege and wonder to explore.

OPPOSITE: At the Family Reunion, a Black food festival, chef Nyesha Arrington offers a dish of Seoul chicken with pecan dukkah, gochujang pimento cheese, and a corn cake.
PAGES 294-295: Attendees celebrate Black food history at the 2023 Food & Wine Family Reunion presented by Kwame Onwuachi at the Salamander Middleburg resort in Virginia.

Acknowledgments

Mom and Dad, thank you for making me who I am. This big wide world is less scary because of you. To my BFFs, thank you for walking beside me and holding me in your light.

To all the culinarians, experts, bakers, bar professionals, chefs, and food folks who let me pick your brain and interview you, pointed me in the right direction, gave your support, and paved the way for this book, my deepest thanks. You are an integral part of this project and your work is a continuation of a long legacy of community, excellence, and creativity that makes Black foodways so special.

Finally, a special thanks to the team at National Geographic who helped make this book a reality, including Allyson Johnson, Nicole Miller Roberts, Katie Dance, Susan Blair, Adrian Coakley, Elisa Gibson, Jerome Cookson, and Michael O'Connor, as well as illustrator Andrea Pippins, photographer Farrah Skeiky, food stylist Nichole Bryant, prop stylist Emilie Fosnocht, digital technician Travis Marshall, and lighting assistant Matt Dandy.

Select Sources

Marc Aronson and Marina Budhos, *Sugar Changed the World: A Story of Magic, Spice, Slavery, Freedom, and Science* (Clarion Books, 2010).

Cornelia Walker Bailey, interview by Cornelia Walker, Georgia Black Fishermen oral history project (NOAA Voices Oral History Archives), August 27, 2009.

Edward E. Baptist, *The Half Has Never Been Told: Slavery and the Making of American Capitalism* (Basic Books, 2016).

Scott Alves Barton et al., "The Original Innovators," *Food & Wine,* July 7, 2021.

William R. Black, "How Watermelons Became a Racist Trope," *The Atlantic,* December 9, 2021.

Jennifer Hill Booker, "Fighting Stereotypes, One Dinner at a Time," JamesBeard.org, February 14, 2017.

Anne L. Bower, ed., *African American Foodways: Explorations of History and Culture* (University of Illinois Press, 2008).

Lean'tin L. Bracks and Jessie Carney Smith, eds., *Black Women of the Harlem Renaissance Era* (Rowman & Littlefield, 2014).

Larry Buchanan, Quoctrung Bui, and Jugal K. Patel, "Black Lives Matter May Be the Largest Movement in U.S. History," *New York Times*, July 3, 2020.

Judith A. Carney, *Black Rice: The African Origins of Rice Cultivation in the Americas* (Harvard University Press, 2001).

Judith A. Carney and Richard Nicholas Rosomoff, *In the Shadow of Slavery: Africa's Botanical Legacy in the Atlantic World* (University of California Press, 2009).

Christian Woman's Exchange of New Orleans, *The Creole Cookery Book* (1885; repr. Hermann-Grima/Gallier Historic Houses and the Historic New Orleans Collection, 2017).

Freda DeKnight, *A Date With a Dish: Classic African-American Recipes* (Dover, 2014; originally published as *The Ebony Cookbook: A Date With a Dish*, 1962).

Electronic Encyclopedia of Chicago, "Map of Pullman Company Rail Network, 1885," Chicago Historical Society.

Farley Elliott, "Witness the Renaissance of LA's Black Barbecue Scene," Eater LA, August 12, 2021.

Rufus Estes, *Good Things to Eat, as Suggested by Rufus: A Collection of Practical Recipes for Preparing Meats, Game, Fowl, Fish, Puddings, Pastries, Etc.* (1911; repr., LSC Communications, 2021).

Abby Fisher, *What Mrs. Fisher Knows About Old Southern Cooking: Soups, Pickles, Preserves, Etc.* (1881; facsimile ed. with historical notes by Karen Hess, Applewood Books, 1995).

Adrian Florido, Sarah Handel, and Megan Lim, "How Black Activists Used Lynching Souvenirs to Expose American Violence," NPR, February 8, 2022.

Paul Freedman, *American Cuisine: And How It Got This Way* (Liveright, 2019).

Eugene D. Genovese, *Roll, Jordan, Roll: The World the Slaves Made* (Random House, 1972).

Robert L. Hall, "Food Crops, Medicinal Plants, and the Atlantic Slave Trade," in *African American Foodways: Explorations of History and Culture,* ed. Anne L. Bower (University of Illinois Press, 2008).

James Hancock, "Sugar and the Rise of the Plantation System," *World History Encyclopedia,* last modified June 18, 2021.

Jessica B. Harris, *Beyond Gumbo: Creole Fusion Food From the Atlantic Rim* (Simon & Schuster, 2003).

———, *High on the Hog: A Culinary Journey From Africa to America* (Bloomsbury USA, 2011).

———, "Migration Meals: How African American Food Transformed the Taste of America," Eatingwell.com, February 8, 2021.

———, "Prosperity Starts With a Pea," *New York Times,* December 29, 2010.

Dana Hatic, "A Brief History of Pecan Pie," Eater, November 23, 2016.

Karen Hess, *The Carolina Rice Kitchen: The African Connection* (University of South Carolina Press, 1992).

High on the Hog: How African American Cuisine Transformed America, "The Rice Kingdom," season one, episode two, Netflix.

Chala June, "Cheryl Day Just Wrote the Definitive Book on Southern Baking," *Bon Appétit,* October 26, 2021.

Naa Oyo A. Kate, *White Burgers, Black Cash: Fast Food From Black Exclusion to Exploitation* (University of Michigan Press, 2023).

Sarah Lohman, *Eight Flavors: The Untold Story of American Cuisine* (Simon & Schuster Paperbacks, 2016).

Syreeta McFadden, "Uncovering the Roots of Caribbean Cooking," *The Atlantic,* June 1, 2021.

Claude McKay, *Home to Harlem,* ed. Richard Yarborough (Northeastern University Press, 1987).

Adrian Miller, *Black Smoke: African Americans and the United States of Barbecue* (University of North Carolina Press, 2021).

———, *The President's Kitchen Cabinet: The Story of the African Americans Who Have Fed Our First Families, From the Washingtons to the Obamas* (University of North Carolina Press, 2017).

———, *Soul Food: The Surprising Story of an American Cuisine, One Plate at a Time* (University of North Carolina Press, 2013).

Frederick Douglass Opie, *Hog and Hominy: Soul Food From Africa to America* (Columbia University Press, 2008).

Gabrielle Nicole Pharms, "Drinks Innovators of the Year: Fawn Weaver and Victoria Eady Butler," *Food & Wine,* March 15, 2022.

Donna Battle Pierce, "Freda DeKnight: A 'Hidden Figure' and Titan of African-American Cuisine," NPR, February 16, 2017.

Mary Randolph, *The Virginia Housewife, or Methodical Cook* (1824; repr. Marula, 2017).

Etha Robinson, "Tea Cakes and Black History: Reclaiming a Legacy," National Geographic Education Blog, February 1, 2022.

Malinda Russell, *A Domestic Cookbook: Containing a Careful Selection of Useful Receipts for the Kitchen* (1866; repr. Facsimile Publishers, 2007).

Sarah Rutledge, *The Carolina Housewife* (1847; facsimile ed., American Antiquarian Cookbook Collection, 2013).

Marcus Samuelsson, *Yes, Chef: A Memoir* (Random House, 2012).

David S. Shields, *The Culinarians: Lives and Careers From the First Age of American Fine Dining* (University of Chicago Press, 2017).

———, *Southern Provisions: The Creation and Revival of a Cuisine* (University of Chicago Press, 2015).

Elazer Sontag, "Meet the Southern Chef Spreading the Word of Gullah Geechee Cuisine," GrubStreet.com, June 16, 2018.

Frank X. Tolbert, *A Bowl of Red* (Texas A&M University Press, 1993).

Townsends, "Food of the Enslaved: Barbecue, Featuring Michael Twitty." YouTube, www.youtube.com/watch?v=GwkRWIwZ43A.

Michael W. Twitty, "How Rice Shaped the American South," BBC.com, March 8, 2021.

Kevinisha Walker, "The Vibrant and Complex History of Black Oyster Culture," Thrillist.com, July 30, 2021.

Psyche A. Williams-Forson, *Building Houses Out of Chicken Legs: Black Women, Food, and Power* (University of North Carolina Press, 2006).

William C. Whit, "Soul Food as Cultural Creation," in Bower, *African American Foodways*.

Maps & Illustrations Credits

MAPS CREDITS

U.S. Food Regions
Richard Pillsbury, Georgia State University; Lou Sackett and David Haynes, *American Regional Cuisines: Food Culture and Cooking* (Pearson, 2011).

African Food Origins
Emily C. Sousa and Manish N. Raizada, "Contributions of African Crops to American Culture and Beyond: The Slave Trade and Other Journeys of Resilient Peoples and Crops," *Frontiers in Sustainable Food Systems* (December 2020).

Civil Rights
Kenneth T. Andrews and Michael Biggs, "The Dynamics of Protest Diffusion: Movement Organizations, Social Networks, and News Media in the 1960s Sit-Ins," *American Sociological Review* (October 2006); Southern Regional Council, "The Student Protest Movement: A Recapitulation" (September 1961).

Rice
Daniel Hanks, aquatic ecologist, Environmental Research South, Weyerhaeuser Company.

Barbecue
Adrian Miller, *Black Smoke* (University of North Carolina Press, 2021); Tasteatlas.com.

ILLUSTRATIONS CREDITS

2–3, Brent Hofacker/Adobe Stock; 4, Laura Murray, Bon Appetit © Conde Nast; 6, Clay Williams; 9, Gordon Parks/Library of Congress Prints and Photographs Division, LC-DIG-fsa-8d23343; 10, Rachel Seidu; 13, "Bar-b-que," 1942, Lawrence, Jacob (1917–2000)/Terra Foundation for American Art, Chicago/Art Resource, NY/© 2024 The Jacob and Gwendolyn Knight Lawrence Foundation, Seattle/Artists Rights Society (ARS), New York; 14–5, Marianna Massey/Getty Images; 16, "The Huastec Civilisation," detail showing the cultivation of the millenarian plant and natives making various corn dishes, 1950/Rivera, Diego (1886–1957)/Palacio Nacional, Mexico City, Mexico/Bridgeman Images/© 2024 Banco de México Diego Rivera Frida Kahlo Museums Trust, Mexico, D.F./Artists Rights Society (ARS), New York; 19, Westend61/Achim Sass/Alamy Stock Photo; 20, Shava Cueva/Stocksy; 21, "The Virginia House-Wife" by Mary Randolph, printed by Davis and Force, 1824, Washington/Library of Congress Rare Book and Special Collections Division, Elizabeth Robins Pennell Collection; 23, "Corn Shucking in the Moonlight," 1890–1910 (detail), Williams, Mary Lyde Hicks (1866–1959), courtesy the North Carolina Department of Natural and Cultural Resources; 25, Berenice Abbott/Getty Images; 27 (UP), "The Old Plantation (Slaves Dancing on a South Carolina Plantation)," attributed to John Rose, ca 1785–95/Abby Aldrich Rockefeller Folk Art Museum, Williamsburg, Virginia/Pictures from History/Bridgeman Images; 27 (LO LE), Russell Lee, Library of Congress Prints and Photographs Division, LC-DIG-fsa-8a23625; 27 (LO RT), Shilpa Iyer/Stocksy; 28, Evi Abeler/Offset; 29, ferrantraite/iStock/Getty Images; 33, Bettmann/UPI via Getty Images; 34–5, Farrah Skeiky; 39, JLMcAnally/Stockimo/Alamy Stock Photo; 40–1, "Cotton Plantation, Progress of Cotton No. 1," pub. 1840/Barfoot, James Richard (1794–1863)/Private Collection/Bridgeman Images; 42, Hunter McRae/The New York Times/Redux; 44, Collection of the Smithsonian National Museum of African American History and Culture; 45, Gregory Manchess © 2024; 46, page 82 from "Inventory of Negroes at Berry Plain Plantation," 1855/© Virginia Historical Society, Richmond, Virginia/Bridgeman Images; 49, Bettmann/Getty Images; 50, Private Collection/© Don Troiani. All rights reserved 2024/Bridgeman Images; 51, photographs in Carol M. Highsmith's America Project in the Carol M. Highsmith Archive, Library of Congress, Prints and Photographs Division, LC-DIG-highsm-67701; 52, Russell Lee/Library of Congress Prints and Photographs Division, LC-DIG-fsa-8a28763; 54, dankadanka/Getty Images; 57, "In the Vegetable Garden," 2000 (detail), courtesy the Estate of Nathaniel Kato Gibbs (1948–2018); 58, Heami Lee; 61, "Cotton Pickers," 1945/Benton, Thomas Hart (1889–1975)/The Art Institute of Chicago/Art Resource, NY/© T.H. and R.P. Benton Trusts/Licensed by Artists Rights Society (ARS), New York; 62, Sahil Ghosh/iStock/Getty Images; 65, Duet Postscriptum/Stocksy; 66, "Section Old Market," Charleston, SC, SCHS Postcard Collection, South Carolina Historical Society; 69, "Charleston Square," 1872 (detail view). Charles J. Hamilton/The Colonial Williamsburg Foundation. Museum purchase; 70, Collection of the Smithsonian National Museum of African American History and Culture; 71, Isabelle Souriment/Hans Lucas/Redux; 72, Kennedi Carter/National Geographic Image Collection; 74, Akasha Rabut; 75, Sarah Bird; 76, "Sunup," 1955 (detail)/Gwathmey, Robert (1903–1988)/Philadelphia Museum of Art/The Louis E. Stern Collection, 1963/Bridgeman Images/© 2024 Estate of Robert Gwathmey/Licensed by VAGA at Artists Rights Society (ARS), NY; 79, Joe Raedle/Getty Images; 81, Library of Congress, Manuscript/Mixed Material, LC-MSS-27748-180; 83 (UP), Earth Pixel LLC/Alamy Stock Photo; 83 (LO LE and LO RT), Hunter McRae/The New York Times/Redux; 84, Adam Kuehl, courtesy Telfair Museums; 85, Jeremiah Hull, courtesy Telfair Museums; 87, British Library/Science Source; 88, Library of Congress Prints and Photographs Division, LC-USZC4-7917; 90, Tim Graham/Alamy Stock Photo; 93, detail of illustration from "Voyage Pittoresque et Historique au Bresil," 1835/Debret, Jean Baptiste (1768–1848)/Bibliothèque nationale, Paris, France/Bridgeman Images; 95, Nadine Greeff/Stocksy; 96–102, Farrah Skeiky; 104–5, Jim Wilson/The New York Times/Redux; 106, "Field Workers," ca 1948–1951 (detail)/Wilson, Ellis (1899–1977). Gift of the Harmon Foundation (1967.57.31). Smithsonian American Art Museum, Washington, D.C./Art Resource, NY; 108, Collection of the Smithsonian National Museum of African American History and Culture; 109, Alice Moseley courtesy the Alice Moseley Folk Art Museum; 110, Photographs in the Carol M. Highsmith Archive, Library of Congress, Prints and Photographs

Division, LC-DIG-highsm-14233; 113, courtesy Special Collections and University Archives, University Libraries, Virginia Polytechnic Institute and State University; 114, Library of Congress Manuscript Division, Carter G. Woodson Collection, container I:10; 115, "Migration Series, Panel 1," 1940–41/Lawrence, Jacob (1917–2000)/The Phillips Collection, Washington, D.C., USA, acquired 1942/Bridgeman Images/© 2024 The Jacob and Gwendolyn Knight Lawrence Foundation, Seattle/Artists Rights Society (ARS), New York; 116, Jack Delano/Library of Congress Prints and Photographs Division, LC-DIG-fsa-8c02701; 118, Tony Cenicola/The New York Times/Redux; 119, George Karger/The Chronicle Collection/Getty Images; 120, Collection of the Smithsonian National Museum of African American History and Culture. Gift of the family of Becca Nu'Mani; 121, Richard Saunders/Pictorial Parade/Archive Photos/Getty Images; 122, Lars Plougmann; 124, Bill Waterson/Alamy Stock Photo; 125, Paul Natkin/Archive Photos/Getty Images; 126, Steve Schapiro/Corbis via Getty Images; 128, © Atlanta Journal-Constitution. Courtesy Special Collections and Archives, Georgia State University Library; 130, Marvin Joseph/The Washington Post via Getty Images; 133, Ducho Dennis/It's About Time Archive; 134–8, Farrah Skeiky; 141, Sonia Berengueras/Addictive Stock Creatives/The Picture Pantry; 142, Farrah Skeiky; 144–5, Carmen Chan; 146, Clay Williams; 149, Cori Carter; 150, Maryanne Gobble/Stocksy; 153, The Ron Finley Project; 154, Danielle Levitt/AUGUST; 156, Jim Heaphy; 157, Chia Chong; 158, Kendall Bessent/Kintzing; 159, Sirena Singleton; 161, Eric Lee; 163, "Pepper-Pot: A Scene in the Philadelphia Market," 1811 (detail)/John Lewis Krimmel (1786–1821)/Philadelphia Museum of Art, 125th Anniversary Acquisition. Gift of Mr. and Mrs. Edward B. Leisenring, Jr., 2001; 164, T.J. Kirkpatrick/Redux; 167, Jonathan Cooper; 168, Collection of the Smithsonian National Museum of African American History and Culture; 169, Photographer Robert H. McNeill, courtesy Susan P. McNeill; 170, Scott Suchman; 172, "Saturday Night," 1935/Motley Jr., Archibald J. (1891–1981)/© Chicago History Museum/© Estate of Archibald John Motley Jr. All rights reserved 2025/Bridgeman Images; 173, Rey Lopez; 174–80, Farrah Skeiky; 182–3, Lelanie Foster; 184, Rinne Allen/The New York Times/Redux; 186, Collection of the Smithsonian National Museum of African American History and Culture; 187, Henry P. Moore/Library of Congress Prints and Photographs Division, LC-DIG-ppmsca-11398; 188, Richard Ellis/Alamy Stock Photo; 190, "Loading a Rice Schooner," ca 1935 (detail)/Smith, Alice Ravenel Huger (1876–1958)/Gibbes Museum of Art/gift of the artist (1937.009.0024); 193, Leah Flores/Stocksy; 195, courtesy Orange County (Virginia) Historical Society; 196, Sean Locke/Stocksy; 199, courtesy Stuart A. Rose Manuscript, Archives, & Rare Book Library, Emory University; 200, Lauren Carnes/Stocksy; 202, Mike Norton via flickr (CC by 2.0); 204, Kirk Jordan/Arkansas Department of Parks, Heritage and Tourism; 207, Russell Lee/Library of Congress Prints and Photographs Division, LC-DIG-fsa-8a24459; 208, "Ed Walker Cleaning Fish," 1982/Bates, David (b. 1952)/© Dallas Museum of Art, Texas, USA/gift of Mr. and Mrs. Claude Albritton III, John C. Tatum, Jr., Mrs. John W. O'Boyle, Elizabeth B. Blake, Mr. and Mrs. I. D. Flores III, and two anonymous donors/Bridgeman Images; 211, Bettmann/Getty Images; 213, CWP, LLC/Stocksy; 215, AP Photo; 216, Orsolya Bán/Stocksy; 218, "The Ideal Bartender" by Tom Bullock, 1917; 219, Marion Post Wolcott/Library of Congress Prints and Photographs Division, LC-USF34-052483-D; 221, Peter Frank Edwards/Redux; 222, Clay Williams; 225, Ryan Dearth; 226, Farrah Skeiky; 229, Brie Williams; 230-1, Farrah Skeiky; 234, © 2011 Tom Kates Photography; 237, Kat Wilson; 238, Johnny Autry; 241, Dave Rossman; 242, Farrah Skeiky; 245, Anthony Werhun; 246, Rey Lopez; 249, T.J. Kirkpatrick/Redux; 250, Farrah Skeiky; 253-4, Peter Frank Edwards/Redux; 257-8, Farrah Skeiky; 261, Kevin Marple Photo; 262-6, Farrah Skeiky; 269, Nicholas Karlin; 270-9, Farrah Skeiky; 281, Casey Kelbaugh/The New York Times/Redux; 282, Farrah Skeiky; 285, Amy Dickerson; 286-9, Farrah Skeiky; 290, Harris Jeter; 293, Farrah Skeiky; 294-5, Clay Williams; 296, Farrah Skeiky; back cover (UP LE), Farrah Skeiky; (UP RT), Bettmann/Getty Images; (LO LE), "The Old Plantation (Slaves Dancing on a South Carolina Plantation)," attributed to John Rose, ca 1785-95/Abby Aldrich Rockefeller Folk Art Museum, Williamsburg, Virginia/Pictures from History/Bridgeman Images; (LO RT), Shilpa Iyer/Stocksy.

General Index

Boldface indicates illustrations.

A

Ackee 92
Adichie, Chimamanda Ngozi **10**
"African American" (term) 11
Alabama 60, 108, 111, 127, 129, 160
Alcohol 121, 197, 218
Alexander, Cato 218
Ali, Ben 128
Ali, Muhammad 121
Ali, Virginia 128, **130,** 131
"America" versus "United States" 8
American cuisine
  Black contributions to 9–11, 32, 56–59, 76, 166, 185, 223, 224, 235
  definition of 11–13
  immigrant influences on 12, 24–25, 32, 162–165
  Indigenous roots of 18–21
  and wealth 76–77
Angelou, Maya 197
Anju (restaurant), Washington, D.C. 171
Antigua, West Indies: sugarcane **87**

Arkansas: barbecue restaurant **202,** 202–203, **204,** 205
Arlington, Virginia: restaurant 268
Armstrong, Louis 117, 125, 168
Atlanta, Georgia: restaurants 127–128, **128,** 129, **149**
Augustin, James 70, 111
Aunt Jemima (character) 112

B

Bailey, Cornelia Walker 209
Bailey, Mashama 157, **157**
Baked goods 13, 127, 214–217. *see also* Biscuits; Bread; Cakes; Pies
Baking, southern, art of 214–215, 217, 284
Baltimore, Maryland 70–71, 111, 132
Banneker, Benjamin 171
Baptist, Edward E. 47, 77
Bar professionals 172–173, 218, 291
Barbecue 117, 148, 198–205
  barbecued chicken **230–231,** 232
  barbecued pork 125, **200,** 202, 205
  celebrated Black pitmasters 203, **203**
  Native American techniques 198–199, 205
  regional styles 201, 203
  sauce 201, 205, 276
  spit roasting 199, **199**
Barreto, Angel 171–172
Barton, Scott Alves 212
Bauhaus Biergarten, Springdale, Arkansas 236
BayHaven Restaurant Group 228
Ben's Chili Bowl, Washington, D.C. 128–131, **130**
Benton, Thomas Hart 61
The Birth of a Nation (film) 197
Biscuits 94, **138,** 139, 215, 217, 284
Black, William R. 64
Black Culinary History (organization) 244
Black-eyed peas **2–3,** 54, 56, 63, 148, **150,** 192, 265
Black history
  influences on American cuisine 9–11, 32, 125, 185, 194, 255, 280
  of Washington, D.C. 168–171
  see also Civil rights movement; Enslavement; Great Migration; Harlem Renaissance; Jim Crow era; Segregation

306 • AMERICAN SOUL

Black Lives Matter 129, 160, **161**
Black Panther Party 132
Black pepper 12
Black pride movement 116, 120
"Black" (term) 11
BlaqNmilD (producer) **183**
Bonner, Daisy 224
Booker, Jennifer Hill 123, 236, **237,** 239
Booze, Jermond 155
Bracey, Day 166
Brazil
   sorghum 92
   sugar-mill workers **93**
Bread 26, **170,** 194, 201, **215.** see also Cornbread
Bread pudding 50, 74, **102,** 103
Brewing 218
Brown, Tabitha 151
Buffalo Soldiers 73
Bullock, Tom 218, 291

C

Cajun cuisine 26, 29
Cakes
   hoecakes 22
   pound cake 127, **180,** 181
   sweet potato cake **282,** 283
   tea cakes **216,** 217
California
   gold rush 73, 76
   sriracha hot sauce 25
   see also Los Angeles; Oakland; San Francisco
Callaloo 92
Capitalism 77, 91, 123, 148, 161
Caribbean region
   and Cajun cuisine 29
   cassava 92, 118, 163
   introduced plants 56
   plantains 92, 118, 163

slave trade 24, 44, 47, 88, 92, 163
   sugar plantations 56, **87,** 87–88, 92
   trading ties with Philadelphia 162–163
   Trinidadian cuisine 247
   yams 92, 210
Carney, Judith A. 53, 55, 191, 192
Carolina Gold rice **188,** 191
The Carolina Housewife (Rutledge) 21, 59, 61–62, 80–81, 194, 217
Cassava 54, 92, 118, 163
Catfish 64, 208
Cattle drives 53, 73
Centennial Exhibition 89
Charleston, South Carolina 51, 53, 66–68
   enslaved person's tag **50**
   fishing operation 112, 207, 209
   market **66,** 68, **69,** 188
   pastry cooks 67–68, 214–215
   rice 50, 188, **188,** 191
   wealth 50, 188, 191
Charlotte, North Carolina
   bars and restaurants 228, 291
   food and wine festival 166
Chattel slavery 47, 48, 107, 123, 148
Chesapeake Bay region 206–207
Chicago, Illinois 111, 115, **125,** 127, 203
Chicken
   barbecued chicken **230–231,** 232
   cashew chicken 12
   chicken croquettes 113, 140, **141**
   chicken purloo 256, **257**
   jerk chicken **170**
   see also Fried chicken

Chickens 194–195, 197
Chigul (comedian) **10**
Chilies 54, 67, 135, 259
Chinese immigrants 12, 24, 25, 251
Chitlin Circuit 124, 128
Chitlins (chitterlings) 107, 118, 122, **122,** 125, 284
Choctaw 29
Chop Suey (restaurant), New York, New York **25**
Church functions 195, 212
Civil rights movement 107, 108, 116, 120–129, 148, 151, 169, 236
Civil War, U.S. 48, 108
Claiborne, Jenné 149
Clark, William 87
Clarksdale, Mississippi: bar **219**
Clinton, Bill 205
Club From Nowhere 127
Coast Salish people 21
Coca-Cola 63
Cocktails 173, 218, 291, 292, **293**
Coffee 55, 63, 86, 88, 159, 163
Cole, Nat King 128
Cole, Pinky 151
Collard greens **15,** 92, 123, **150, 263,** 264
Collier, Gregory and Subrina 228, **229,** 232
Colonial America
   diasporic culinary exchange 162–164
   enslavement 44–47
   sugar production 86–91
Colonialism 18, 19, 21, 44–48, 91, 297
Compère Lapin (restaurant), New Orleans, Louisiana 164
Compton, Nina 164
Congri 92

Cookbooks, early 58, 61–67, 80–81, 112, 217
   by Black authors 64, 66, 113, **113**, 194, 217
   Native American dishes 19, 21
   by wealthy white women 61–62, 194
Coon Chicken Inn restaurants 197
Corn **20**, 21, 22, **23**, 109, **196, 238, 274–275**, 276
Cornbread 11, 22, **34–35**, 36–37, **150**, 193
Cotton Club, Harlem, New York 118
Cotton gin, invention of 77
Cotton pickers **40–41**, 50, **52**, 60, **61, 76**, 77, 203
Cotton plantations **40–41**, 60, 89
Cowboys, Black 32, 53, 73–75, **75**
Cowpeas 54, 56, 192
Creole cuisine 26–29
Croquettes 113, 140, **141**, 278, **279**
Curaçao, West Indies: sorghum 92
Currence, John 161
Curry, Kevin 260, **261**, 264
Cxffeeblack (company) 159

D

Davis, Angela 148, 151
Day, Cheryl 185, 284, **285**, 287
Dean, Lillian Harris 118
Debret, Jean-Baptiste 92
Dennis, Benjamin "BJ" 185, **221**, 252–256, **253, 254**
Detroit, Michigan 115, 155, 236, 280
Direct-action campaigns 127
Distilling 159, 218, 292
Dōgon (restaurant), Washington, D.C. 171
Domestic workers 107, 109, 111–112, 125, 248

Downing, Thomas 71, 73, 209
Du Bois, W. E. B. 117, 118
Duck 111, 232, **242**, 243

E

EatOkra (app) 159
Edwards, Anthony 159
Edwards, Janique 159
Eggplant 54, 55, 59, **98–99**, 100
Ehikhamenor, Victor **10**
Ellington, Duke 117, 128, 169
Elliott, Farley 117
Emancipation Proclamation 109
Enslaved peoples
   food rations 22, 56, 59, 123, 148, 153, 195, 218
   gardens 48, 55–56, **57**, 62, 64, 67, 78
   plantation inventory **46**
   punishments inflicted on 191, 205
   shackles **44**
   slave auctions 48, **49**
   tag of enslaved person **50**
   treatment of 48
   wealth generated by labor of 32, 43, 50, 76–78, 89, 198
   work regimes 48, 91
Enslavement, colonial expansion and 44–48
Estes, Rufus 113, **113**
Ethiopia: coffee 63
Ethiopian cuisine 17, 165
Ethiopian immigrants 164–165

F

Family Reunion (food festival) 166, **167, 294–295**
Fanner baskets **186**, 191
Farm-to-table movement 123

Feed The Malik (blog) 147
Field peas 56, 58, 191, 192 **230–231**, 232, 265
Fields, Mary 75
Filipino cuisine 248, 251
Finley, Ron 153, **154**, 155
First Nations groups 21
Fish and seafood **5**, 71, 92, 112, 206–209, 278. see also Catfish; Oysters; Salmon; Shrimp
Fisher, Abby 75–76, 159
Fishing 71, 112, 123, 153, 206–209
Flatbreads 21, 24
Floyd, George 161
Fonio 165
Food activism 132
Food apartheid 86, 151, 152, 153, 260
Food crop origins: map 63
Food deserts 152
Food festivals 166, **167**
Food theft 59, 197
Forced feeding 59
Francis, Dick 218
Franklin, Aretha 125, **125**, 169
Free Breakfast for Children Program 132, **133**
Freedman, Paul 26
French cuisine 29, 80, 236
Fried chicken **14–15**, 194–197, **196**, 268
   brined **271**, 272
   fast food 166, 268
   fried-chicken sandwiches 268
   history of 107, 116, 194–195, 197, 268
   racial stereotypes 116, 119, 197, 205, 268
Fuller, Nat 66, 68
Fusion cuisines 17

G

Gantt Cottage, St. Helena Island, South Carolina **42,** 43
Gardens
  community gardens **153,** 155
  of enslaved peoples 48, 55–56, **57,** 62, 64, 67, 78
  and plant-based traditions 123
  and sharecropping system 109
Georgia
  black belt regions 60
  Gullah Geechee community 209
  pecan production 89
  rice growing 188
  slavery 47, 108
  see also Atlanta; Savannah
Georgia Black Fishermen oral history project 209
Ghana 44, 164, 280
Gibbs, Nathaniel 56
Gillie's Seafood, Charleston, South Carolina, **159**
Gilmore, Georgia 127
Good Things to Eat, as Suggested by Rufus (Estes) 113, **113**
Gordonsville, Virginia: waiter carriers 195, **195**
Goudia, Ederique 155, 233
Grand Central Hotel, Deadwood, South Dakota 75
Grant, Jerome 248, **249,** 251
Great Migration 114–119, 148, 169, 185, 193, 197, 206, 212
  class-related and racial struggles 116–117, 201
  spread of southern cuisine 107, 115–117
Green, Nancy 112
Green, Nathan "Nearest" 159, 292
Greens, as culinary staple 192–193
Gregory, Dick 148, 151

The Grey (restaurant), Savannah, Georgia **157**
Grits 116, 125, 206
Grubbs, Hannah Queen 284
Guinea squash. *see* Eggplant
Gullah Express food truck **144–145**
Gullah Geechee 43, 58, 147, 209, 235, 252, 255, 256
Gumbo 7, 13, 26, **28,** 29, 38, 59, 62, 206
Gwathmey, Robert 76

H

Harlem, New York
  direct-action campaigns 127
  restaurants **13, 104–105, 110,** 117, **121,** 280
  street vendors 64, 117, 118, **211**
Harlem Renaissance 117–119, **118, 119**
Harper, Rock 268, **269,** 272
Harris, Jessica B. 10, 11, 47, 76, 111, 116, 157, **222,** 223
Hazelton, Justin **290,** 291, 292
Hemings, James 80–81
Henderson, Renata 159
Henson, Lexius 111
Hibiscus 55, **226,** 227, 291
Historic Charleston City Market, Charleston, South Carolina 188
Hoecakes 22
Hontzas, Timothy 160–161
Hooker, George 73
Hooks, Matthew 75
Hoppin' John **2–3,** 56, 92, 116, 191, 192, 255, **262,** 265
Horses **72,** 73, **74,** 75
Hoskins, Dionne 209
Hot sauces 13, 25, 67, 116, 165
Houston, Texas: restaurants 240

Hualapai peoples 21
Huastec civilization **16**
Huckleberry 21
Hughes, Langston 117, **119**
Hurst, Devon **183**
Hurston, Zora Neale 117
Huy Fong Foods 25

I

Icehouses 78–79
The Ideal Bartender (Bullock) 218, **218**
Ighodaro, Osas **10**
Immigration: impacts on American cuisine 12, 24–25, 32, 162–165
Indentured servitude 53, 89
Indigenous peoples 17–25, 44, 47, 67, 68, 87, 92, 205, 244

J

Jalapeño peppers 25, 135, 176, 259
Jamaica 67, 92
Jambalaya 255, **258,** 259
James Beard Foundation 123, 128, 156, 160–161, 223, 228, 236
Jamestown, Virginia 55
Jazz music 117, 118, 125
Jean, Marie 201
Jefferson, Thomas 80–81
Jim Crow era 108–113, 114, 124, 127, 240
Johns Island, South Carolina: farm **221, 254**
Johnson, Joseph "JJ" 280, **281,** 283
Johnson, Lyndon B. 127, 215
Jollof rice 166–167, 191, 255
Jones, Bartholomew 159
Jones, James 202, 205

Jones, Walter 202
Jones' Bar-B-Q Diner, Marianna, Arkansas **202,** 202–203, **204,** 205
Joseph Fields Farm, Johns Island, South Carolina **221, 254**
Juke joints 124
June, Chala 214

K

Kaepernick, Colin 151
Kale 192, **193**
Kansas City–style barbecue 201, 203
Kearney, KJ 158–159, **159**
Kentucky
　barbecue styles 203
　slavery 47
King, B. B. 125
King, Martin Luther, Jr. 43, 127, 128, 129, 131, 132
Kola nuts 53–54, **54,** 55, 63
Korean food 171
Krimmel, John Lewis 163

L

Lawrence, Jacob 13, 115
Lee, Canada **119**
Lee, Eliza 66, 67
Lee, John 67
Leslie, Charles C. 112, 207, 209
Lewis, John **128**
Livestock industry 53, 73
Lohman, Sarah 25
Lorem Ipsum (bar), Charlotte, North Carolina 291
Los Angeles, California
　barbecue scene 117
　　community garden **153,** 155
　　street festival 166

Louisiana
　Cajun and Creole cuisine 26
　gumbo 26, 29
　hot sauce 67
　oystermen **27, 207,** 209
　plantations **51,** 89, **90,** 91, 92, 155
　slavery 89, 91, 108
　sugar production 89, 91, 92
　see also New Orleans
Lowcountry cuisine 252, 255
　hoppin' John 192
　okra soup **58,** 255
　purloo 255, 256, **257**
　red rice 191
　seafood 206
Lucille's (restaurant), Houston, Texas 240
Lynchings 108–109, 114, 124, 205

M

Macaroni and cheese 13, **16,** 59, 80–81, **96,** 97, 113, 150
Madrid, Frozine 111
Maize **16,** 21, 30, 54
Malcolm X 121, **121**
Mali 44, 165
Malik, Anela **6**
"Mammy" stereotype 68, 112
Maple syrup 18, 21, 30
Maps
　food crop origins 63
　food regions of the United States 30–31
　historic rice fields of South Carolina 189
　regional barbecue styles 203
　restaurants involved in civil rights movement 129
　sit-in movement: sites of protest, 1960–61 129

March on Washington for Jobs and Freedom (1963) **126,** 128, 129, 131, 151
Marshbanks, Lucretia 75
McKay, Claude 118
Memphis-style barbecue 201, 203, 232
Mexican immigrants 24
Michelin Guide 171, 240
Middle Passage 45, 47, 53, 62, 63, 67, 188, 210
Migration. see Great Migration; Immigration
Miller, Adrian 10, 22, 67, 168–169, 193–194, 198, 201–202, 212, 224, **225**
Millet 54, 55, 56, 63, 92
Mississippi 60, 108. see also Clarksdale
Mitsitam Native Foods Cafe, National Museum of the American Indian, Washington, D.C. 248
Mixologists 172–173, **173,** 218, 228, **290,** 291
Molasses 88, 163
Montgomery bus boycott (1955–56) 127, 129
Monticello, Virginia 80, 81
Morgan, Charity 151
Moseley, Alice 109
Motley, Jr., Archibald 172
Mount Vernon, Virginia 78–79, **79**
Muhammad, Elijah 121
Murray, Nellie 111
Museum of Food and Drink, New York, New York 223
Museum of the African Diaspora, San Francisco, California 151

N

Nation of Islam (NOI) 120–122

National Museum of African American History and Culture, Washington, D.C. 223, 248
Native Americans 22, 30, 53, 89, 191, 198–199, 205
Nelson, Thérèse 244, **245**
New Orleans, Louisiana 26, **29,** 67, 111
   dinner party **181–182**
   oystermen **27,** 209
   restaurants 129, 164
New Year's food traditions 5, 56, 151, 191, 192, 251, 262
New York, New York
   Black southern migrants 115
   Chinese restaurant (1930s) **25**
   oyster houses 70, 71, 73
   see also Harlem
Newton, Huey P. 132
Nigeria 44, 58, 164, 165, 280
North Carolina
   barbecue styles 203
   plantation **23**
   see also Charlotte

O

Oak Alley Plantation, Vacherie, Louisiana. 89, **90,** 91
Oakland, California 115, 132, 280
Oaxaca, Mexico: corn **20,** 21
Obama, Barack 131
Obi-Uchendu, Ebuka **10**
Okra 26, **27,** 29, **39,** 54, 56, 61–63, **146**
Okra soup **58,** 59, 118, 255
Olga, Louisiana: oystermen **207**
Onwuachi, Kwame 164, **164,** 166, 171, 297
Opie, Frederick Douglass 10, 118, 125, **234,** 235
Owens, George Welshman 82

Owens-Thomas House & Slave Quarters, Savannah, Georgia 82–85, **83–85**
Oxtail 165–166
Oyster jar **70**
Oystermen 9, **27,** 206, **207,** 209
Oysters 67, 70, 71, **71,** 111, 209, 278

P

Pancake mix and syrups 112
Parks, Rosa **126,** 151
Pasadena, California 115
Paschal's, Atlanta, Georgia 127–128, **128**
Pastry cooks 66–68, 214–215
Peanuts 54, 62, **62,** 116
Pecans, history of 89
Pepper pot 58, **134,** 135, **163,** 163–164, 263
Pepper sauces 67
Philadelphia, Pennsylvania
   African migrants 164, 165
   Black southern migrants 115
   Caribbean cuisine 163–164
   colonial era 162–163
   19th-century Black caterers 70, 111
   pepper pot hawkers 163, **163**
   restaurants 70, 165
Phyno (rapper) **10**
Pickett, Bill 73
Pickled watermelon rinds 64, 117–118, 136, **137**
Pies
   apple cream pie 288, **289**
   lemon cream pie **142,** 143
   sweet potato pie 86, 212, 284
Pig's feet 68, 113, 116, 117, 118, 122, 125, 224
Pilau 255
Pine Bluff, Arkansas 201

Pink, Willie B. **75**
Pitmasters 9, 200, 201, 202, **203**
Pizza 12
Plant-based traditions
   gardens and 123
   innovation in 151
   see also Veganism; Vegetarianism
Plantains 54, 92, 118, 163
Plantations
   cotton plantations **40–41,** 60, 89
   inventory of enslaved persons 47
   music and dancing **23, 27**
   rice plantations **187,** 191
   sugar plantations 56, **87,** 87–89, 91, 92
   see also Oak Alley Plantation; Whitney Plantation
Pleasant, Mary Ellen 76
Point Comfort (Fort Monroe), Hampton, Virginia 47
Political discourse, and Black food 124–132
Pork
   barbecued pork 125, **200,** 202, 205
   chitterlings **122**
   as dietary staple 59, 109, 116
   greens cooked with 193
   jerk pork lumpia **200,** 201
   and Nation of Islam 121, 122
   pork chops 116, 148
   pork loin roast **266,** 267
Portugal: colonial exploration and expansion 44, 87, 186
Posey, Hercules 78–80
Possum 122
Potato salad **4, 270,** 273
Potatoes 18, **19,** 116
Pound cake 127, **180,** 181
Prime, Peter **246,** 247

Prosser, James 70
Pullman porters 113, 114
Purloo 255, 256, **257**

Q

Queen Mother's Kitchen, Arlington, Virginia 268

R

Radical Reconstruction 108, 114
Railroads 73, 113, 195
Randolph, Mary 21, 58, 64
Randolph, Patsy 117–118
Rastafarians 148–149
Red rice **4,** 92, 191
Reeves, Bass 73
Rent parties 118
Republic Theatre, Washington, D.C. **169**
Rice Coast 188
Rice dishes 92, 255
    chicken purloo 256, **257**
    dirty rice 233
    hoppin' John **2–3,** 92, 191, 255, 265
    jambalaya 255, **258,** 259
    jollof rice 166–167, 191, 255
    pilau 255
    red rice **4,** 92, 191
    rice and peas 92, 255
    rice waffles **174,** 175
Rice growing 186–189, **187, 189,** 191
Rivera, Diego 17
Robinson, David **126**
Robinson, Etha 217
Robinson, Jackie **126**
Robinson, Kapri 173, **173**
Robinson, Rachel **126**
Roman, Jacques Telesphore 89
Roosevelt, Franklin 224
Roosevelt, Theodore 218
Rosomoff, Richard Nicholas 53, 55, 64, 191, 192
Ross, Jr., Freddie **182–183**
Roux 29
Rum 88, 163
Russell, Malinda 64, 66
Rutledge, Sarah 80–81

S

Sacred Heart Church, San Francisco, California **133**
St. Helena Island, South Carolina
    cottage **42**
    food truck **144–145**
    praise house 43
St. Louis, Missouri 115, 203
Salads **184, 263,** 264. *see also* Potato salad
Salmon 18, 30, 278
Saltfish 92
Samuelsson, Marcus 10, 166
San Francisco, California
    Black southern migrants 115
    children's free breakfast **133**
    Museum of the African Diaspora 151
Sapelo Island, Georgia 209
Sassafras 19, 29
Savannah, Georgia
    bakery 284
    museum 82–85, **83–85**
    restaurant 157
School Breakfast Program 132
Seafood. *see* Fish and seafood
Seale, Bobby 132
Second Middle Passage 77, 89
Segregation, racial 73, 107–109, 114, 124, 127, 153, 171, 173
Senegal 44, 92, 165, 280
Senegambia 73
Seymour, Sally 66–67
Sharecropping 109, **109**
Shark, fried **5**
Shields, David S. 67, 71, 73, 80
Ships, slave-trading 45, **45,** 47, 53, 55, 59, 63, 67, 188, 210
Shoebox lunches 197
Shrimp
    fried shrimp **5**
    gumbo **28**
    Jambalaya **258,** 259
    shrimp and grits 206
Shuttlesworth, Fred **126**
Simms, Benjamin Franklin 111
Simms, Hilda **119**
Slave trade. *see* Transatlantic Slave Trade
Slavery, institution of 44–48, 59, 60, 70, 77, 89, 197. *see also* Enslaved peoples
Smiley, Charles Henry 111
Smith, Alice Ravenel Huger 191
Smith, Joshua B. 70
Smith, Lucille Bishop 240
Social control 59
Social media 7, 147, 151, 157–160, 166, 244, 260
Son of a gun stew 101, 248
Sorghum 54, 56, 63, 92
Soul food
    and African American identity 11
    plant-based traditions 123
    rejection of, by Nation of Islam 120–122
    vs. southern food 120, 122–123
    stigma 120–123, 194
South Carolina
    barbecue styles 203
    Gullah Geechee cuisine **4,** 43, 235, 255

map showing historic rice fields 189
plantations **27, 187**
rice production 188, 189, 191
slavery 47, 66, 78, 108, 187
see also Charleston; Johns Island; St. Helena Island
Southern cuisine
art of baking 214–215, 217, 284
building blocks of 60–68
and civil rights movement 235
plant sources 148, 192–193
vs. soul food 120, 122–123
spread of, during Great Migration 107, 115–117
Southern Poverty Law Center 120
Spices 67, 212, 214
Springfield, Missouri: cashew chicken 12
Sriracha sauce 13, 25, 167
Stone, Martel 171
Storytelling, food 7–13, 157, 297
Sugar 86–91
Sugar plantations 56, **87,** 87–89, 91, 92
"Superfoods" 165, 193, 212
Sustainability 112, 160, 165, 209
Sweet Home Cafe, National Museum of African American History and Culture, Washington, D.C. 248
Sweet potato biscuits 94
Sweet potato cake **282,** 283
Sweet potato hash 212, **213**
Sweet potato pie 86, 212, 284
Sweet potatoes 54, **95,** 118, 210, 212
Sylvia's (restaurant), Harlem, New York **104–105, 110**

T

Tabasco sauce 67
Tacos 21, 24–25
Tanner, Alethia 169
Taro 92
Tassili's Raw Reality Café, Atlanta, Georgia **149**
Tea cakes **216,** 217
Tea drinking 88
Temple 7 (restaurant), Harlem, New York **121**
Terry, Bryant 151
Tervalon, Esperanza **72**
Tex-Mex 25
Texas
barbecue 203
Black cowboys 73, 74, 75
food festival 166
slavery 108
see also Houston
Thiam, Pierre 165
Thomas, Haile 151
Thomas Downing Oyster House, New York 70, 71, 73
Tipton-Martin, Toni 112
Tobacco 45, 47, 50, 77, **106**
Tomatoes, origin of 18
Trail of Tears 73
Trains 77, 195, **195,** 197
Tran, David 25
Transatlantic Slave Trade 11, 24, 26, 44–48, 54–55, 61, 88, 159, 186
Trinidadian cuisine 247
Tully, Thomas R. 68
Twain, Mark 122
Twitty, Michael W. 10

U

Underground Railroad 73
"United States" versus "America" 8

V

Vanilla 12–13
Vegan chili 178, **179**
Veganism 123, 148–151, 165, 193
Vegetarianism 123, 148–149, 151, 165
Velez, Paola 164
Virginia
barbecue 199, 203
food festival **294–295**
slavery 47, 108
waiter carriers 195, **195,** 268
see also Arlington; Monticello; Mount Vernon
The Virginia Housewife (Randolph) 21, **21,** 58, 61–62, 64, 194, 217

W

Waiter carriers 195, **195,** 268
Washington, Booker T. 117
Washington, D.C. 168–173
African migrants 164–165
bars and bartenders 168, 172–173, **173,** 218
Black history 168–169
Black Lives Matter protests 129, **161**
Caribbean restaurants **164,** 171, 247
Ethiopian restaurants 165, 171
March on Washington (1963) **126,** 128, 129, 131, 151
museum cafés 248
racial segregation 128, 131, 169, 171
restaurant worker (1942) **9**
U Street area 128, 169, **169**
see also Ben's Chili Bowl; White House
Washington, George 78–79
Watermelon 55, 63, 64, **65, 184**

Watermelon rinds, pickled 64, 117–118, 136, **137**
Wealth generation, and enslaved Black labor 32, 43, 50, 76–78, 89, 198
Weaver, Fawn 166
West Africa
  brewed drinks 218
  cattle raising 73
  crops 62, 92
  fishing practices 206, 209
  food traditions 22, 61, 64, 67, 165
  gumbo 7, 26
  native plants 53, 56, 92, 165, 192, 291
  plant-based diets 148
  rice dishes 92, 166, 191, 255
  rice growing 186–188, 191, 255
  yams 210, 212
West (region), U.S. 32, 48, 73–76, 115, 248
Whit, William C. 54, 189
White, Maunsel 67
White House, Washington, D.C.: Black cooks 169, 173, **215,** 224
Whitney Plantation, Wallace, Louisiana **51,** 91, 155
Williams, Chanel "Tootie" **182**
Williams, Chris 240, **241,** 243
Williams, Mary Lyde Hicks 22
Williams-Forson, Psyche A. 195
Wilson, Ellis 107
Wilson, Renae 13, 259, 265, 267, 273, 277, 278, 288
Wright, Raphael 155
Wright, Zephyr **215**

Y

Yams 54, 55, 92, 118, 210, 212

Recipe Index

Boldface indicates illustrations.

A
Apple Cream Pie 288, **289**

B
Baked Beans, Southern **275,** 277
Baked Eggplant **98–99,** 100
BBQ Chicken and Field Peas **230–231,** 232
BBQ Sauce, Corn Ribs With **274,** 276
Beans
   Hoppin' John **2–3**
   Son of a Gun Stew 101
   Southern Baked Beans **275,** 277
   Succotash With Tarragon and Crème Fraîche **238,** 239
   Vegan Chili 178, **179**
Beef
   Dirty Rice 233
   Gumbo 38, **39**
   Pepper Pot **134,** 135
   Son of a Gun Stew 101
Beverages
   F.U.B.U. Cocktail 292, **293**
   Hibiscus Aid **226,** 227
Biscuits
   Buttermilk Biscuits **138,** 139
   Sweet Potato Biscuits 94, **95**
Black-eyed peas
   Hoppin' John **2–3, 262,** 265
   Vegan Chili 178, **179**
Blackberry Cobbler **286,** 287
Boiled Turnips and Greens With Smoked Turkey 177
Bread Pudding **102,** 103
Breads
   Hot-Water Cornbread **35,** 37
   Southern Skillet Cornbread **34,** 36
Brined Fried Chicken **271,** 272
Butter beans, Succotash With Tarragon and Crème Fraîche **238,** 239
Buttermilk Biscuits **138,** 139

C
Cakes
   Pound Cake **180,** 181
   Sweet Potato Cake With Cream Cheese Mousse and Candied Pecans **282,** 283
Candied Pecans, Sweet Potato Cake With Cream Cheese Mousse and **282,** 283
Chard, Collard Green Medley Salad **263,** 264
Cheese, Macaroni and **96,** 97
Chicken
   BBQ Chicken and Field Peas **230–231,** 232
   Brined Fried Chicken **271,** 272
   Chicken Croquettes 140, **141**
   Chicken Purloo 256, **257**
   Dirty Rice 233
Chili, Vegan 178, **179**
Chutney, Peach and Peppa 176
Cobbler, Blackberry **286,** 287
Cocktail, F.U.B.U. 292, **293**
Collard Green Medley Salad **263,** 264
Corn
   Corn Ribs with BBQ Sauce **274,** 276
   Succotash With Tarragon and Crème Fraîche **238,** 239
Cornbread
   Hot-Water Cornbread **35,** 37
   Southern Skillet Cornbread **34,** 36

Cream Cheese Mousse, Sweet Potato Cake With, and Candied Pecans **282,** 283
Cream pies
    Apple Cream Pie 288, **289**
    Lemon Cream Pie **142,** 143
Crème Fraîche, Succotash With Tarragon and **238,** 239
Croquettes
    Chicken Croquettes 140, **141**
    Oyster and Salmon Croquettes 278, **279**
Crowder beans, Hoppin' John **2–3, 262,** 265

D
Desserts
    Apple Cream Pie 288, **289**
    Blackberry Cobbler **286,** 287
    Bread Pudding **102,** 103
    Lemon Cream Pie **142,** 143
    Pound Cake **180,** 181
    Sweet Potato Cake With Cream Cheese Mousse and Candied Pecans **282,** 283
Dirty Rice 233
Drinks
    F.U.B.U. Cocktail 292, **293**
    Hibiscus Aid **226,** 227
Dry rub, Memphis 232
Duck, Upright Roasted **242,** 243

E
Eggplant, Baked **98–99,** 100

F
Field Peas, BBQ Chicken and **230–231,** 232
Fried Chicken, Brined **271,** 272
F.U.B.U. Cocktail 292, **293**

G
Ginger, fresh
    Hibiscus Aid **226,** 227
    Peach and Peppa Chutney 176
    Pickled Watermelon Rinds 136, **137**
Greens
    Boiled Turnips and Greens With Smoked Turkey 177
    Collard Green Medley Salad **263,** 264
Gumbo 38, **39**

H
Hibiscus Aid **226,** 227
Hoppin' John **2–3, 262,** 265
Hot-Water Cornbread **35,** 37

J
Jambalaya **258,** 259
Jerk Pork Lumpia **250,** 251

K
Kale, Collard Green Medley Salad **263,** 264

L
Lemon Cream Pie **142,** 143
Lumpia, Jerk Pork **250,** 251

M
Macaroni and Cheese **96,** 97
Memphis dry rub 232
Meringue topping 143
Mousse, Cream Cheese, Sweet Potato Cake With, and Candied Pecans **282,** 283

N
Navy beans, Southern Baked Beans **275,** 277

O
Okra, Gumbo 38, **39**
Oyster and Salmon Croquettes 278, **279**

P
Peach and Peppa Chutney 176
Peas, Field, BBQ Chicken and 232
Pecans, Fried, Sweet Potato Cake With Cream Cheese Mousse and **282,** 283
Pepper Pot **134,** 135
Peppers
    Peach and Peppa Chutney 176
    Pepper Pot **134,** 135
Pickled Watermelon Rinds 136, **137**
Pies
    Apple Cream Pie 288, **289**
    Lemon Cream Pie **142,** 143
Plant-based meat, Vegan Chili 178
Pork
    Jerk Pork Lumpia **250,** 251
    Pork Loin Roast **266,** 267
Potatoes
    Pepper Pot **134,** 135
    Southern Potato Salad **270,** 273
Pound Cake **180,** 181
Pudding, Bread **102,** 103
Purloo, Chicken 256, **257**

R
Rice
    Chicken Purloo 256, **257**
    Dirty Rice 233
    Hoppin' John **2–3, 262,** 265

Jambalaya **258,** 259
Rice Waffles **174,** 175
Roast, Pork Loin **266,** 267
Roasted Duck, Upright **242,** 243

S
Salads
    Collard Green Medley Salad **263,** 264
    Southern Potato Salad **270,** 273
Salmon
    Oyster and Salmon Croquettes 278, **279**
Sauces
    BBQ Sauce 276
Sausage
    Gumbo 38, **39**
    Jambalaya **258,** 259
Seafood
    Jambalaya **258,** 259
    Oyster and Salmon Croquettes 278, **279**
Shrimp
    Jambalaya **258,** 259
Skillet Cornbread, Southern **34,** 36
Smoked Turkey, Boiled Turnips and Greens With 177
Son of a Gun Stew 101
Southern Baked Beans **275,** 277
Southern Potato Salad **270,** 273
Southern Skillet Cornbread **34,** 36
Stews
    Gumbo 38, **39**
    Pepper Pot **134,** 135
    Son of a Gun Stew 101
Succotash With Tarragon and Crème Fraîche **238,** 239
Sweet potatoes
    Pepper Pot **134,** 135
    Sweet Potato Biscuits 94, **95**
    Sweet Potato Cake With Cream Cheese Mousse and Candied Pecans **282,** 283
Swiss meringue topping 143

T
Tarragon, and Crème Fraîche, Succotash With **238,** 239
Turkey, Smoked, Boiled Turnips and Greens With 177
Turnips and Greens, Boiled, Smoked Turkey With 177

U
Upright Roasted Duck **242,** 243

V
Vegan Chili 178, **179**

W
Waffles, Rice **174,** 175
Watermelon Rinds, Pickled 136, **137**

About the Author

ANELA MALIK is an award-winning influencer, videographer, host, and writer who focuses on embracing nuance, imperfection, and joy on her platform Feed The Malik. Her work explores topics ranging from the role of food in our lives and relationships to cultural expectations related to travel to Black-owned businesses and Black stories. Anela is also a curious traveler, perpetual language student, awkward dancer, and curse-word connoisseur.

About the Recipe Developer

RENAE WILSON is a southern-born, Brooklyn-based culinary cook and storyteller with roots stretching from South Carolina to East Texas. A U.S. Navy veteran, she traded her uniform for an apron, using her GI Bill to study at the Institute of Culinary Education in New York. Renae's career is as rich and varied as her cooking—she's a published recipe developer, private chef, cookbook tester, and magazine test kitchen alum. Her Dear Henry pop-ups in Brooklyn are a love letter to southern cooking, where every dish is a blend of soul, tradition, and warmth, with a touch of razzle-dazzle. For Renae, food is more than sustenance—it's a way to connect, to share joy, and to make others feel cherished. When she's not in the kitchen, she's budget-traveling the world (always eating), dancing, camping, crocheting, or indulging in a bit of well-deserved tomfoolery.

Since 1888, the National Geographic Society has funded more than 14,000 research, conservation, education, and storytelling projects around the world. National Geographic Partners distributes a portion of the funds it receives from your purchase to National Geographic Society to support programs including the conservation of animals and their habitats.

National Geographic Partners, LLC
1145 17th Street NW
Washington, DC 20036-4688 USA

Get closer to National Geographic Explorers and photographers, and connect with our global community. Join us today at nationalgeographic.org/joinus

For rights or permissions inquiries, please contact National Geographic Books Subsidiary Rights: bookrights@natgeo.com

Text Copyright © 2025 Anela Malik. Compilation Copyright © 2025 National Geographic Partners, LLC. All rights reserved. Reproduction of the whole or any part of the contents without written permission from the publisher is prohibited.

NATIONAL GEOGRAPHIC and Yellow Border Design are trademarks of the National Geographic Society, used under license.

Succotash With Tarragon & Crème Fraîche recipe from *Dinner Déjà Vu: Southern Tonight, French Tomorrow*, by Jennifer Hill Booker. © 2017 by Jennifer Hill Booker, used with permission of the publisher, Pelican Publishing Company, Inc.

ISBN: 978-1-4262-2240-5

Printed in China

25/RRDH/1